The Croydon, Oxted & East Grinstead Railway

by
David Gould

THE OAKWOOD PRESS

© Oakwood Press & D. Gould 2003

British Library Cataloguing in Publication Data
A Record for this book is available from the British Library
ISBN 0 85361 598 5

Typeset by Oakwood Graphics.
Repro by Ford Graphics, Ringwood, Hants.
Printed by Inkon Printers Ltd, Yateley, Hants.

Dedication

To R.W. Kidner, whose original book *The Oxted Line* (1972) provided the groundwork for and inspired the writing of the present volume.

Front cover: Ex-LBSC 'E4' class 0-6-2T No. 32581 arrives at Oxted with a train from Tonbridge in July 1960. *Derek Cross*

Rear cover: Brighton-built 2-6-4T No. 42070 crosses Riddlesdown viaduct with a train for Tunbridge Wells in September 1959. *Derek Cross*

Published by The Oakwood Press (Usk), P.O. Box 13, Usk, Mon., NP15 1YS.
E-mail: oakwood-press@dial.pipex.com
Website: www.oakwood-press.dial.pipex.com

Contents

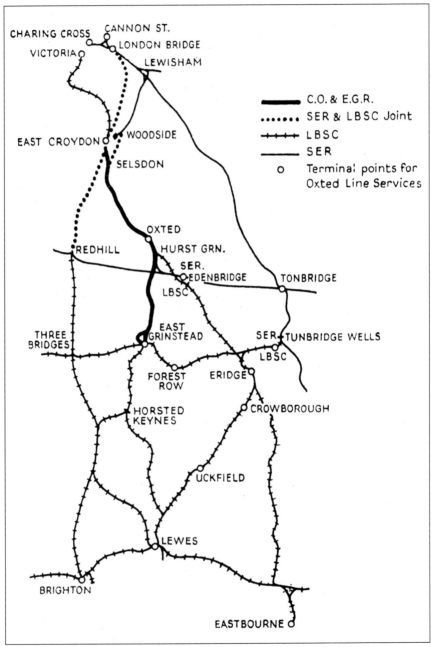

Oxted lines and connections (*see also detailed map on page 16*).

Introduction

Why should the Oxted line, amongst so many in the southern counties, deserve a history? After all, it is nowadays just another suburban electric railway whose trains look the same as those anywhere else in the south. But it was not always so. Long after all the other lines into London had been electrified steam traction was retained and the line definitely had the status of a secondary main line. Even when diesel trains took over the sense of being 'different' and somewhat special did not entirely disappear.

The origins of the line lay in two companies, the Surrey & Sussex Junction (S&SJ) and the Croydon, Oxted & East Grinstead (CO&EGR), both having unusual features: no engine ever turned a wheel for the Surrey & Sussex Junction, and the Croydon, Oxted & East Grinstead was a joint committee of two other railway companies. But, more than that, it was a railway in the round, for no narrow straits confined its traffics. It took away lime from Oxted and bricks from Lingfield, and brought in coal for ample firesides. Racehorses and bananas both received special treatment. Bookmakers mingled with well-connected families going to their country seats. Even today, it is more than merely a commuters' line, for there is an appreciable leisure traffic (mainly shoppers) and journeys are still made between some of the intermediate stations.

What is generally referred to as 'the Oxted line' is really a service of trains rather than an actual line. The Croydon, Oxted & East Grinstead Railway , which is the main subject of this work, is only part of that service and, because this was a link line rather than a branch with a terminus, the CO&EGR is inextricably mixed up with earlier and later developments.

Railway history to the south of London is complicated, partly because certain lines from London Bridge southwards were built in the infancy of railways, and partly because the area was for decades disputed territory between the London, Brighton & South Coast Railway (LBSCR) and the South Eastern Railway (SER).

For example, an Oxted train leaving London Bridge starts out on the approximate site of the London & Greenwich (opened in 1836) as far as Corbetts Lane Junction, Bermondsey, and from there travels over the former London & Croydon Railway (1839) to Norwood Junction, where the London & Brighton (1841) commenced. However, the same lines formed the main line of the South Eastern Railway, which had running powers from London Bridge to Coulsdon, and the portion of the Brighton line between Coulsdon and Redhill was actually owned by the South Eastern, the Brighton having running powers. The SER opened its main line between Redhill and Dover in stages between 1842 and 1844.

Originally the SER had wanted its line to Tonbridge to run via Croydon, Purley, Wapses Lodge (Caterham), Oxted and Edenbridge. The 1836 scheme included a tunnel of 528 yards at Riddlesdown, upon which work began in July 1837 (according to *Herapath's Railway Journal*, April 1837) but ceased about six months later, the tunnelling equipment being moved to Tonbridge. The Oxted tunnel was to have been 2,706 yards in length and there were inclined planes of 1 in 150 at Riddlesdown and 1 in 100 at Oxted. Unfortunately the South Eastern was required by Parliament to enter London over the Brighton Railway route via Redhill, as it was then thought that not more than one railway into London from the south would ever be required. Thus were sown the seeds of antipathy between the Brighton and South Eastern companies; the running of trains owned by both railways over a single set of tracks caused endless trouble, with each company blaming the other for causing late running.

The SER was not unmindful of East Grinstead, and the official South Eastern Railway map of 1846 showed a branch line to the North Sussex town from a junction with the Redhill to Dover line at Crowhurst Lane End, where land had been taken and a delivery siding set up. From here the line would have run a little west of the later route through Lingfield and ended on the Felbridge road not far from the site of the second (1866) East Grinstead station.

Because there was a clear conflict of interest, in 1848 the SER and the London, Brighton & South Coast Railway (constituted two years previously by amalgamation of the London & Croydon and London & Brighton) signed an agreement, the effect of which was that the territory north of the Redhill-Tonbridge line and east of the London-Brighton line was South Eastern territory, and all the rest was Brighton territory. A further agreement of 1864 had introduced a rather more friendly atmosphere, but the projection in that year of the Surrey & Sussex Junction Railway, with LBSCR backing, threatened to start trouble all over again. This line, which received its Act on 6th July, 1865 (28-29 Vict. c. 379), was to run from Croydon via Oxted to Groombridge, where it would join the East Grinstead-Tunbridge Wells line then under construction. It traversed 'South Eastern territory' between Croydon and Edenbridge.

The South Eastern replied with a projected London, Lewes & Brighton Railway, jointly with the London, Chatham & Dover Railway. This scheme never got further than its Act (29-30 Vict. c. 318, 1866) as the Chatham lost interest. It was not to be until 1899 that the two companies would come to an agreement to be worked jointly by a Managing Committee, known as the South Eastern & Chatham Railway.

London Brighton & South Coast Railway.

Eridge to

OXTED

Chapter One

The Surrey & Sussex Junction

Construction of the Surrey & Sussex Junction began, the contract having been let to Messrs Waring, and rapid progress was made with the works. A good deal of heavy engineering was carried out, including the boring of Oxted tunnel, 1 mile 506 yards in length. This was done by the then normal method of sinking shafts from the surface at intervals of about 200 yards. The tunnel curves gently eastwards for most of its length. The other two shorter tunnels, Riddlesdown and Limpsfield, were also bored, and the few roads then existing were bridged, except for the Maidstone road at Oxted. No attempt was made to bridge the Riddlesdown chalkpit (then half its present size), but the four-arched viaduct north of Woldingham seems to have been completed. This was carried out in brick, but when the joint companies later bridged the chalkpit and the Maidstone road valley the viaducts were made of wrought-iron lattice girders resting on brick piers. An example of an original S&SJ bridge is the partially broken one south of Oxted tunnel, which carried the approach road to the Oxted limeworks over the shallow cutting.

Things did not go well with the Surrey & Sussex Junction. During this period many railways were in trouble and in 1866 there was a great financial panic following the Overend & Gurney bank failure. The S&SJ troubles were many: there were some irregularities over land deals, and also labour troubles. There was a serious riot at Edenbridge in 1869 because of the importation by the contractor, Waring, of large numbers of Belgian navvies. Friction between the LBSCR and SER also arose as the LBSC claimed that the line did not contravene the 1864 agreement because it merely joined up two parts of the LBSCR's own line, thus shortening the distance from London to East Sussex in the same way that the SER was doing with its 'New Main Line' between New Cross and Tonbridge. There were long and tedious negotiations and the Duke of Richmond was asked to arbitrate. The result was that an Act of Parliament was obtained in 1869 to transfer ownership of the S&SJ to the LBSCR. This company, however, believed it would cost £1½-£2 million to complete the line and that traffic would be meagre. It therefore asked for powers to abandon the works, but the request was refused. A penalty of £50 per day for failing to complete the line was imposed, with a limit on the penalty of £32,250. The Brighton, which was at that time financially over-extended, partly as a result of expenditure on unprofitable lines, preferred to pay the maximum penalty, and so the Surrey & Sussex Junction powers automatically lapsed.

And there it was: few people imagined that the line would ever open since the works had definitely been abandoned. The embankments became overgrown, the tunnel mouths obscured by shrubs and vegetation. Everywhere the grass grew and the saplings sprouted along the unballasted trackbed. The 1872 Ordnance Survey six-inch map indicates single track in position for about 400 yards south from what was later Selsdon station, probably left there by the contractors.

No doubt in time many locals forgot the railway, and although anyone trudging the long half-mile from the hamlet of Oxted to the church would be aware that up in the woods there was a tunnel, there was not much to show.

It was the same with another abortive LBSCR line, built at the same time: the Ouse Valley Railway, abandoned in 1868. This took off from the south end of the Ouse viaduct, on the Brighton main line, heading for Eastbourne direct via Lindfield and Uckfield. For this line, however, there was to be no rescue, and its cuttings and embankments still lie sleeping and forgotten in the woods and meadows of East Sussex.

Marden Park viaduct in 1884. This is an example of a Surrey & Sussex Junction Railway structure.

Chapter Two

A Fresh Start

Several railway schemes affecting the Oxted area were mooted in the 1870s. The most ambitious was the Metropolitan & Brighton in 1875, for a line beginning at Penge (London, Chatham & Dover Railway) and Beckenham (South Eastern Railway) and running by way of Warlingham village, Caterham, Godstone, East Grinstead, Lindfield and Clayton to Brighton. There would have been a viaduct over the Woldingham valley and a tunnel through the Down emerging at a point near the present Caterham station. The Caterham & Godstone Valley actually obtained an Act (39-40 Vict. c. 99) in July 1876 to build a line from Caterham to Godstone, Oxted and Westerham, but this company was dissolved four years later without anything having been built. The SER revived its proposal for a line from Wapses Lodge (where the present Caterham roundabout is) via Oxted and Edenbridge to Tonbridge.

None of these schemes came to fruition. Nevertheless, there was no denying the fact that half a railway already existed between Croydon and Oxted and beyond. In June 1878 an Act was passed (41-42 Vict. c. 72) for a Croydon, Oxted & East Grinstead Railway, and in the same year agreement was reached that this line would be jointly owned by the LBSCR and the SER as between South Croydon Junction and Crowhurst Junction North, where a spur line was to join the SER 'old main line' (*see map page 16*). From Crowhurst Junction North southwards it would be purely LBSCR property.

Also in 1878 the LBSCR acquired the Lewes & East Grinstead Railway, whose Act had been obtained in August 1877. Construction of this line (by the contractor Joseph Firbank) was forging ahead, and it was intended that it should make end-on connection at East Grinstead with the CO&EG, so that the whole set-up could provide an alternative route between London and Brighton. The contract for the CO&EG was let to Joseph Firbank, and it seems that work on reconstructing the old Surrey & Sussex Junction was begun in 1881. The *East Grinstead Parish Magazine* reported in December that 'The work on the northern section by Oxted and Croydon is now being pushed forward, as the Contractors gain possession of the remaining plots of land necessary for the various works.'

By then other connections had been planned, and in time were executed. The Woodside & South Croydon Railway obtained its Act in 1880 and was acquired jointly by the LBSCR and the SER in 1882, and the Oxted & Groombridge Railway Act was passed in August 1881, acquisition of this line by the LBSCR occurring in 1884. The Croydon, Oxted & East Grinstead was no longer just a simple line.

The first section to be opened was the Lewes & East Grinstead, on 1st August, 1882, following an official inspection for the Board of Trade by Colonel Yolland on 21st July. The station building at East Grinstead, whose architect was T.H. Myres of Preston, was uncompleted and it is recorded that a temporary ticket box was in use. Now Firbank could give his undivided attention to the CO&EG:

The works on the northern section to Croydon and London are being rapidly proceeded with including deep cuttings, bridges and connections, both on the loop [i.e. the St Margaret's Loop at East Grinstead] and the main lines. (*East Grinstead Parish Magazine*, August 1882.)

An unfortunate accident occurred in Riddlesdown tunnel on 1st August, when a ballast train and another containing shift men collided on the single track. Ten of the men were seriously injured. There was a clear breach of the rules, as fresh ballast was not supposed to be sent down the line after 5.30 pm, and the group of navvies had been waiting for the arrival of the last lot of ballast. When the down train failed to show up they decided to set off up the line for Croydon in wagons that had previously been emptied of ballast.

The joint line was engineered by Fred D. Banister, the LBSCR's Engineer, and Francis Brady, the SER's. Banister was responsible for the section between Crowhurst and East Grinstead. Resident engineers in charge of the works were George Lopes and A. Steinheauser. In May 1883 the Brighton invited tenders for the construction of station buildings, station masters' houses, platform canopies and footbridges at Dormans and Lingfield. Both these stations were well-built in the Brighton's lavish style, but the stations on the joint line all had timber weatherboarded single-storey structures.

Several locomotives were in use by the contractors, including saddle-tank engines named *Grinstead*, *Oxted*, *Croydon* and *Cliftonville*. This last was a Hunslet 0-6-0 saddle-tank of 1876 (No. 165) which had been used on the Cliftonville Spur contract (Preston Park to Hove) and worked on the Oxted line contract from 1880 to 1884.

The LBSCR timetable of 1883 showed the CO&EG as a dotted line, though no reference was made to forthcoming opening. The stations marked included one at Crowhurst, just south of the brickworks, and Oxted appeared as 'Limpsfield', but Dormans was not marked. There never was a station at Crowhurst.

Another accident of sufficient seriousness to be reported in the local press occurred on 2nd October, 1883, in the deep and curving cutting of the St Margaret's loop. A workmen's train of two wagons containing about 30 men returning to East Grinstead after leaving work in the afternoon was being propelled by a locomotive, when it struck a stationary wagon on the line. The driver's view had been blocked by the number of men standing in the wagons, which were lower-slung than the LBSCR wagon, whose buffers crushed the end of the contractor's truck and caused severe injuries to three or four men.

At the time of the opening of East Grinstead High Level and Low Level stations, 15th October, 1883, an announcement had been made that the line north would be opened on 1st November, but this prediction was wildly optimistic. It was not until 18th February the following year that a long and arduous inspection was completed by Major-General C.S. Hutchinson, in company with J.P. Knight (General Manager of the LBSCR) and several Directors. A special train carried them from Croydon to East Grinstead, the examination taking about 1½ hours. Although everything was pronounced to be satisfactory and in good working order, there were in fact several requirements to be carried out. However, there was no objection to opening for passenger traffic.

A special Directors' inspection train ran from Victoria to Brighton over the new line on 26th February conveying Major-General Hutchinson and various

This is the building at Oxted station that was used as the residence of the contractor's foreman in 1883, later becoming the ganger's cottage. Disused by July 1987, it was demolished shortly afterwards. *Author*

LBSCR officers and Directors. The General Manager and traffic superintendent (W. Williams), along with the Deputy Chairman (Ralph L. Lopes) were there, as were the Mayors of Eastbourne, Brighton and Gravesend, no doubt all eagerly awaiting the slap-up luncheon held at the new station refreshment rooms at Brighton, and at the LBSCR's expense.

Hutchinson said that the works were very substantial and well suited to heavy traffic. The *East Sussex News* reported that 'Tuesday's trip by the new line occupied nearly two hours, including stoppages at all stations, and was safely accomplished amidst brilliant sunshine, that would have done no discredit to the month of May.'

The Croydon, Oxted & East Grinstead was opened to passenger traffic on Monday, 10th March, 1884. There were only four trains each way between Brighton and London Bridge via Oxted, plus four South Eastern trains each way between London Bridge and Oxted (for details of train services see later). Fares from East Grinstead to London Bridge at opening were

	First	Second	Third
Singles	5s. 8d.	4s. 1d.	2s. 6d.
Returns	10s. 0d.	7s. 4d.	4s. 9d.

East Grinstead was something of a 'railway town' even at the opening, with services to Three Bridges (line opened on 9th July, 1855), Tunbridge Wells (line opened on 1st October, 1866) and Lewes. The new route to London was six miles shorter than that via Three Bridges, but some passengers continued to use this route to get the benefit of fast trains from there to London. Anyone wishing to be in London early had no choice, for the first up train via Lingfield was not until 8.07 am, but to Three Bridges there was a departure at 6.45 am.

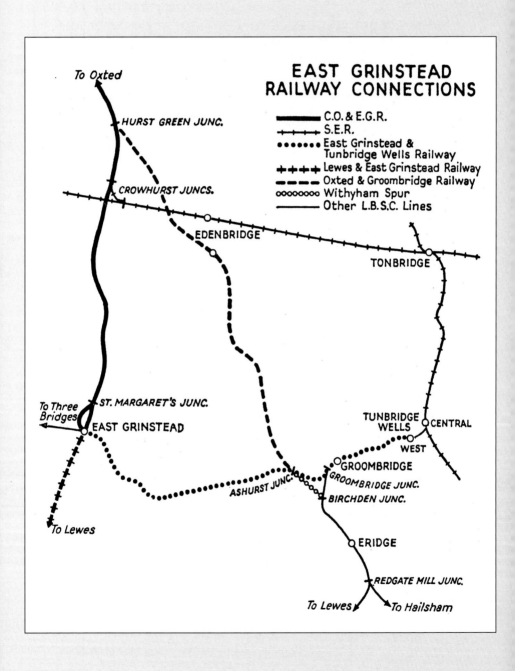

**EAST GRINSTEAD
RAILWAY CONNECTIONS**

———— C.O. & E.G.R.
+++++ S.E.R.
••••••• East Grinstead &
Tunbridge Wells Railway
+++++ Lewes & East Grinstead Railway
– – – Oxted & Groombridge Railway
ooooooo Withyham Spur
———— Other L.B.S.C. Lines

To Oxted

HURST GREEN JUNC.

CROWHURST JUNCS.

EDENBRIDGE

TONBRIDGE

St. MARGARET'S JUNC.

To Three Bridges

EAST GRINSTEAD

To Lewes

ASHURST JUNC.

TUNBRIDGE WELLS

CENTRAL

WEST

GROOMBRIDGE

GROOMBRIDGE JUNC.

BIRCHDEN JUNC.

ERIDGE

REDGATE MILL JUNC.

To Lewes

To Hailsham

Directors of the Croydon, Oxted & East Grinstead Railway Board had been appointed, these being Samuel Laing, Jonas Levy and Ralph L. Lopes to represent the Brighton, and Lord Brabourne, James Byng and Alexander Beattie to represent the South Eastern. John Shaw of the SER was appointed Secretary and Allen Sarle of the LBSCR was Treasurer. Brady and Banister, the joint Engineers, reported to this Board, which held its meetings alternately at the LBSCR and SER London Bridge offices. The strict observance of an 'equal shares for both companies' is something at which to marvel!

Firbank continued to be responsible for the maintenance of the joint line for one year after the opening, until 10th March, 1885. After this, the LBSCR assumed responsibility for the section between South Croydon and Selsdon Junction and from a point south of Upper Warlingham station to Crowhurst Junction. The SER was responsible for maintaining the whole of the Woodside & South Croydon (opened on 10th August, 1885), the CO&EG to a point south of Upper Warlingham, and the Crowhurst spur. This spur had been inspected by Major-General Hutchinson on 6th June, 1884, and trains began using it on 1st August.

In August 1885 Firbank sent in his account: the original contract amount was £185,000 but he wanted a further £44,150 for extras. The Board had no intention of paying that amount, and the engineers recommended that he be paid only £10,000 more. In December two buildings at Oxted station were purchased from Firbank for £140, and in February 1886 he was paid £2,604 for the construction of Selsdon Road, Sanderstead, Upper Warlingham and Oxted stations. Marden Park station (later Woldingham), a later addition, was started during the period of Firbank's 'tenure', and he built it for £1,500.

The three new iron viaducts were, it seems, designed by Henry Wallis; at all events he made the drawings. These viaducts had special chairs on the outer rails carrying guard rails slightly above rail level in order to ensure that any derailed vehicles remained upright.

A further inspection of the line was made by Major-General Hutchinson on 14th April, 1885, as one of his requirements the previous year was that the girders of the Riddlesdown viaduct should be strengthened; this had now been done.

The following description of the line is taken from *Life of Joseph Firbank*, by F. McDermott (1887):

Running South, from Croydon, the first obstacle the engineers had to meet was the vast chalk-pit at Kenley - worked from time immemorial for lime-burning operations - which had to be crossed by a handsome wrought- iron lattice girder viaduct, on brick piers, in five spans, two of 55 feet and three of 100 feet each, the total height from the road level being 59 feet. Near Marden Park, the beautiful seat of Sir Robert Wm. Clayton, Bart., a richly-wooded valley is crossed by a fine brick-arched viaduct, of four spans, each 40 feet wide, 51 feet high from the surface of the roadway to rail level. Another short run brings us to Oxted Tunnel, 2,266 yards in length - the longest tunnel undertaken by Mr Firbank. In cutting this tunnel heavy springs were tapped at the junction of the chalk with the gault, or grey chalk, formation. Pumps could only just keep this water under control, and, when the tunnel was finished, arrangements had to be made for running the constantly-flowing stream away. This was successfully accomplished.

McDermott ignores Oxted viaduct (which has three spans), but goes on to give a description of Cook's Pond. It was 'a magnificent wrought-iron lattice girder viaduct of five spans, each 125 feet in width, with a brick arch of 12 feet span at each abutment, and an extra elliptical arch of 30 feet span at the southern extremity'. From ground to rail level the height was 65 feet.

The whole of the joint line was heavily engineered, much of it running along the eastern side of the Caterham valley. There was a long climb for down trains, much of it at 1 in 100, to a 'summit' just north of Oxted tunnel; and for up trains an eight-mile climb from Lingfield to that summit. These gradients made for slow schedules.

The final addition to the network was the Oxted & Groombridge, opened from Hurst Green Junction to Edenbridge Town on 2nd January, 1888, and extended to Ashurst Junction on 1st October the same year. At last the Brighton had a competitive route from London to Tunbridge Wells, only five miles further than the South Eastern's, and it took the opportunity to put on a really excellent service of trains.

This line had been part of the old Surrey & Sussex Junction, but before it could be opened a great deal of work needed doing. The contractor was Joseph Thomas Firbank, eldest son of the CO&EG contractor. Markbeech tunnel (between Hever and Cowden, on the line from Hurst Junction to Ashurst Junction) had been only partly made when the works were abandoned in 1869; most of the timber supports had rotted and rubbish that had fallen down the shafts had to be cleared away. When completed the tunnel was 1,338 yards long. The station buildings at Edenbridge Town, Hever, Cowden and Ashurst were in the same attractive style as those at Lingfield and Dormans.

Pre-opening shot of Dormans station, looking south in 1884. The main station building, at the top of the bank, is 'detached' from the down platform.

Chapter Three

The Line Described

The following description of the line covers the whole period up to date; some items may therefore appear to be out of context, but are better dealt with in the geographical context.

South Croydon Junction has been remodelled on two occasions. When opened there were only two tracks on the main line for the use of both South Eastern and LBSCR trains. The 'local line', on the west side of the 'through line', was extended from South Croydon to Stoats Nest (later renamed Coulsdon North) on 5th November, 1899, and in 1908 the 'down relief line' from Norwood Junction through East Croydon to South Croydon was laid and connected to the Oxted line and the down through line at South Croydon Junction. On 2nd June, 1958, the down relief line became reversible between Windmill Bridge Junction and South Croydon, and six up Oxted line trains used it each day. The great value of this reversible line was that trains from Oxted to London Bridge no longer needed to cross the paths of down trains from Victoria at any point. However, in 1985, the junction was altered again, the reversible line becoming solely a down line once more and the connection from the up Oxted line to this line was taken out. What had been the through lines became the local lines, and a connection from the up Oxted line to what had been the down through line was put in, this now becoming reversible; it was used chiefly by trains terminating at East Croydon.

The Croydon & Oxted Joint climbs sharply from South Croydon at 1 in 83 to Selsdon (11⅜ miles from London Bridge - Selsdon Road until 30th September, 1935), built in the vee where the Woodside & South Croydon Railway (W&SC) came in on the down side. Opened on 10th August, 1885, the station was very badly sited, being only a short distance from South Croydon but nowhere near Selsdon. The 1882 LBSCR Act contained a clause for a deviation of the W&SC to join the CO&EG further south, but a condition of the Wigsel Trust in selling the land at what became the present junction was that a station must be built there. The SER, for its part, wanted the station to be closer to the main line. The W&SC platforms fell into disuse on 1st January, 1917, when the W&SC service was suspended, the line remaining semi-derelict for 18 years. Most Oxted trains continued to use their side of the station, and on 30th September, 1935, the station was fully re-opened and a service of electric trains was inaugurated on the W&SC. The third rail was carried through to Sanderstead on the Oxted line to enable trains to terminate there, although some reversed at Selsdon. There was a half-hourly service to and from Charing Cross via the Mid-Kent line.

Latterly the off-peak service ran only between Sanderstead and Elmers End, although there were still peak trains through to Charing Cross and Cannon Street. The off-peak service was discontinued in November 1959, and some years later the service degenerated into a two-car shuttle train, peak-hours only, between Elmers End and Selsdon or Sanderstead. The Oxted line platforms were used less and less, and on 15th June, 1959, trains ceased to call there; there

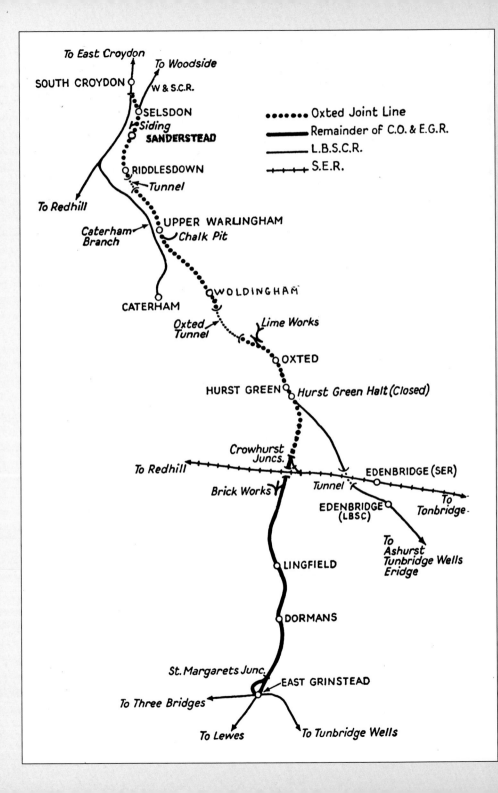

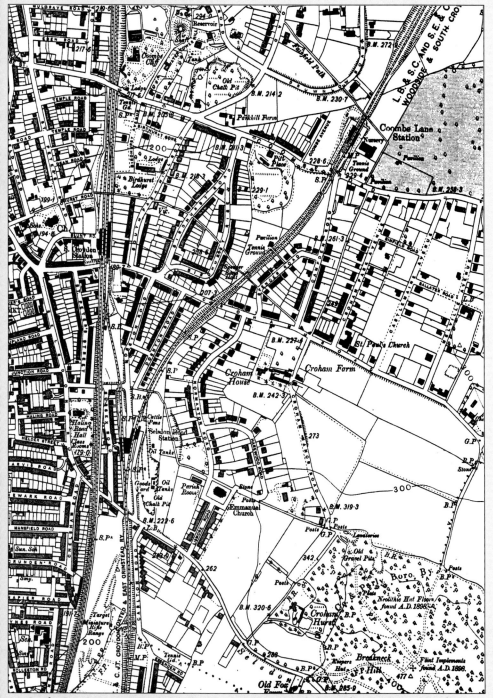

South Croydon station and Selsdon Road station also showing the line from Lewisham approaching from the north-east and the the main line to Brighton running parallel with the Oxted line to the south. *Reproduced from the 6", 1911 Ordnance Survey Map*

Selsdon Road station from the north, about 1922. The Woodside & South Croydon platforms are in the centre and the Croydon & Oxted platforms are to the right.

H.J. Patterson Rutherford Collection

The 10.45 am London Bridge to Tunbridge Wells West via East Grinstead passes through Selsdon on 7th May, 1955, with class '4PT/FT' No. 42066 (built at Brighton in October 1950); Three Bridges duty number 675 is displayed. The LBSCR semaphore signalling here was replaced by power signalling during the night of 7th/8th May, 1955.   *D. Cullum*

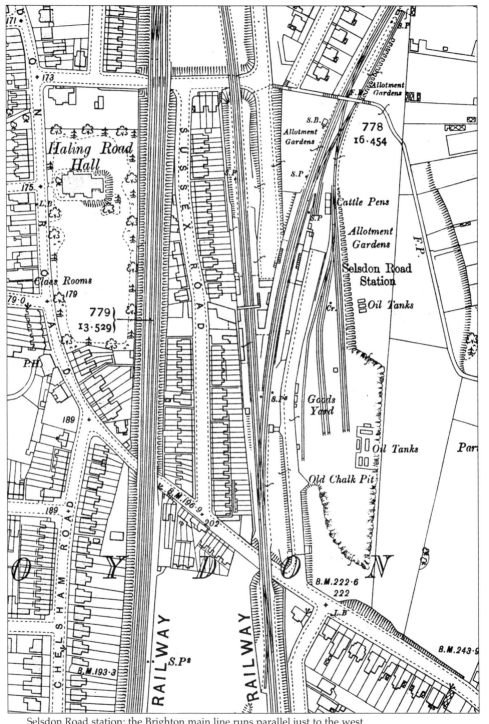

Selsdon Road station; the Brighton main line runs parallel just to the west.
Reproduced from the 25", 1913 Ordnance Survey Map

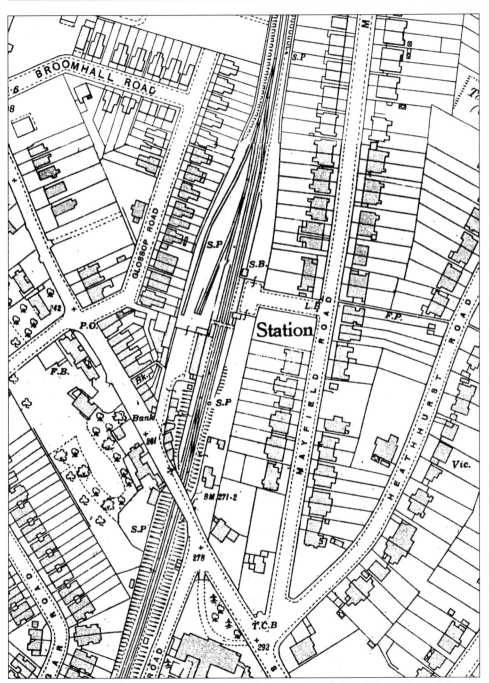

Sanderstead station.   *Reproduced from the 25", 1933 Ordnance Survey Map*

had been only three up and one down morning trains using the station. A few years later these platforms were partly demolished and later still the main station building was taken down and the bay platform on the down W&SCR platform filled in.

Patronage of the W&SC declined almost to zero, as Selsdon station in particular became a most uninviting place, with only a tiny hut from which tickets were sometimes sold. However, the W&SC survived the spate of line closures in the 1960s, not succumbing until 13th May, 1983, the last day of service.

A siding for the Anglo American Oil Co., installed in 1894, continued in use after closure of the station; it was noted in 1932 that the down W&SC line through the station, and the sidings, were well polished but the up line was rusty, and the North signal cabin was in use to operate the points in the sidings. After the 1983 closure most of the track was lifted, but the down line remained to give access to the sidings. This connection was severed in the mid-1990s.

Beyond Selsdon the gradient eases to 1 in 110/100. Just beyond the junction, on the up side, a siding led to a factory owned by Blackwell's and National Roofings (in use by 1934); and train-ferry wagons were to be seen there up to about 1960, when it ceased to be used. The points were removed in 1969.

Sanderstead station (12¼ miles) had weatherboarded buildings which, along with the platform canopies, remained almost totally unaltered until 5th June, 1986, when the up-side building was damaged by fire. Demolition soon followed, and in September 1987 an unusual brick-built structure with deep overhanging eaves was the replacement, with a small shelter on the down platform. There were crossovers at both the north and south ends of the station; the north crossover and up sidings were installed in May 1889. Freight traffic here was withdrawn on 20th March, 1961, and the sidings lifted when the platforms were lengthened about 1963. The north crossover was removed in 1980, but the south crossover, which had long ago been resited south of the road bridge, remained for reversing electric trains; the third rail continuing on the down line for about a quarter of a mile beyond the crossover. The bridge carrying Sanderstead Road over the railway was renewed on 8th February, 1970.

The gradient continues at 1 in 100 for another 1¾ miles. The next station, Riddlesdown (13½ miles from London Bridge), was not opened until 5th June, 1927; a somewhat unreal place at the time but soon the Down was covered with houses and there was a small parade of shops near the station. The Southern's timber platform structures were replaced by larger brick buildings in the late 1950s and these remain. Access to the station is by ramps both sides.

There is no break in the gradient, which continues through Riddlesdown tunnel, 836 yards long; the tunnel's outline is that of an inverted 'U' and there are two ventilating shafts. Beyond the tunnel the track levels out for a quarter of a mile before continuing its rise at 1 in 264. The line here is built along the side of the hill, so that there is a cutting on the down side but an embankment on the up; at milepost 14¾ there is an iron viaduct on brick piers built right across a lime works, and passengers are given an impressively close view of the chalk pit. The kilns were almost underneath and a narrow gauge track, used by

A postcard view of Sanderstead station with the station staff in attendance..

John Alsop Collection

Sanderstead signal cabin, on the down platform. The timber valancing of the platform canopy was in the style used for all the joint-line stations. 13th May, 1983.   *Author*

Two views of the engineers installing a new bridge over the line at Sanderstead station on Sunday 8th February, 1970. *(Both) Author*

Riddlesdown station, showing Southern Railway platform shelters, soon to be replaced by slightly more substantial buildings.   *Lens of Sutton*

A Victoria to Tunbridge Wells train pauses at Riddlesdown station, which was built on a gradient of 1 in 100. 'LM4' 2-6-4 tank engine No. 42103 of Tunbridge Wells heads the train, which comprises a Maunsell three-corridor set 'B'.   *Lens of Sutton*

wagons for tipping material from the top of the kilns, passed under the viaduct. The works closed about 1969, but the overgrown track could still be glimpsed from the trains for many years afterwards. A public footpath crosses the line immediately south of the viaduct, providing a splendid vantage point for photography of trains as they cross the viaduct. Also at this point since 1965 has been the boundary between Greater London and Surrey.

Upper Warlingham (15⅜ miles) must surely hold the record for the most absurd station name in Surrey. Since the village of Warlingham is several hundred feet above and a mile distant from the station, a more sensible name for it, as suggested by Jeoffry Spence back in 1952, would be *Lower* Warlingham. The station is actually in Whyteleafe; indeed the destination shown in timetables of London Transport's bus route 115 was 'Whyteleafe Upper Warlingham Station'.

Until May 1884 the station was plain 'Warlingham', but Sir George Balfour MP had complained to the South Eastern Chairman about the confusion with another station of that name on the Caterham branch in the valley and made the reasonable suggestion that the Oxted line station be called 'Whyteleafe'. Nevertheless, 'Upper' Warlingham it became, and when a station called Whyteleafe was opened on the Caterham branch in January 1900 the opportunity to give the Oxted line station an accurate name was lost. When Warlingham station, which was even worse-sited, came up for renaming on 11th June, 1956, the attractive name 'Portley Wood' suggested by the local council was ignored and an unimaginative 'Whyteleafe South' was substituted. As there was now no Warlingham station the name 'Upper Warlingham' became even more pointless, but still it remains. Between January 1894 and September 1900 it was shown in the timetables as 'Upper Warlingham and Whyteleafe'.

The station was substantial, with coal sidings on both up and down sides; Charringtons had offices on the down side at the London end of the station, which was built on the side of the hill. The footbridge, which was fully glazed and roofed, with tongue-and-groove boarding inside the lattice girders, not only connected the platforms but provided access for pedestrians between the high ground east of the station and the station forecourt an the western side. The glazing and roof of the bridge were removed in the mid-1950s. The usual weatherboarded structure was provided as the station building on the up side, and a substantial canopy; on the down platform later the canopies were rebuilt but the timber building was still in use in 2002. In Joint days this station and Selsdon Road were staffed by the South Eastern. A house for the station master was built in 1893. Freight facilities were withdrawn on 4th May, 1964, and most sidings were lifted except for a reserve layby at the down end, up side, normally locked but capable of taking a failed three-car train if required. This loop siding was removed in June 1977.

Immediately south of the station, by a trailing connection from the down line, was a siding leading to a chalk pit. This was laid in November 1886 and brought into use a month later for the use of Frederick Nichols, lime, coal and cement merchant, who paid for the siding's installation. In 1930 it was dealing with about six wagons per month, but by 1934 the siding was out of use. The quarry,

Former SER class 'F1' 4-4-0 heads an afternoon London Bridge to Tunbridge Wells train across Riddlesdown viaduct in September 1932. Stock comprises two SR utility vans, an LBSCR 6-wheel brake van and an LBSCR three-coach bogie set.

An afternoon Victoria to Tunbridge Wells train enters Upper Warlingham station in the mid-1930s, with class 'B1' 4-4-0 No. 1443 of Stewarts Lane Shed and an ex-SECR three-coach set.

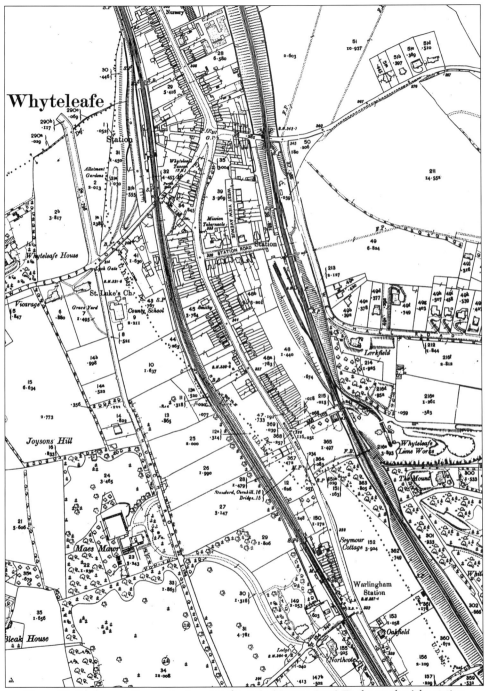

Upper Warlingham station can be found at the end of Station Road. To the south of the station is the line into the lime works. The railway to the west of the Oxted line is the Caterham branch. Two stations on the Caterham branch can be seen on this map, Whyteleafe (*top*) and Warlingham (*bottom*). *Reproduced from the 25", 1913 Ordnance Survey Map*

The weatherboarded up-side station building at Upper Warlingham. Although the signboards are headed 'Southern Railway' the picture was taken in early BR days; the timetable posters are graced by 'double sausage' totems.   *Lens of Sutton*

A much more recent view at Upper Warlingham shows a pair of 'VEP' units, No. 3905 and 3901, arriving at Upper Warlingham with an East Grinstead train on 25th January, 2003.   *P. Barnes*

now owned by the Riddlesdown Lime & Fuel Co., remained but eventually, after many years of disuse, a housing estate was built in it.

Beyond Upper Warlingham the gradient steepens again to 1 in 100 through Woldingham, with a brief level section between mileposts 16 and 16¼. A public footbridge a quarter of a mile south of Upper Warlingham was removed in 1971 and just beyond milepost 16¼ was the boundary north of which the South Eastern was responsible for the maintenance of 'way and works' and south of which the Brighton had the responsibility. The evidence remained in the shape of South Eastern & Chatham Railway (SECR) cast-iron mileposts and metal bridge number plates on the section of line maintained by the SECR, and LBSCR wooden mile- and gradient posts on the southern section. These were mostly replaced by standard concrete posts in early BR days.

Between mileposts 16½ and 16¾ the railway passes over a fine brick-built four-arch viaduct, from which there are good views of the Downs, the continuous built-up area at last being left behind. The scenery around Marden Park station (17⅛ miles; opened in July, 1885 and renamed Woldingham in January 1894) is among the finest to be seen from a train in Surrey. The main station building was on the down side, with a generous canopy and small waiting room on the up platform. Land for the station, plus a contribution of £500 towards its construction, was given by one John Morris in 1884, but no inn, public house or refreshment room was to be built there. The platforms were 400 ft long, and there was a single siding trailing off the down line and leading to a horse and carriage dock, which was 120 ft long. Another siding was later added, but was lifted about 1976. The former dock siding remained because of its use for a motorised trolley with light trailers employed on tunnel maintenance, but in November 1984 even this siding was lifted, leaving only a crossover on the running lines.

Because of the 1 in 100 gradient through the station, catch points were put in 237 yards north of the down home signal. Although it is stated that opening was on 1st July, 1885, there may have been some delay for in June the LBSCR informed the Board of Trade: 'We propose opening Marden Park Station on Wednesday, 15th July'. If so, it was still in advance of the official BOT inspection, which was made by Major-General C.S. Hutchinson towards the end of July. The signal cabin had been in use since March 1885, and a house for the station master was built in 1892. The footbridge connecting the platforms was replaced by the Southern Railway by one in concrete, later fully roofed and glazed; the glazing was however removed some time after 1960. Apart from recent renewal of the canopies, Woldingham station remained pretty much as built, and was still remarkably isolated; a fact reflected in the average number of daily passengers (600 in 1978). In Joint Line days Woldingham was staffed by the Brighton, as was Sanderstead.

The summit of the line is reached just beyond milepost 17½, just over a quarter of a mile beyond Woldingham, and the down grade, which will carry the line down to the level of the Eden water-meadows at Lingfield, starts as 1 in 132 through the long Oxted tunnel, which at 2,266 yards in length is joint holder, with Clayton on the Brighton main line, of the record for being the longest tunnel on the LBSCR. It is unusual in two ways: firstly, it is built mostly

The down-side station building at Woldingham, from the approach road; the village itself is nearly a mile away at the top of a very steep hill, leading off to the left.

Woldingham Supply Stores Series

Woldingham station, with LBSCR-type nameboard. Both the down starting signal (in the foreground) and the up starting signals are on immensely tall posts with co-acting arms for good visibility.   *Lens of Sutton*

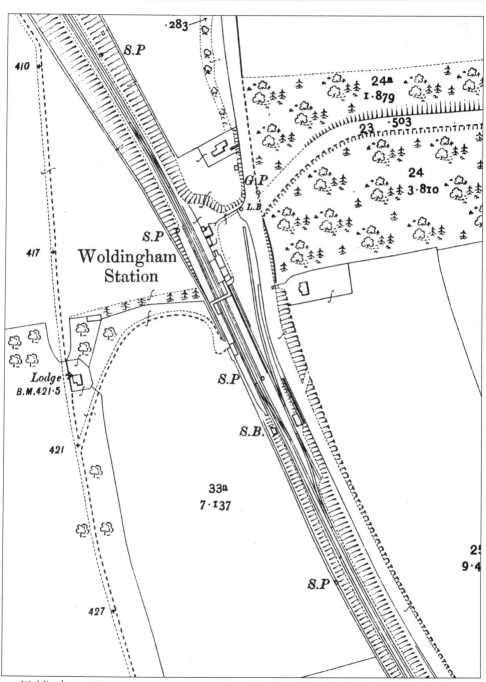

Woldingham station. *Reproduced from the 25", 1912 Ordnance Survey Map*

A 1947 view of Woldingham station.   *John Alsop Collection*

A nine-car demu pauses at Woldingham station on its slow journey from Uckfield and East Grinstead (combined at Oxted) on 18th February, 1984. 3H unit No. 1102 forms the rear portion.

Author

on a curve; and secondly, the tunnel outline varies. The northern two-thirds of the tunnel has an inverted 'U'-shaped outline whilst the southern end is built to the more conventional horseshoe outline. There are seven ventilating shafts.

Oxted tunnel was 'inherited' from the Surrey & Sussex Junction, and seems not to have been built to the highest standards, for it has given a great deal of trouble over the years. In June 1917 it was closed for several weeks owing to part of the roof falling in, and on 29th April, 1919, there was a further collapse after the passage of the 2.49 pm Oxted to London. After repairs the line was reopened on 7th May, 1919. In 1920 a decision was made to carry out extensive repairs, a single line was laid through with scaffolding either side and the engineers had possession from 7th February, 1921, until normal service was resumed on 1st December, 1921. Only at business times and all day each Saturday were trains permitted through during the period of repairs.

In recent times the tunnel wall began to 'bulge' in several places until BR, worried about the close proximity of the wall to the trains, decided to ensure that passengers could no longer lean out of the windows. In June 1989 the droplights were either screwed up so that they were openable only a few inches, thus making the carriage interiors unbearably hot in summer, or else the droplights had horizontal bars placed across them, so that passengers felt they were being carried in a mobile jail.

Upon leaving Oxted tunnel the train passes the partially-broken abutments of an overbridge that was bombed during World War II, and then the site of the Oxted Greystone Lime Company's siding, first laid in May 1885 at that company's expense. This was on the down side, with no connection from the up line. The locomotive working the private line was housed in a wooden shed beside a gate marking the boundary between the railway siding and the lime company's line, and there was a water tank there. In 1930 the sidings dealt with about 10 wagons daily, but regular traffic appears to have ceased about 1939. The tracks were left in place, however, and periodically cleared of undergrowth until 1969, when the line from the siding up to the limeworks was lifted. BR lifted its part of the siding in February 1971.

Just beyond here the down grade steepens to 1 in 100, but the headlong dash of the train, which is travelling faster than at any other point since leaving Croydon, is all too soon arrested for the stop at Oxted station (20¼ miles). Until the 1980s this station was remarkably little altered, but since 1987 it has been quite unrecognisable to one who knew it previously, as everything apart from the actual platforms has changed.

The 1884 station building, of timber construction and on the up platform, was given a crust of pebble-dash on the road-approach side in late Southern or early BR days, presumably in an effort to make it look more modern. This was not perhaps the best idea, for when many years later some of the cement began to fall off the timber corner-posts, they could be seen to be quite rotten. On both platforms there were generous canopies, with decorative valancing, which on the up platform was later trimmed - presumably to give clearance to high-roofed carriages when they were introduced in 1907. The station building was demolished in January 1987, and for a few months temporary waiting rooms in the shape of two electric trailer coaches in the up bay were used. The

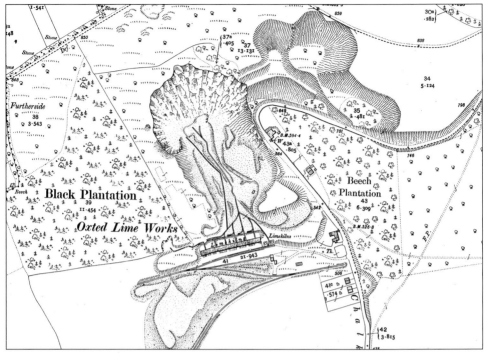

Oxted lime works.

Reproduced from the 25″, 1912 Ordnance Survey Map

A Sentinel shunting locomotive at Oxted lime works in 1933.

L.T. Catchpole

Oxted lime works line, note the engine shed at the junction with the main line.
Reproduced from the 25", 1933 Ordnance Survey Map

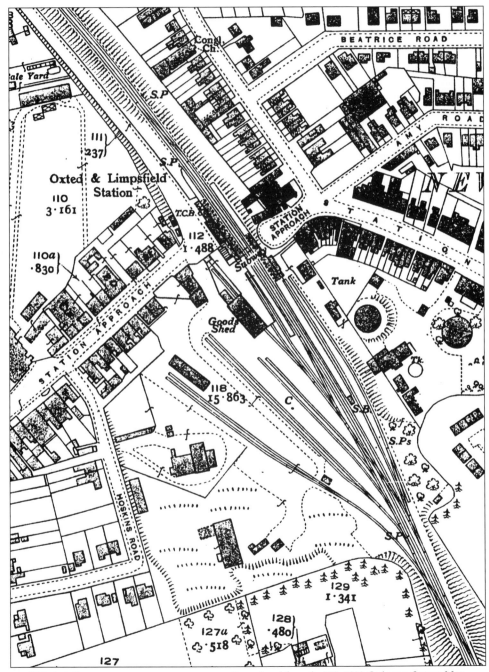

Oxted station.   *Reproduced from the 25", 1933 Ordnance Survey Map*

Two postcard views along the platforms at Oxted station. *(Both) John Alsop Collection*

View of Oxted station looking south from the down platform, with the station staff lined up for their photograph. The nameboard is another one provided by the LBSCR.   *Lens of Sutton*

The bookstall, Oxted station.   *John Alsop Collection*

new building, in brick with deep wooden eaves in the same style as that at Sanderstead, was ready for use in September 1987. Other noteworthy buildings were the large brick-built goods shed (demolished October 1988), the station master's house, the ganger's cottage and, between them, a water tank atop a brick-built tower.

The cottages had been built by the contractor, Joseph Firbank, to serve as his offices and foreman's residence. The larger building contained six rooms and became the station master's house in 1885. The smaller was a quaint single-storey building containing four rooms with a felt roof later replaced by pantiles, and became the district ganger's residence. Both buildings were removed at the time of the station reconstruction; the water tank, upon which was mounted an air-raid siren which latterly continued in use as a fire alarm for the Oxted fire brigade, disappeared soon after the end of steam working.

In 1889 the down platform was lengthened and a new siding leading to a bay was installed; the siding, which was 179 yards long, was inspected by Major-General Hutchinson for the Board of Trade on 18th October, 1889. The water crane needed to be moved to the down end of the extended platform.

Shortly after the station opened a gas works was erected east of the line by the Oxted & Limpsfield Gas Co., who wanted a siding built so that coal could be brought in. However, it was not until 1892 that the gasworks siding was installed, connecting with the down bay road, and it was inspected by Major-General Hutchinson in April of that year.

In October 1896 several alterations were made to the track layout: the south crossover leading to the up sidings was taken out and replaced by a new crossover immediately south of the old one, and in addition two more goods yard sidings were laid. An existing crossover north of the new one was converted to a double slip to give additional access to the same sidings.

There appears never to have been a run-round for the downside bay road. Push-and-pull trains terminating at the up platform generally ran past the up starting signal, reversed on the north crossover, ran through the down platform and reversed into the bay, though trains sometimes propelled direct from the up platform over the south crossover and into the bay. In about 1963 the platforms were lengthened at the London end and the facing points giving entry to the up-side bay were taken out. Freight services were withdrawn on 6th January, 1969, and the extensive coal and delivery sidings were removed apart from one used to stable trains awaiting their times, or to berth defective trains. The former gasworks siding, also occasionally used to stable a train, was lifted in May 1986 ; during the last years of steam operation the locomotive waiting to take on the rear portion of the 6.10 pm from Victoria always stood in this siding.

The line next crosses another iron viaduct on brick piers and almost immediately plunges into Limpsfield tunnel (550 yards), such a sudden change in levels is remarkable in south-east England. Hurst Green station (21¼ miles) was opened on 12th June, 1961, to replace Hurst Green Halt, formerly a wooden structure on the south side of the road opened on 1st June, 1907. Hurst Green station is absolutely typical of its period, when the Southern Railway influence was still strong: acres of concrete (the platforms can hold 12 coaches) and, when

Oxted Station. L. B. & S. C. Rly.

Down train at Oxted. The unidentified locomotive is bearing a strange headcode, being the one for Three Bridges and Tunbridge Wells during the 1910-17 period. In the up bay is a cattle wagon, well lime-washed; on the up platform a wheelbarrow, and on both platforms are milk churns.

South end of Oxted station showing the sidings and connection to the up line c.1910. A 'balloon' trailer appears to leaving from the down bay platform, propelled by a 'Terrier'.

new, the clean-lined buildings (in brick) were tricked out with plenty of green panels and the platform lights had SR hexagonal shades. BR fully had the intention of dividing down trains and joining up trains here, and staff rooms were provided, but the scheme was never implemented. Oxted remained the place for terminating, joining and dividing trains.

There is no trace of Hurst Green Halt, whose platforms (later replaced by concrete ones) had direct access from the road bridge by means of steep steps. Hurst Green Junction, where the branch to Edenbridge Town and Tunbridge Wells diverges to the left, is passed and the line continues on a falling gradient of 1 in 100 past Crowhurst Junction North, with the spur to the Tonbridge line diverging left. This was built with the CO&EG line and used by South Eastern trains. The last scheduled train, a morning up, should have run on 10th June, 1955, but because of a drivers' strike the likelihood is that the train ran for the last time on Friday, 27th May. After this, the spur was heavily used on several occasions when Sevenoaks tunnel was under repair and weekend trains from Hastings to London travelled either via Crowhurst or Redhill. The spur fell into disuse in January 1965 and by 1970 the points had been removed at both the North and South junctions, the rest of the track being lifted a year or two later. From time to time there have been demands for an interchange station here, with platforms on both the South Eastern and East Grinstead lines, but road access would be difficult. Even back in 1884 a station was proposed, and the landowner (Henry Kelsey) was prepared to donate land required for a station and its approaches.

As the CO&EG line passes beneath the SER Redhill-Tonbridge line there is a noticeable dip and the gradient changes to 1 in 200 climbing until milepost 24, where there is another 'summit' in a deep cutting, after which the grade is falling again almost as far as Lingfield. At milepost 24½ is the site of the private siding for the Sussex Brick & Estates Company, controlled from Lingfield Intermediate signal cabin until August 1958, and by a ground frame subsequently. In 1930 about six wagons daily were being dealt with, conveying coal inwards for firing the kilns and bricks outwards. The coal wagons ran down to Lingfield on the pick-up goods and were shunted into the brickworks on the afternoon up goods, loaded wagons of bricks being removed at the same time. Later the bricks went by road, and in the late 1960s when the works changed from coal to oil fuel the siding fell out of use. Production of bricks ceased in 1980 and later one of the two tall chimneys was demolished, but the place remained as a store for bricks.

The line has been straight for 2¾ miles (the longest straight section on the Oxted line) but on the approach to Lingfield there is a reverse curve. It is fortunate that the line here is on a low embankment, for the Eden brook overflows at least twice every year and the fields hereabouts are regularly flooded. This never bothers the trains and, after passing over a level crossing (once provided with a gateman who lived in the adjacent railway cottage) for the private road leading to Park Farm, we enter Lingfield station (26¼ miles).

Most of the sidings were on the up side, and they were brought into use in July 1884, some four months after the station opened. Included were a dock road and a crossover at the London end of the platforms. A further crossover at

Hurst Green station under construction in 1960, showing the immensely long concrete up platform half completed. *Lens of Sutton*

Hurst Green station up-side station building in the 1960s; the station was opened on 12th June, 1961. *Lens of Sutton*

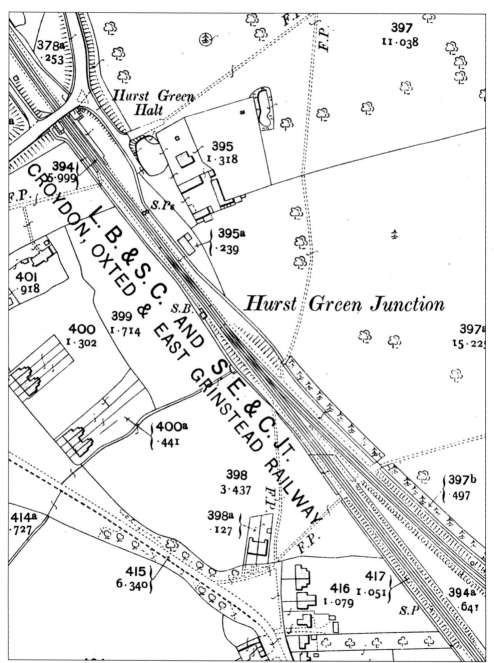

Hurst Green Halt and Hurst Green Junction.

Reproduced from the 25", 1912 Ordnance Survey Map

Hurst Green Halt, probably when new in 1907; 'Terrier' No. 677 with a 'balloon' auto trailer is working a Tunbridge Wells to Oxted via Edenbridge service.

A view of Hurst Green Halt looking north, with a rail motor in the down platform.

John Alsop Collection

Hurst Green Junction signal cabin - another LBSC example. On 31st January, 1953, it was passed by the 9.56 am Tunbridge Wells West to Oxted push-and-pull train, headed by class 'H' 0-4-4 tank engine No. 31517, working Tunbridge Wells duty No. 669.

D. Cullum

the down end was installed seven years later, but it was in 1894, four years after the opening of Lingfield Park racecourse, that the station was extensively altered.

The down platform was widened to 24 ft and effectively converted into an island by laying a bay road with connection from the down line at the down end; additionally a 600 ft siding was laid next to it. There was not at first a direct entry to this new platform from the London end of the station, so that any trains using it had to pass through the station and set back into the bay. The up platform was lengthened at the south end, and a new terminal island platform, intended to be used for up race specials, was built between the up running line and the goods yard. There was no direct connection between the down running line and this new platform so trains using it had first to be shunted there. An existing siding connecting with the up line had to be realigned and new connections laid, and finally, to cater for the racegoers, an additional footbridge with extra-wide stairways was installed at the south end of the station.

These alterations were inspected and brought into use in May 1894. Later that year the down bay road was extended northwards to make connection with the down line so that trains from London could enter the new platform direct. Major-General C.S. Hutchinson made his inspection in November 1894. More sidings were laid in 1898.

Crowhurst Junction, where the Oxted line passes under the Redhill-Tonbridge line.

Reproduced from the 25", 1912 Ordnance Survey Map

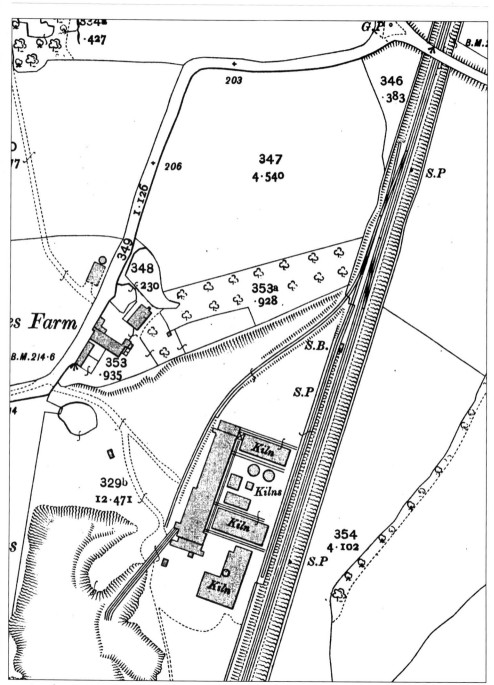

Crowhurst brickworks.   *Reproduced from the 25", 1912 Ordnance Survey Map*

Down end of Lingfield station in the early 1900s, after the conversion of the down platform into an island in 1894. There is an occupation crossing immediately south of the platforms.

The up side station building at Lingfield: 'Brighton' domestic architecture at its best. 19th May, 1961.   *D. Cullum.*

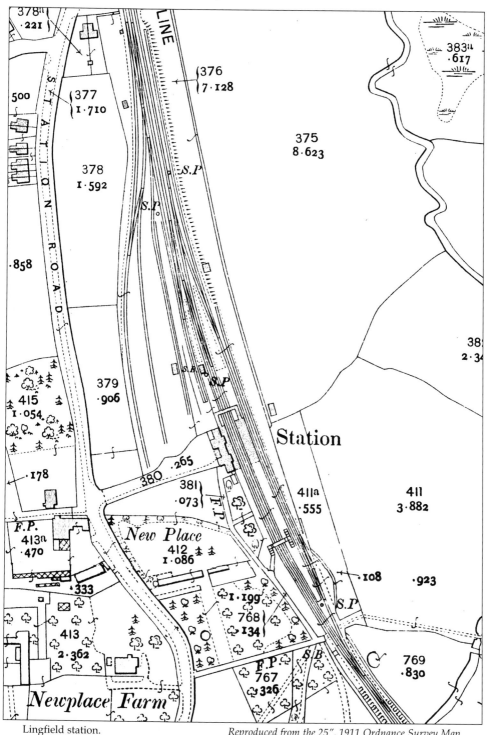

Lingfield station.

Reproduced from the 25", 1911 Ordnance Survey Map

The south footbridge at Lingfield station, erected in 1894 for race traffic, dismantled in April 1982 and transferred to Sheffield Park station, Bluebell Railway. Work had begun on dismantling by 16th April, 1982.   *Author*

Class '4' 4-6-0 No. 75069 of Stewarts Lane enters Lingfield on 19th May, 1961, with the 1.47 pm Tunbridge Wells to Victoria, a regular working for one of these engines. Stock comprises three-corridor set No. 544 and Bulleid four-corridor set No. 90, which worked as far as East Croydon where it formed the 3.44 pm down. The 'covered way' on the right led to the racecourse.   *D. Cullum*

Lingfield station was featured in the *Southern Railway Magazine* in July 1938 when it was stated that there were two hunting stables in the vicinity and that there was much traffic in foals and brood mares to and from Newmarket. Shawlands Cattle Farm handed over a good deal of traffic, and a photograph showed two lines of cattle vans and horse boxes on each side of the loading platform that had been built in 1894. Race traffic was of great importance for many years, with specials not only from London but also from Brighton. They declined in the 1960s, and in the 1970s race traffic was carried mainly in scheduled trains. There was a separate exit at the south end of the up platform, manned on race days, leading to a covered way along which the punters walked to and from the racecourse. In the 1980s the roof was removed and on 25th April, 1982, the south footbridge - which had been disused and boarded across for four years - was taken down and transported to the Bluebell Railway for re-erection at Sheffield Park station.

Goods traffic at Lingfield ceased on 5th August, 1968, except for banana traffic. In 1958, Geest had set up a ripening shed by the sidings at the London end, up side, and a daily train of refrigerated vans carried the traffic until 1st October, 1971, when road transport was used instead. The sidings were removed after 1974, as was the track on the east side of the down platform and the canopy on that platform; fortunately the handsome brick station building on the up platform remained, and it is now 'listed'. The south crossover was lifted in December 1980 but the north crossover was left in place as Lingfield is sometimes used as a terminus when engineering works cause the closure of the line southwards.

Immediately on leaving Lingfield the train has some serious climbing to do: the grade is 1 in 70, which is maintained with only short respite to St Margaret's Junction. Dormans (27¾ miles) serves both Dormans Park and the village of Dormans Land quite adequately. Also served are the Homes of St Barnabas (built between 1900 and 1910), a retreat for retired clergymen located just west of the station.

The station building is 'detached' from the down platform, connected to it by a staircase (renewed in October 1980) and level with the road that crosses the railway here. A ramp leads down to the up platform. Canopies were removed from both platforms in the 1970s. There were sidings on both up and down sides, the up siding being used for coal deliveries to the Homes of St Barnabas, but both disappeared many years ago. The station building has a family likeness to that of Lingfield, but as the station is lightly used the booking office is closed for most of the day. As the road is rather narrow here, a separate concrete bridge for pedestrians was erected alongside the road bridge and completed by May 1965.

The line soon enters a deep cutting - which was an arboreal splendour until 1987 - and passes the site of an overbridge that was blown up in July 1977. Then the site of Dormans Park siding is passed. This was on the up side at the only possible place, where the line is at ground level after leaving the cutting and before going on to the embankment that precedes Cook's Pond viaduct, and was only 120 yards in length. It was laid in 1887 for the Bellagio Estate Company, which was developing the area later known as Dormans Park. There

A view of the station building at Dormans, and Blackberry Lane. Even today the station is quite isolated.

Dormans station on 19th May, 1961, still with its footbridge, which was later replaced by a public bridge nearer to the road bridge.   *D. Cullum*

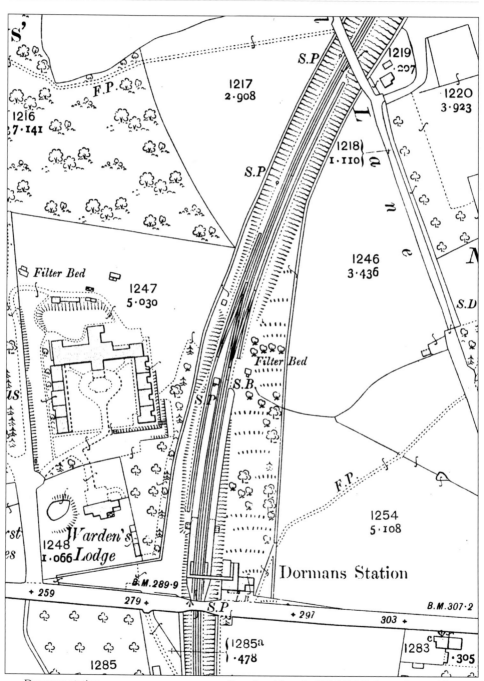

Dormans station.

Reproduced from the 25", 1912 Ordnance Survey Map

3D unit No. 1309 working a London Bridge to East Grinstead service enters Hurst Green. Note the 'low-tech' wooden destination board held in its wall-bracket. 30th November, 1981.

Author

Cook's Pond viaduct from the west side in 1890. Each of the five spans is 125 ft long and the height to rail level is 65 ft.   *F.Frith & Co.*

was a four-lever ground frame controlled by Annett's Key from Dormans signal cabin. The Bellagio Estate Co. failed in 1893 and two years later what had been the club-house was altered into the Dormans Park Hotel. The siding remained in use for coal delivery, approximately two wagons per week being dealt with in 1930. The hotel was closed to the public in 1939.

The line levels out to cross Cook's Pond viaduct - the most splendid of the three iron viaducts with brick piers, of which this example has six. The pond was drained to allow construction of the bridge and was still dry in 1885; as there were many hop gardens in the vicinity a contemporary writer assumed that the land over which the viaduct passed would be brought under cultivation, but by 1890 the pond had filled again and has so remained. It is a superb location, and the views from the viaduct are very fine.

The gradient resumes at 1 in 70, and at an overbridge between mileposts 29 and 29¼ the line crosses the boundary into Sussex. At milepost 29½ is St Margaret's Junction, and the gradient eases to 1 in 132. The double-line loop to the High Level platforms at East Grinstead diverged right until 1st January, 1967, and the 'main line' continues into the Low Level station, now used by all trains, although between 1959 and 1962 only three down trains per day were scheduled to take this route, all others using the loop into the High Level. The junction was named after a nearby Anglican convent; now put to other uses, the buildings and the chapel tower are visible on the east side of the line.

The platforms of the Low Level station (30 miles from London Bridge) are all that remain now, but East Grinstead once had a very substantial station, the third to be built. The first was a terminus for the trains from Three Bridges opened in 1855, later the site of the top goods yard; the old station house, in sandstone, still exists although much altered structurally. In 1866 the station was resited further east, by London Road, for the extension of the Three Bridges line to Tunbridge Wells, and remained open until 1883. The third station was the combined low- and high-level one - 'a somewhat remarkable two-decker station', as described by J. Francis in the *Railway Magazine* in 1914 - built for the opening of the Lewes & East Grinstead Railway in 1882 and in anticipation of the Croydon, Oxted & East Grinstead Railway. The station was fully opened on 15th October, 1883, only temporary arrangements having been in force since August 1882, and the 1866 station closed on the same date. The main station building was in the architectural style of others on the Lewes & East Grinstead; but Lingfield and Dormans, being built later, were in a new style which was followed in the stations on the line from Hurst Green Junction to Ashurst Junction.

The upper storey of the station building was almost certainly timbered with plaster infill, upon which were impressed flower patterns. Later this was all covered with hung tiles. There was a separate refreshment room with a lantern roof. The High Level comprised two island platforms with the tracks arranged down, up, down, up - not the best layout for interchange of passengers. The buildings here were timber and the platforms were timber-planked where they passed over the tracks below. Western and eastern staircases connected all the platforms, and there was a refreshment bar on each of the island platforms. In the 1880s a noted feature of the station was its ornate flower displays seen to by the station master, George Mitchell.

East Grinstead station.

Reproduced from the 25", 1910 Ordnance Survey Map

EAST GRINSTEAD
SIMPLIFIED LAYOUT

East Grinstead station, viewed from the north and showing the High Level (line to Tunbridge Wells to left and that to Three Bridges to right) and the Low Level. 27th May, 1955. *D. Cullum*

The main station building at East Grinstead Low Level, together with a fair complement of staff and idlers. *A. Harding, East Grinstead*

In 1891 an overbridge connecting the Low Level platforms was constructed and the western staircase to the High Level platforms fell out of use; from 1958 the footbridge was no longer required and was removed soon afterwards.

In addition to the connection given by the St Margaret's loop there was a single-track spur leading from a point south of the station to the sidings occupying the site of the 1855 station, and trains were shunted from Low Level to High Level by way of this spur, but no scheduled trains ever used it. Since there was a shorter route from Lewes to Groombridge via Uckfield there would have been no need for a through running line at this point.

The Lewes & East Grinstead was closed in June 1955 (last train ran on 28th May), re-opened on 7th August, 1956, and closed again on 17th March, 1958. After this only a few trains used the Low Level down platform, and none at all departed from the up. The Three Bridges to Ashurst Junction line was closed on 2nd January, 1967, and the High Level fell out of use. The up platform at Low Level was reinstated, certain trains departing there from during busy times, whilst the down platform could be used for both arrivals and departures.

The 1882 station building was demolished in November 1971 and an unremarkable single-storey prefabricated structure was put in its place in 1972. Two concrete footbridges were built: one in 1970 connecting the platforms and one in 1972 providing access to and from the high-level car park which was built on land to the west side of the High Level station, of which there is no trace. Contractors for demolition and reconstruction were J. Longley of Crawley, a firm with much experience of building stations. A Californian restaurant owner, Robert Freeman, purchased several fittings from the old station, including 18 cast-iron pillars, 40 ft of valancing, 11 gas lamps, eight nameboards, 18 cast-iron brackets and the coloured glass from the fanlight over the down-side waiting-room door.

Most of the sidings in the Low Level goods yard remained for many years after the withdrawal of freight services (10th April, 1967), being used variously for berthing corridor set trains or ballast wagons when required. However, all were removed in 1987 and, following track alterations, a single siding leading off the running roads south of the station is all that remains for berthing an electric train. North of the station, in conjunction with platform lengthening, the single crossover was removed and the two tracks dwindle to one and then open out to two again: a cheap way of allowing trains to arrive and depart from either platform without having both a facing and a trailing crossover.

Further changes to East Grinstead station are likely, for the Bluebell Railway hopes to build an interchange station south of the BR one by the year 2006 for its trains and, as a token of good faith, erected a board in 1987 containing the words 'Site for future Bluebell Railway station'.

Chapter Four

Through the Years on the Oxted Line

The line's first 20 years showed little change, either in the trains or the district served. The number of trains was increased, but despite complaints about the inadequacy of the service it actually was sufficient for an area that had no towns between Croydon and East Grinstead. Another source of complaint was unpunctuality; since the schedules were so slow there really seemed no excuse for late running. In 1895 the 8.45 am from East Grinstead was due in London at 10.07, but rarely arrived till a few minutes before the 9.18 up, which waited 13 minutes at Oxted and was due at 10.32. Some trains were slower than in 1884.

All the stations were more-or-less badly sited and it was only in later years that the villages came up to meet the stations; this has not yet happened at Woldingham or Dormans, which to this day sit in splendid isolation. From Croydon to Upper Warlingham there is mostly suburban sprawl, much of it created in the 1930s until checked by the war.

Oxted is the place that has seen the greatest change, whilst still retaining its own identity. Until the railway came, Oxted was chiefly an agricultural place. It was 'Acstede' in the 11th century, 'Ocstede' in the 13th century and 'Oxtede' in the 15th, the name meaning 'place of oaks'. Population in 1876 was nearly 1,200 and by 1891 it had risen to 1,500. In *Handbook to the environs of London* (1876), James Thorne stated that in the High Street there were 'some tolerable shops, and many poor and dirty cottages'. The oldest house was the Bell Inn (16th century), and among the 'three or four public houses' was the George Inn (18th century). The church, easily visible from the railway, was a mixture of styles, with a squat Norman tower and several later additions; it was renovated and re-roofed in 1877.

An 1892 guide book was still dismissing Oxted as 'a mere hamlet, with a railway station', although nearby Limpsfield was distinguished by a good church, which had been restored in 1872. The new roads leading to Oxted station were made first - Station Road West and Station Road East - and by 1896 some shops had been built on the south side of Station Road East and several houses on both sides of the road north of the station. Between the station and Hoskins Road there was a large sandpit worked by Hall & Co. The part of Oxted around the station was generally known as New Oxted, and for years had something of the character of a large village or small town - no one was quite sure. The original village, half a mile west of the station, became Old Oxted and was quite definitely a village. Between the station and the old village a new hotel, the Hoskins Arms, was built during 1886/7, its proprietor being Charles Hoskins Master. By the end of 1886 the Oxted & Limpsfield Gas Co. had erected its gas works and it is recorded that there were now five lamps in the village instead of only two!

Black's *Guide to the County of Surrey* (4th ed. 1892) reveals some of the places of interest a railway traveller might have investigated, although it is lukewarm about other places and much of the scenery. Sanderstead ('Sandy Place'), which had a 15th-century church, also boasted a house with Bradshaw connections: not the Railway Guide man, but 'Bradshaw the regicide'. Riddlesdown (which had no station) was then 'a favourite resort with tired Londoners', and the Rose & Crown, at the junction of the road from the top of the Down with the Caterham-Croydon road, was recommended. Marden Park was not as extensive in 1892 as it had been, but was still over 700 acres, with 'long drawn avenues and noble timber'. Woldingham church was briefly dismissed as 'a modern building of no interest'. Warlingham did rather better with its small flintstone church 'standing in a lonesome meadow, and sheltered by three lofty yews'.

Much of the countryside between Hurst Green Junction and East Grinstead was given over to hop-growing. The ancient church at Crowhurst, which is visible from the train about half a mile west of the railway, was singled out for mention, as was its huge yew tree. The finest building visible from Lingfield station was the 17th century New Place, a sandstone house; and the church, situated in the village proper, was considered worthy of extended mention, with its tombs and brasses to Sir Reginald Cobham. But the countryside hereabouts was 'rather devoid of interest, being but slightly undulated'.

That was also the opinion held by W.R. Pepper, who in his *History and guide to East Grinstead and its environs* was somewhat disparaging about Dormans Land in 1885:

> Once more resuming our travels by rail [from Lingfield], we pass more hops, glide through more cuttings, and after a short ride reach Dormans . . . The village itself is evidently of modern date and has nothing in particular calling for notice . . .
>
> Another short trip by rail brings us to the town of East Grinstead. There is nothing to particularise in the journey, except that we pass over the finest iron-constructed viaduct on the line, which is scarcely noticeable from our carriage . . . We get plenty of hop gardens on our route . . . Passing under a line of rails that runs between Tunbridge Wells and Three Bridges, we enter the Low Level Station, and here again is another marked improvement in the building of the stations.

Grinstead, founded by Gilbert d'Aquila, Lord of Pevensey, in the 13th century, had been laid out as a market town with a wide High Street; 'East' was later added to avoid confusion with a village of the same name in West Sussex, this becoming West Grinstead. 'Greenstede' as a name had been in use in the 11th century, however, and means 'pasture clearing'. Notable buildings are the 17th century Sackville College (an almshouse) and the late 18th/early 19th century parish church, whose tower is visible for miles. Until the 1880s the town comprised the High Street and little else, but the coming of the direct railway encouraged expansion and London Road became built-up with several shops and businesses.

In the 18th century communication between the town and London was by horse-drawn coach. James Batchelar, of the Dorset Arms, ran a service between Brighton, Lewes, East Grinstead and London from May 1756, the fare from East Grinstead to London being six shillings. The journey took all day, the southbound trips being on Mondays, Wednesdays and Fridays and the northbound journeys on Tuesdays, Thursdays and Saturdays. In June 1762 a rival, J. Tubb, started a new 'flying machine' service from Charing Cross to Brighton via East Grinstead with an altogether superior conveyance, and within a few years he had bought out the long-established Batchelar. By 1815 two coaches daily served East Grinstead, one from London terminating there and the other running through between the Borough and Brighton. From London to East Grinstead took five hours, with another five hours from there to Brighton.

A local daily service was operated between East Grinstead Dorset Arms and Godstone station on the recently opened SER main line from 5th October, 1842, and was made twice daily from 16th May, 1849. Also between 1849 and 1855 a coach ran between East Grinstead and Three Bridges on the Brighton main line. After the opening of the Three Bridges-East Grinstead railway there was no requirement for coach services, which were not only very slow but extremely expensive.

From 25th March, 1906, George Frederick Stone and Harold Hewitt Nutt, co-partners and cab proprietors, had the exclusive right to ply for hire at East Grinstead station forecourt, for which privilege the Brighton charged them a quarterly rent of £2 10s. Nutt Bros, as the business later became, had premises at the bottom of Station Road, just north of the bridge where the High Level station crossed the road; they ran livery stables, horse cabs, broughams and other carriages, and from 1914 began using motor cars, which could be hired, and these replaced horse-drawn vehicles within a few years. Their regular advertisement in the *ABC Railway Guide* read: 'Taxi Cabs can be hired to meet any train at this station by telegram or telephone No. 12 to Nutt, Station Road, East Grinstead'. Upon the death of Harold Nutt in 1948 his son Kenneth took over the business, running it as 'Nutt's Garage' until 1966.

In the 1880s East Grinstead's population was about 5,500 and during the next decade it increased to just under 6,000. Fred Banister, the LBSCR's Engineer, on a visit to East Grinstead in March 1895 said that his company could not be expected to spend a great deal of money for the benefit of what was only a small town, and to run fast trains to London from there was impossible. The company had to think of its 62,000 shareholders and to improve services only at places where there was likely to be a good return.

The local worthies were duly incensed, and in June 1895 held a meeting about ways to secure a better train service. At this time there were eight trains each way via Oxted, and nine each way via Three Bridges. It seems that passenger traffic was 10 times what it was in 1887, but the service had not been increased to any great extent. To put the Brighton's nose out of joint a suggestion was made that goods be sent by the South Eastern, and moreover that railway could be petitioned to run its trains from Crowhurst Junction to East Grinstead. But it never did.

W.V.K. Stenning, who owned a timber yard adjacent to East Grinstead station, said that when the shorter route to London had opened he had refused to pay charges for his goods to be carried based on the distance via Three Bridges, and had accordingly had them reduced. Stenning thought it a disgrace that the 30 mile journey could not be accomplished in less than 1¼ hours. A special train for the Prince of Wales had taken only 40 minutes and, while Stenning didn't expect to receive quite such consideration, he did think a morning train could cover the distance in 45 or 50 minutes. During one week some of the best trains were taken off three days out of the six and passengers had been turned out at all sorts of stations.

Things had not changed a great deal 90 years later!

The Brighton merely shrugged off the threats of East Grinstead to boycott its trains, and continued providing the same service until 1907, when at last improvements were made. What spurred the LBSCR to action was the threat of the motorbus, which had begun to ply some of the roads of Surrey and Sussex, and was beginning to make inroads on the railway's receipts, 1907 being a bad year.

So, as the buses were 'road motors', the railway's response was to invent 'rail motors'. Originally the steam engine and the carriage were an integral unit but, as this was not very successful, the Brighton next built single carriages, open saloons with swing-over seat-backs and a driving position at one end, these being coupled to ordinary 'A1X' 'Terrier' locomotives, fitted for push-and-pull or 'auto' working. These trains entered service on 1st June, 1907, working local all-stations services additional to the normal trains and serving unstaffed 'halts' at Hurst Green and Monks Lane (near Edenbridge) which were opened the same day. Platforms of these halts were only 100 feet long and seven feet wide, and as built did not even boast waiting shelters.

The auto-trains were much cheaper to operate than conventional trains, so at last the service could be improved at little extra cost, the improved service itself attracting extra custom. The new cars had exceptionally high elliptical roofs which gave rise to the nickname 'Balloons'. Some were allocated to Tunbridge Wells and class 'A1' Nos. 667 and 682, plus 'A1X' Nos. 673 and 677, were based there to work them. Originally the motor gear was mechanically operated, but from 1912 a more efficient compressed-air system was used, and this was adopted as standard by the Southern Railway for all its push-and-pull trains.

From about 1914 the auto-trains became two-coach and several more new vehicles were built which reverted to the old arc-roof profile. Later still, when more push-and-pull trains were required, they were rebuilt from old carriages. The 'Terriers' were soon replaced by motor-fitted 'D1' 0-4-2 tank locomotives.

Steam railcars did, however, work on the Woodside & South Croydon Joint line. Since opening, this line had been worked on a somewhat odd principle: in the even years, commencing 1st July, the SER was responsible for the working, and in the odd years, from 1st July, it was the LBSCR's turn to work all the trains. This system continued, so that in 1912, for example, Oxted line passengers would have seen a South Eastern & Chatham railcar at Selsdon Road, and in summer 1913 an LBSCR one.

From June 1907 the status of the Oxted line was enhanced by the introduction of a fast train, complete with Pullman car, between Crowborough and London Bridge via Groombridge. The up train left Crowborough at 8.45 am and was booked to take 80 minutes on the journey; the down train left London at 4.50 pm. There were through carriages to and from Tunbridge Wells. E.A. Langridge in 1965 recalled that the 4.50 was formed of the latest elliptical-roofed stock, roofboarded 'The Crowborough Express'. The Pullman, however, ceased to run after 1908.

On 20th May, 1910, the funeral of King Edward VII was held. The LBSCR ran a Sunday service, but there was a special train at 6.00 am from Tunbridge Wells to Victoria via Edenbridge Town, returning at 4.10 pm; ordinary fares were charged.

In 1914 the Withyham spur (between Ashurst Junction and Birchden Junction near Eridge, *see map page 12*), which although built in 1888 had never been opened, was relaid with double track and opened on 7th June, 1914. This improvement was made because of the growing population of Crowborough and Jarvis Brook, and direct trains between London and Uckfield, Lewes, Heathfield and Eastbourne, no longer reversing at Groombridge, began to run. Eridge became an important point for attaching and detaching through portions, as did Ashurst, where Tunbridge Wells portions were shed in the down direction or attached in the up. For this a new up refuge siding for passenger trains had to be laid at the end of Ashurst station.

Oxted was now served by 49 down and 43 up trains every day, Monday to Friday. Of these 67 were LBSCR and 25 were provided by the SECR - 13 down and 12 up. Three SECR trains each way ran via the Woodside & South Croydon, the others going via East Croydon. Four LBSCR trains did not call at Oxted: the 3.45 and 6.03 pm from Victoria and the 8.02 and 9.55 am from Eastbourne.

During World War I troop trains ran to Crowborough Camp, but little else disturbed the line until January 1917, when services were severely reduced, the SECR service discontinued, and fares were increased by 50 per cent. The Woodside & South Croydon was closed, but a few Oxted line trains continued to call at Selsdon Road in spite of this. On the night of 15th June, 1917, about 10 feet of the roof of Oxted tunnel collapsed, a further 50 feet bulging dangerously, and the tunnel had to be closed for two weeks or more for repairs. The only other wartime incident recorded was on 22nd April, 1918, when an aeroplane crashed on the line between Sanderstead and Upper Warlingham, blocking the line for half an hour. The machine was reduced to ashes and the airman burned to death.

Both the Brighton and the SECR were in a pretty poor state after the war, and a prolonged coal strike in 1921 did not help matters; an emergency train service had to be introduced which was worse than that provided in 1917. And for most of 1921 Oxted tunnel was closed (except during business hours) for heavy repairs.

In 1923 the railways of Britain were compulsorily 'grouped' under the Railways Act of 1921, and the LBSCR and the SECR found themselves in the Southern group. The Croydon & Oxted Joint was joint no longer, but train services continued to run as in pre-Grouping days, except that for a while one Tunbridge Wells train each way was extended to and from Cannon Street. The main outward change was in the livery of the trains, which were painted sage green with yellow lettering. This was more cheerful than the dark brown of the LBSCR locomotives and carriages, and the dark grey locomotives and brown carriages of the SECR. The old liveries did not entirely disappear until 1929.

Right from the start the Southern stood for 'bigger and better' housing estates, and it co-operated with the builders by adding new stations for the resulting commuters. Every line that was electrified was soon accompanied by

East Grinstead station foreman Joseph Hollingsworth by the steps of the North signal cabin about 1921.   *C.E.K. Nutt*

East Grinstead ticket collector Jock Goyle poses on the down platform of the Low Level station just under the bridge that carried the High Level lines. *C.E.K. Nutt*

Afternoon London Bridge to Tunbridge Wells train entering Oxted with ex-SER 'B1' 4-4-0 No. 1446 displaying a New Cross Gate duty number and a seven-coach 'long set' of ex-SECR bogies. Class 'D1' 0-4-2 tank No. 2224 waits in the down bay with a motor train that will connect with the train from London.

Lens of Sutton

rows of 'semis' and, although the Oxted line was not electrified until many years later, it too had houses built beside it from Sanderstead to Upper Warlingham, and on Riddlesdown after a station had been opened there in 1927. Houses were built at Oxted also, especially north of the station as far as the limeworks. The village began to look like a detached part of suburbia. In Station Road West, however, some of Oxted's finest buildings were erected around 1930, designed by members of the Williams family: Mock Tudor, but of the highest quality, with timber framing that looked as though it actually supported the structure, the timber itself being exquisitely carved. Most notable in this style was the Plaza Cinema (still functioning in 2002). The bank in Station Road East (A. Bentley Williams) was also of a high architectural standard. The population of Oxted at this time numbered about 3,800.

In 1925 a light electric railway, to run from Orpington to Sanderstead and to be worked as part of the Southern Electric system, was independently promoted. One of the promoters was Lt-Col H.F. Stephens of rural light railway fame. The route would have been 'V'-shaped, the mileage nearly 15½, and it would have run via Biggin Hill, Tatsfield and Chelsham, with gradients up to 1 in 40. Negotiations dragged on and, although a Light Railway Order was granted in 1928, work was never started on construction owing to lack of finance. The Southern Heights Light Railway, as it was called, was for a time shown as a dotted line on the maps displayed in carriage compartments, but the powers lapsed in 1930, and the SR Board - which initially had been quite enthusiastic about the scheme - lost interest, mainly because of expected complications when pooling of receipts in the London area began in 1933 - the year the London Passenger Transport Board was set up.

Part of the Caterham Valley at Whyteleafe , where the Caterham and Oxted railways ran close together for two miles (although on different levels), had some similarities with the valleys of South Wales, where one commonly found two or even three lines sharing the same valley. But it was a feature not often found in the South-East. When the Caterham branch was electrified (25th March, 1928) the inhabitants of Whyteleafe had the choice of walking down to the valley bottom for the benefits of electric trains (quick, clean but uncomfortable) or up the hill to Upper Warlingham station for steam (slow but comfortable). Possibly the only other place where a similar choice of traction could be made - at least during the early 1960s - was Helensburgh, on the Clyde coast.

By 1930 virtually the whole of the suburban area was served by electric trains and eight years later electrification of all the ex-LBSCR main lines was complete - except for the Oxted line. It is said that certain influential gentlemen living around Woldingham liked it just the way it was, knowing that electric trains would soon be followed by floods of houses all over the Downs; and that somehow the residents prevailed upon Waterloo not to electrify; whatever the reason, the line had now assumed its role of 'odd man out' which it was to hold until 1987. The timetable changed little; no attempt was made by the Southern Railway to run a regular-interval service, although this was a *sine qua non* where electric trains were concerned. Even when the Woodside & South Croydon was re-opened with electric trains - which were projected over the Oxted line as far

Class 'D' 4-4-0 No. 1738 (built at Ashford in 1902) enters East Grinstead Low Level with the 12.03 pm Victoria to Brighton on 3rd March, 1934.

H.C. Casserley

as Sanderstead (30th September, 1935) - there was little or no change. Some Oxted trains may have connected at Sanderstead with those from Charing Cross; others did not.

Electrification of the Eastbourne main line in 1935 released a certain amount of modern corridor stock, some of which began to appear on the Oxted line. Set No. 465 or 466, reduced from eight to six coaches, worked the 12.20 pm (Saturdays) from London Bridge to Tunbridge Wells.

Use of the line for filming purposes does not seem to have been made often. In October 1935 scenes for a film entitled *Strictly Illegal* were shot at Woldingham station and near the north portal of Oxted tunnel. Maunsell corridor 3-set No. 226, hauled by a 'C2X' class 0-6-0 goods locomotive, was featured in scenes showing people clambering along the footboard of one of the third brakes. In October 1960 scenes were shot at East Grinstead for the Tony Hancock film *The Rebel*, and also (it is thought) at one of the stations on the Woodside & South Croydon.

During World War II a reduced service ran; two peak trains each way were cut out, as well as several slack-hours services, and the last down train left Victoria at 8.02 pm. There were no Services' depots on the line, and the heavy troop train traffic from the North and Midlands to the Channel ports was sent via Kensington, Clapham Junction, Redhill and Tonbridge in preference to the more steeply-graded route via Oxted and Crowhurst Junction. Some troop specials did run via Oxted, however: one such was noted on 15th July, 1944, when a 'K' class 2-6-0 locomotive worked 10 corridors (including two London & North Eastern vehicles) down through Oxted around midday.

Station nameboards were removed, making it very difficult for passengers (and possibly German spies) to identify their station in the blackout that was enforced. This blackout was the cause of many accidents, and it was not unknown for passengers to step out of their compartment on the wrong side. Canopy supports had bars of white paint sloshed over the green to render them more visible in the gloom, the chequered effect presumably being more effective than solid white.

The Southern tried very hard to revert to its former high standards after the war, and painted as many locomotives as possible in its brilliant malachite green; especially notable were the two 'J' class passenger tanks based at Tunbridge Wells from January 1946 and which appeared in green in the middle of that year. However, the Government of the day decided that the State could run the railways better than the companies could and, after Nationalisation became effective from 1st January, 1948, the main outward change for several years was that locomotives again were black and some carriages were red. The Southern's modernisation plans, announced in 1946 (which included electrification of the Oxted line), were quietly forgotten by the new masters.

For several years the Oxted line, as operated by the Southern Region of British Railways, seemed to be frozen in the style of BR's predecessors. The same trains continued running to the same old untidy timetable and serving the same unchanging stations. The Railway Executive was wedded to steam, and when the 'I3' class 4-4-2 tanks - the mainstay of the services - wore out they were replaced by new 2-6-4 tank locomotives built at Brighton to a London, Midland

& Scottish Railway design. Later, Brighton built most of the BR Standard 2-6-4 tanks, mostly for other Regions, but 13 were allocated to the Oxted line from the start. They were superb engines, very suitable for working suburban trains, and in the 1950s most Oxted trains were worked by one or other of these types. In December 1959 the LMS-designed engines were exchanged for an equivalent number of BR 2-6-4 tanks.

In 1955 BR announced its Modernisation Plan, which included the abolition of steam as soon as possible and in that year the Oxted line's timetable was at last tidied up. Although in the business hours demand for Victoria trains was growing and that for London Bridge trains was declining, BR did not respond; no more trains could be squeezed through East Croydon anyway. So the peak-hour trains were unchanged and still there were more London Bridge services than Victoria ones in the morning and evening.

Three years later, the Southern Region had every intention of replacing steam by diesel-electric trains as a temporary measure, and of electrifying the line in 1964. The objections to the steam locomotive now included its poor acceleration, a shortage of skilled firemen, and the non-availability of large lumps of coal (it was officially stated that the steam locomotive did not perform well on small coal).

Also promised were greater reliability, speed, regularity and accommodation; replacement of semaphore signals by multiple-aspect colour lights on the busiest section; station accommodation modernised and platforms lengthened and the replacement of Hurst Green Halt by a new station.

In the mid-1950s house-building in the area began to cause a rapid increase in passengers, particularly from East Grinstead, whose population had shot up from 7,900 in 1931 to 10,950 in 1951. In 1937 there were 588 season-ticket holders; 20 years later there were 7,539. They felt they were entitled to a better train service and BR agreed, although it could not work an overnight miracle. One thing that was done in 1958 was to alter the dividing point of the 6.10 pm from Victoria to Oxted instead of East Croydon, giving East Grinstead the benefit of through carriages, in place of a push-and-pull connection from Oxted.

This change in the timetable brought to an end an interesting ceremony at East Croydon. The locomotive waiting to work the rear (slow) portion of the 6.10 used to stand for a time in the siding alongside Hall's depot at the north end of the station. At about 6.15 it would move out and the station announcer would call out 'engine for Croydon, please', whereupon as the engine came down the relief road to a point beyond the road bridge at the south end a shunter came out from the inspector's office on platform 5/6, putting on a pair of leather gloves, and stepped down to the ground frame then controlling the 'post office' sidings. After the shunter had telephoned the signal cabin the points under the road bridge would be moved; he would set the trap-points, and the locomotive would move into the 'post office' loop. It then usually worked its injectors to the interest of bystanders, and the 'H' class in particular obliged with suitable noises and massive ejections of water and steam from drain-cocks. The 6.10 then arrived, the rear three coaches were detached and, in order not to delay departure the buckeye coupler on the rear coach of the front portion was left in the horizontal position instead of being dropped, and the retractable buffers were not pulled out. Thus were precious seconds saved. After the main portion of the train had moved off, the locomotive left the 'post office' loop, backed on to the waiting rear portion, which eventually got away.

During 1960 work began on constructing Hurst Green station as part of 'British Railways Modernisation'. Like some of the stations built by the LBSCR it was designed in a burst of optimism, with platforms for 12-car trains (which never materialised) and a full complement of staff. With increased housing development in the area, it soon became a busy station after opening on 12th June, 1961, and in particular it was very popular with residents wishing to go shopping in Oxted (it provided a faster, more direct and cheaper alternative to the local bus service).

Once the electric trains for the Kent Coast lines had been completed, Eastleigh carriage works could turn its attention to building the promised diesel-electric multiple units for the Oxted line. The first of these were ready by April 1962, by which time the days of steam on the last unelectrified suburban line south of London were drawing to a close. Most passengers probably were not sorry, but the enthusiasts among them could only reflect that it was nearly 35 years since the last steam train for Caterham had left London Bridge, and in comparison the Oxted line had had a good run under steam.

Erosion of the Oxted line network had begun with the closure of the Lewes-East Grinstead section in 1958, but it was in the 1960s that the greatest damage was inflicted. First to go was the Eridge to Hailsham line, whose closure was approved by the Ministry in February 1965 and effected from 14th June, 1965. A Hailsham-Eastbourne service was retained for a time. The effect was to cut off Oxted from the popular seaside resort of Eastbourne. Next came the Three Bridges-East Grinstead-Ashurst Junction line, closure being approved in February 1966 and effected from 2nd January, 1967; the main effect of this was to cut off East Grinstead from the rest of Sussex.

In December 1966 plans were announced to close all the remaining east-branch lines: Hurst Green-Tunbridge Wells West-Grove Junction and Ashurst Junction-Uckfield-Lewes. Here, however, objections to closure prevailed and the only parts that the Minister would allow to be closed were Uckfield to Lewes and Ashurst Junction to Groombridge Junction. The one-time useful Tonbridge-Brighton service was cut back to a less-useful Tonbridge-Eridge service, providing cross-platform interchange in each direction with the Oxted-Uckfield trains at Eridge, an isolated country junction station with four platforms. Ashurst Junction to Groombridge Junction was closed from 6th January, 1969, but the Uckfield to Lewes section maintained a twilight existence, first with a shuttle train, then with buses and taxis, until 5th May, 1969, when Barcombe Mills and Isfield stations were finally closed.

So, having closed the busiest section of the Hurst Green to Lewes line, BR was left with a long and straggling branch whose towns and villages were cut off from the coast and the county town of East Sussex. Edenbridge, Crowborough and Uckfield were the only places of any size on the line, and most commuters at Uckfield probably preferred to drive to the nearest main-line station with a fast service to London.

The 5.36 pm Victoria to Uckfield and East Grinstead at Oxted, with the North Downs behind. 3H unit No. 1117 is the front portion of the train on 3rd May, 1978.   *Author*

The 3.53 pm East Croydon to East Grinstead train, headed by class '33' No. 33 056, heaves its eight-coach load away from Dormans station up the 1 in 70 gradient on 15th May, 1980.

Author

The Tonbridge-Eridge service lasted a surprisingly long time. It lost money heavily and only the minimum work necessary to maintain safety was carried out until September 1982, when closure plans were announced. Despite many objections, the Ministry gave permission for closure; there were about 700 daily journeys on the line during 1984/85, but BR was anxious not to have to renew Grove Junction for the Hastings line electrification. The last passenger trains ran on Saturday, 6th July, 1985. Empty trains to and from Tunbridge Wells West fuel sidings continued until autumn, when they too were discontinued, the fuel sidings and depot were closed and Selhurst became the new fuelling point.

Meanwhile, at the northern end of the Oxted line, the connecting service between Elmers End and Sanderstead had run for the last time on 13th May, 1983; this rush-hours-only service had been very lightly used for several years, possibly because few people were aware of its existence! The trackbed was kept in being, so that any future re-opening (possibly as a light railway) could be facilitated. The formation between Elmers End and Coombe Road was indeed adapted as part of Croydon Tramlink and opened in May 2000.

A perennial problem with the demus was wheelslip on autumn leaves on the track. As the brakes were applied for a station stop the wheels would lock, slide along the rails with an ominous hissing sound and create a flat patch on the tread. On leaving the station the wheels on the motor bogie would spin madly as they lost adhesion on the slippery rails and then one would hear the damaged wheel going 'bop, bop, bop' at every revolution. Trains would then have to be withdrawn from service for reprofiling of the wheels.

This problem seems to have been unknown in steam days. The locomotives carried sand, which could be sprayed on to slippery rails to give adhesion, but demus never were equipped with sand boxes. Trees which formerly were cut back were allowed to grow, and each autumn the problem increased until at last BR was forced to take some action. In autumn 1974 de-icing unit 002 was equipped with water cannon and, in conjunction with a class '33' locomotive, made daily forays over the Oxted line spraying the line in order to clear away the leaves. This was only partially effective and slipping was still very bad in places, particularly at Woldingham. Unit 002 was employed again in autumn 1975 and 1977; unit 017 in 1976, and 004 in 1978. These were based at Selhurst depot and could be seen during October and November on rail-cleaning duties.

In the 1980s the two-car de-icing and rail-cleaning units were further altered to spray 'Sandite' instead of water. This compound was a jelly-like paste of sand which, it was hoped, would adhere to the rail rather than be blown away in the autumnal breezes. Unit 002 was used in most years, but still there were reports of trains slipping badly, damaging their wheels and motors and losing 15 or more minutes on their journeys. One train took that long to travel from Upper Warlingham to Woldingham, hardly exceeding 4 mph! In the end BR decided (possibly reluctantly) that prevention was better than cure and almost every tree on railway property was destroyed. All the passenger had to look at now was a vista of ugly stumps, but at least the slipping was not nearly so bad.

Patronage of the Oxted line throughout the 1970s remained at a satisfactory level. In October 1978 the average number of daily passengers at various stations was quoted as: 1,600 at Upper Warlingham, 600 at Woldingham, 4,200

A train conveying track panels leaves East Grinstead at 4.04 pm on Sunday 8th July, 1984.

Author

Oxted viaduct on 16th May, 1979 ; the 7.29 am East Croydon to East Grinstead train rumbles over. *Author*

at Oxted, 2,200 at Hurst Green and 920 at Lingfield. A public relations exercise was staged on 24th July, 1980, when Mr Bob Mackmurdie, the divisional manager, travelled on the 8.25 am East Grinstead to London Bridge to find out what people thought of the train service. He was filmed by TV crews. Some passengers felt he should have travelled on an earlier, more crowded train, but he explained that he had no wish to cause disruption, and so deliberately chose a train on which there were spare seats. Other passengers condemned the whole exercise as just a publicity stunt.

From time to time BR issued passengers with questionnaires headed 'What do you want from your train service?' or similar, but the questions were never couched in those terms; all the passenger could fill in was details of the actual journey he was making at the time - which may have been a completely untypical one.

The centenary of the Croydon, Oxted & East Grinstead was celebrated on Saturday 10th March, 1984, in a modest way. At East Grinstead the station was decorated with bunting loaned by the Town Council, and there were photograph displays behind the glass of the booking office, as there was no room in the hall itself. In the afternoon a TV crew arrived to do some filming, but were disappointed to find that it was not the station building itself that was 100 years old. Mr Michael Leppard, the curator of the town museum (which also had displays of railway interest) was interviewed by the TV crew, but it is believed that none of the footage was ever shown. On the Sunday, a railway thanksgiving service was held at Oxted. There was no 'official' recognition of the centenary, and BR took no part in it, but fortunately the station staff raised no objection.

3H unit No. 205012 in Network SouthEast livery unit departs Hurst Green with the 14.04 Oxted-Uckfield service on 26th June, 1993.   *P. Barnes*

So, even though there were times when it looked unlikely, the original CO&EGR did survive for 100 years - not bad for a line that the old LBSCR had paid £32,250 for the privilege of abandoning - and the long awaited electrification of the line, completed in 1987, means that its future is assured.

In recent years passengers have had to accept many changes of name and ownership of their trains. On 10th June, 1986, the Southern Region became part of Network South East, and much red paint was splashed about on stations. On 1st April, 1994, the former Central Division of the Southern Region was renamed Network South Central. When at long last privatisation came it was a French-owned company that took over from 12th April, 1996, the trains - which were repainted white and yellow - being operated by Connex South Central. This company, however, fell somewhat short of expectations and on 26th August, 2001, surrendered its franchise to Govia, who began by using the name South Central and yet another new train livery was introduced: green and grey. New trains were promised for 2004.

South Central 'VEP' No. 3916 at Woldingham on 25th January, 2003 with the 13.08 East Grinstead-Victoria service.   *P. Barnes*

Chapter Five

Train Services

LBSCR

The Croydon, Oxted & East Grinstead was initially provided with just four trains each way, all running through between London Bridge and Brighton. There were departures from London Bridge at 8.10, 11.50 am, 4.10 and 7.27 pm. Up services left East Grinstead Low Level at 8.07, 10.22 am, 2.55 and 8.55 pm. For the 30 mile journey 1 hour 13 minutes was allowed in either direction. On Sundays there were only two trains each way, also continuing through to Brighton or starting from there.

After a few months the first goods services began to run. From July 1884 the existing 7.15 am goods from Brighton to East Grinstead was extended to Oxted, returning at 2.00 pm, and a month later the stations north of Oxted were served by a goods train that left New Cross at 5.00 am and returned from Oxted at 7.15 am.

From June 1885 four additional passenger trains began running between Victoria and Oxted, reversing there. In January 1886 the first of these was extended to Lingfield to form a new service from Lingfield at 8.50 am; in the evening the 5.00 pm Victoria-Oxted was extended to Lingfield, returning at 6.20 pm.

The first regular use of the St Margaret's Loop, whereby trains from Oxted could enter the High Level station at East Grinstead and continue to Tunbridge Wells via Forest Row, was in October 1885, when new fast trains (initially first and second class only) were introduced. These were the 10.00 am Tunbridge Wells to Victoria and the 5.52 pm return. The down train was booked to arrive in East Grinstead in one hour, but it is unlikely that it was ever on time as only three minutes were allowed for the uphill journey from the stop at Lingfield to Dormans, at which it was booked to call for setting down London passengers. By 1905 the schedule had been eased to 65 minutes to allow for additional stops. Over the years the train was slowed down until it became 'all-stations' but East Grinstead's 5.50 lasted as identifiably the same train until May 1978.

Other changes in October 1885 were the withdrawal of the 10.22 am East Grinstead to London Bridge and its replacement by a later train, the 10.30 am Brighton to East Grinstead extended to London Bridge. Three months later the 1.25 pm Brighton to London Bridge was retimed to leave at 2.30 pm (East Grinstead 4.06 pm).

From June 1886 another new train running over the St Margaret's Loop was inaugurated: the 6.45 am Victoria to Tunbridge Wells. A new 8.40 am East Grinstead to Victoria was actually the 8.50 am from Lingfield extended back. This was another long-lived train; from April 1898 it was altered to start its journey at Forest Row, being cut back to East Grinstead again only when the Three Bridges to Ashurst Junction line was closed 69 years later.

Further improvements came in January 1887, when the 5.00 pm Victoria to Lingfield was extended to East Grinstead and Lewes. This was balanced by the extension of the 5.10 pm Brighton-East Grinstead through to Victoria, the 6.17

pm Lingfield to Victoria being discontinued. The 2.30 pm Brighton to London Bridge now ran only between East Grinstead and London Bridge. Now, three years after opening, there were seven trains each way between East Grinstead and London via Lingfield; quite a good service for a still-rural area. The 7.27 pm London Bridge to East Grinstead was still the last train of the day and had ceased to run through to Brighton; however, every summer season from 1887 to 1914 it was extended to Brighton and only during the winter months did it terminate at East Grinstead.

Oxted was served by 15 trains each way during 1887, the year before the opening of the line to Edenbridge Town. These included seven between East Grinstead and London and three between Victoria and Oxted only; also there were five South Eastern services, of which three ran via the Crowhurst Spur and two reversed at Oxted.

The service provided to Edenbridge, when the line there opened on 2nd January, 1888, was lavish, there being 11 trains each way, including two between Oxted and Edenbridge only. There were two goods trains each way. When the line was fully opened to Tunbridge Wells on 1st October, 1888, it provided connections with the Uckfield and Heathfield lines, Groombridge being the interchange station. Initially four fast trains each way between London and Tunbridge Wells included through carriages to or from Eastbourne, attached or detached at Groombridge. These were the 11.15 am, 1.40, 3.45 pm Victoria to Tunbridge Wells and 5.25 pm London Bridge to Tunbridge Wells; and the 8.30, 9.25, 11.10 am and 4.55 pm Tunbridge Wells to Victoria. From June 1889, however, the through carriages were withdrawn from the 1.40 pm down and 4.55 up; and from April 1892 the 8.25 up and 5.26 down ceased to convey Eastbourne portions. The other four trains continued to include through carriages between London and Eastbourne via Groombridge until 1914. The 3.45 pm was the fastest train on the line, being timed to run non-stop to Groombridge in 53 minutes. The 9.25 am up was a fairly fast 1 hr 13 min. Tunbridge Wells to Victoria calling at Groombridge to attach the coaches from Eastbourne, then non-stop to East Croydon, Clapham Junction and Grosvenor Road (where all up trains stopped for the collection of tickets).

In June 1890 East Grinstead was blessed with another train service: 10.45 am from London Bridge, returning at 12.06 pm. From East Grinstead this up train ran only 10 minutes behind the 10.35 am Brighton to Victoria (due to leave East Grinstead at 11.56 am) so was not very sensibly timed, especially as there were no further up trains for four hours. Still, there were now eight trains each way between East Grinstead and London and so it remained for several years, the only additions being various short-workings and late-night down trains that ran only on certain days. On the Edenbridge line there were, since October 1888, 13 trains each way between London and Tunbridge Wells. One of these was a fast train leaving Victoria at 5.00 pm, calling only at Upper Warlingham, Oxted and Hever (to set down first-class passengers only) before being due in Groombridge 62 minutes after leaving Victoria. East Grinstead's fastest up train, the 9.57 am Tunbridge Wells to Victoria, was allowed only 61 minutes from the North Sussex town to London. On the other hand, East Grinstead's gentry were not best pleased by the next alteration, made in July 1891, when the

5.03 pm from Victoria on arrival at Oxted shunted in order to provide an East Grinstead connection for the 5.26 pm London Bridge to Tunbridge Wells. The journey time from Victoria to East Grinstead was consequently increased to a lamentable 1½ hours, and remained so until June 1928, despite endless complaints.

The complete 'business' service during the 1890s was as follows:

Up via Edenbridge: 6.40, 7.30, 8.22 am Tunbridge Wells to Victoria, 9.08 am Tunbridge Wells to London Bridge, 9.28 am Tunbridge Wells to Victoria. *Up via Lingfield:* 6.45 am Brighton to London Bridge, 8.45 am East Grinstead to Victoria, 8.20 am Lewes to Oxted, connecting there with the 9.08 from Tunbridge Wells. *Down from Victoria:* 3.45 pm to Tunbridge Wells, 5.00 to Tunbridge Wells, 5.03 pm to Oxted and Lewes, 5.52 pm to East Grinstead and Tunbridge Wells, 5.55 pm to Tunbridge Wells. *Down from London Bridge:* 4.09 pm to East Grinstead and Brighton, 4.26 pm to Tunbridge Wells, 5.26 pm to Tunbridge Wells.

Various late-night trains included the 10.05 pm Victoria to Edenbridge, which from July 1894 ran to Edenbridge on Mondays, Wednesdays and Fridays, but to East Grinstead on Tuesdays, Thursdays and Saturdays. On Wednesdays from April 1892 a new late train left Victoria for Oxted at 11.40 pm, returning empty. Goods services were revised about 1893, the Brighton-Oxted train being replaced by a New Cross-East Grinstead goods and a separate train between Brighton and East Grinstead.

One of the most interesting trains to run on the Oxted line was a summer-only through service to the coast that began in July 1892. This was the 11.30 am from both Victoria and London Bridge (portions joined at East Croydon) to Seaford, via East Grinstead, Horsted Keynes, Haywards Heath, Lewes and Newhaven. The return was at 3.05 pm by the same route, although the up train called additionally at Oxted. The service ran every year, July to September, from 1892 to 1900; in 1901 the up train was re-routed via the main line and Redhill, the down train continuing to run via East Grinstead. This practice continued every summer until 1907 and possibly later.

A new business train from Oxted to London Bridge at 8.25 am was introduced in January 1905. It was balanced by the 7.00 pm London Bridge to Oxted, the stock being berthed there overnight.

Many new services were introduced in June 1907, being provided by third-class-only single coach 'rail motors' working on the pull-and-push principle. Some of the services had previously been summer-only, but when operated by rail motors they became all-year-round services. The initial motor service, which began on 1st June, 1907, was: 10.15 am and 12.50 pm Groombridge to Oxted, returning at 10.50 am and 1.40 pm; 3.40 and 5.40 pm Tunbridge Wells to Oxted, returning at 4.40 and 6.40 pm. Some of these connected at Oxted with London services, but others connected with nothing, being purely for local use. The motor service was revised in November 1907. Further new trains (normal stock) introduced in June 1907 were an 8.45 am from Crowborough to London Bridge via Groombridge (through carriages from Tunbridge Wells at 8.48 am), due London Bridge 10.05. The return was at 4.50 pm from London Bridge to Tunbridge Wells, the Crowborough carriages being

Class 'H1' 4-4-2 No. 41 (Kitson, 1906) on an East Grinstead to Victoria train crossing Riddlesdown viaduct about 1908.

detached at Groombridge. From October 1907 this train left Victoria at 2.37 pm on Saturdays.

The London 'business' service in 1912, 1913 and 1914 before the opening of the Ashurst spur showed some retimings and an extra train or two, but was similar to that provided in the 1890s.

Up via Edenbridge Town: 6.38, 7.20, 8.12 am Tunbridge Wells to Victoria, 8.46 am Tunbridge Wells to London Bridge (through carriages from Crowborough), 9.22 am Tunbridge Wells to Victoria (through carriages from Eastbourne and Brighton). *Up via Lingfield:* 6.35 am Brighton to London Bridge, 8.40 am Forest Row to London Bridge and Victoria, 8.15 am Lewes to London Bridge, 9.50 am Tunbridge Wells to Victoria via East Grinstead. 8.23 Oxted to London Bridge.

Down from Victoria: 3.45 pm to Tunbridge Wells (non-stop to Groombridge), 4.50 pm to Tunbridge Wells , 5.03 to Oxted and Lewes, 5.50 to Tunbridge Wells via East Grinstead, 6.03 to Tunbridge Wells. *Down from London Bridge:* 4.10 pm to Brighton via East Grinstead, 4.22 pm to Tunbridge Wells, 4.47 (not Saturdays) to Tunbridge Wells and Crowborough, 5.22 to Tunbridge Wells, 6.39 pm (not Saturdays) to East Grinstead, 7.00 pm to Oxted.

Similarities to the service still being provided in the 1960s are becoming evident.

With the opening, on 7th June, 1914, of the Ashurst spur a splendid service of through trains between London and East Sussex was put on, and the tiresome reversal of trains at Groombridge was no longer necessary. The 11.10 am Victoria to Eastbourne and 4.45 pm London Bridge to Uckfield slipped Tunbridge Wells portions at Ashurst. The 9.10 am Victoria to Uckfield and 12.25 pm London Bridge to Uckfield included Tunbridge Wells portions detached at Ashurst. The 4.50 pm Victoria to Brighton, being an individualist, detached its Tunbridge Wells carriages at Edenbridge Town, and the 6.03 pm (not Saturdays) Victoria to Uckfield slipped a Heathfield portion at Ashurst. In the other direction, the 8.16 and 10.20 am Brighton to Victoria included through carriages from Eastbourne, and at Ashurst portions from Tunbridge Wells were added. The 3.10 and 4.46 pm trains from Uckfield to Victoria also included Tunbridge Wells carriages from Ashurst.

The working at Eridge was now very complicated. The 6.52 am from Eastbourne conveyed Victoria and Tunbridge Wells coaches; the 7.05 am from Brighton conveyed London Bridge and Tunbridge Wells coaches. When both trains were at Eridge the Victoria portion of the Eastbourne train was attached to the rear of the London Bridge portion of the Brighton train and the Brighton-Tunbridge Wells portion was transferred to the Eastbourne-Tunbridge Wells portion. The combined London train got away first, followed by the combined Tunbridge Wells one.

Unfortunately these excellent services were short-lived. Because of the Great War, several trains were discontinued. From January 1916 the 4.21 pm London Bridge to Tunbridge Wells, the 6.39 pm (not Saturdays) London Bridge to East Grinstead and the 7.53 am Tunbridge Wells to London Bridge were suspended. On Sundays there were only two trains each way between Brighton, East Grinstead and London Bridge. On 1st January, 1917, the SECR service over the Oxted line was discontinued and Selsdon Road station was closed. It was re-opened and one SECR service each way reinstated on 1st March, 1919.

A Victoria to Tunbridge Wells train at Oxted; class 'D3' No. 371 of 1892, allocated to Tunbridge Wells Shed, takes water, about 1920. The bogie third brake behind the engine was rebuilt from a 6-wheel third and a 6-wheel brake van.

Gorringe

The post-war service saw little improvement, and there were very few through trains between London and East Sussex. Then after two occasions when part of the roof of Oxted tunnel had collapsed the tunnel was closed for permanent repairs from 7th February until 30th November, 1921, except during the business hours and on Saturdays. The engineers had possession on Mondays to Fridays between 10.15 am and 4.55 pm, 8.30 pm and 7.53 am; and on Sunday nights between 12.00 midnight and 7.53 am next morning. At other times single line working through the tunnel was in force. There were separate services between London and Woldingham and between Oxted and points south at slack times, but there were no connecting bus services; passengers from London to Oxted were required to travel by way of the main line to Three Bridges, thence East Grinstead and Lingfield. Some of the Victoria-Brighton via Eridge trains were diverted via Three Bridges and Forest Row.

On 1st December, 1921, normal working through Oxted tunnel was resumed. The full service between London and East Grinstead via Lingfield was as follows:

6.45 am Victoria to Tunbridge Wells, 8.07 am London Bridge to Haywards Heath via Horsted Keynes and Lewes, 10.35 am London Bridge to East Grinstead, 12.00 noon Victoria to Lewes, 12.50 pm (Saturdays) London Bridge to Tunbridge Wells, 4.10 pm London Bridge to Brighton, 5.05 pm Victoria to Lewes, 5.48 pm Victoria to Tunbridge Wells, 7.22 pm (not Saturdays) East Croydon to Horsted Keynes, 7.38 pm London Bridge to East Grinstead and 9.03 pm (Saturdays) Victoria to East Grinstead.

In the opposite direction East Grinstead was directly connected with London by the following:

6.20 am Brighton to London Bridge, 8.38 am Forest Row to London Bridge and Victoria, 8.08 am Lewes to London Bridge, 9.50 am Tunbridge Wells to Victoria, 10.30 am Brighton to Victoria, 1.50 pm East Grinstead to London Bridge, 4.10 pm East Grinstead to London Bridge, 5.03 Brighton to Victoria and 7.45 pm Brighton to London Bridge via Haywards Heath and Horsted Keynes.

Although East Grinstead could be reached by other services, with a change of train at Oxted, the civic dignitaries of the North Sussex town felt that their train service was wholly inadequate, given the increase in population and in business travel. A petition of season ticket holders called for two fast evening trains from London to Oxted and East Grinstead, reinstatement of the late 'theatre' train, a connection at Oxted off the 6.08 pm from London Bridge, and for the 7.48 am East Grinstead to London to be fast from Oxted to East Croydon.

Not a single one of these requests was acceded to!

However, the following summer the LBSCR did unbend slightly, and from 12th June, 1922, a new fast morning train was introduced. Leaving Tunbridge Wells at 8.32 am, it was booked to leave East Grinstead at 9.15 and, calling only at Dormans and Lingfield, it then ran non-stop to London Bridge where it was due at 10.07. The 8.08 am from Lewes was timed to connect with it at East Grinstead. Unfortunately there was no balancing fast train from London in the evening.

The final alterations made before the LBSCR became part of the Southern Railway were that on Wednesdays in December 1922 the 10.30 pm Victoria to Oxted and 11.50 pm Victoria to Woldingham were both extended to East Grinstead for the benefit of theatregoers in London.

South Eastern Railway

As if to emphasise its parity with the LBSCR, the South Eastern put on four trains each way between London Bridge and Oxted from 10th March, 1884, the same number as the Brighton. They left London Bridge at 7.19, 10.49 am, 4.46 and 8.39 pm, returning from Oxted at 9.20 am, 1.55, 6.05 and 9.33 pm. On Sundays, just as the Brighton ran two trains each way, so did the SER. The only difference was that the SER was not allowed to call at any station between London Bridge and East Croydon, or at South Croydon, these being Brighton property; and it was only by special agreement between the companies that the SER was permitted to use East Croydon. All SER Oxted trains called at Sanderstead and Upper Warlingham.

On 1st August, 1884, three of these trains were extended from Oxted by way of the Crowhurst spur to the South Eastern's own Redhill-Tonbridge line. The 7.19 am and 4.46 pm ran through to Edenbridge, and the 10.49 am was extended to Tonbridge. In the up direction the first and third trains started back at Edenbridge (9.15 am and 5.51 pm) while the second started at Tonbridge at 1.20 pm. The fourth train continued to run to and from Oxted. A goods train began operations in October 1884, leaving London Bridge at 6.45 am for Oxted and the Edenbridge line, and returning the same way (Oxted depart 3.35 pm).

In 1887 an additional SER passenger train was put on: 3.51 pm London Bridge to Oxted and 5.42 pm return. The goods train began running by way of the Woodside and Selsdon Road joint line. A year later the SER passenger service was increased to seven trains each way, the new trains being at 9.10 am and 12.21 pm from London Bridge to Oxted and 11.00 am and 2.25 pm from Oxted back to London Bridge. Three each way continued to run over the Crowhurst spur. This service was maintained for several years, with only minor changes in timings. The 1891 tables show that the SER goods train called at Selsdon, Upper Warlingham, Marden Park, Oxted Lime Siding and Oxted; the up train called at the same places but not the Lime Siding, which had no connections to the up line.

Despite the fact that the line was jointly owned, there was never a timetable published that showed both companies' train services in the one table. Passengers and staff alike had to refer to two separate timetables, each issued by the relevant railway company.

By 1906 the service (now South Eastern & Chatham) had been increased but had become 'unbalanced', with more trains in one direction than the other, and a down fast to Oxted (the 4.57 pm from Cannon Street) but no up fast. There were six trains from Cannon Street, four terminating at Edenbridge, one at Oxted and one at Tonbridge; and four trains ran from London Bridge (Low Level), of which three continued through to Tonbridge.

Of the up trains provided, three ran through to Charing Cross. Even one main line service used the Crowhurst spur: starting from Dover Town at 7.05 am it was due to leave Tonbridge at 9.03 am, Oxted 9.33 am and, continuing over the Mid-Kent line, was due into Charing Cross at 10.52. Another unbalanced working was the train due to arrive at Edenbridge at 5.46 pm: this returned to London via Redhill instead of Oxted.

The SECR goods service worked from Bricklayers Arms via the Mid-Kent, Woodside, Selsdon Road, Oxted and Crowhurst Junction to Tonbridge. On

Thursdays for some years up to and during World War I a 'Market Special' cattle wagon train ran from Tonbridge to Croydon. There was no return working, so the locomotive and brake van worked back light, and tender-first as there was no turntable at East Croydon.

The 1914 timetable showed 13 down and 12 up trains, of which three each way ran via Woodside.

In April 1916 the SECR service to the Oxted line via the Mid-Kent was seriously reduced. All that remained were the 2.06 pm (Saturdays) London Bridge to Penshurst, 9.32 pm Charing Cross to Edenbridge, 8.50 am Tonbridge to Cannon Street, 4.38 pm Tonbridge to London Bridge and 5.52 pm Wadhurst to Cannon Street. These were now the only trains running over the Woodside & South Croydon, but not for much longer: on 1st January, 1917, this line was closed to normal passenger traffic and at the same time the service over the Croydon & Oxted was suspended. Goods traffic was worked to Selsdon Road and handed over to the LBSC from that point.

The SECR service was never restored to anything like its pre-war extent. From 1st March, 1919, one train a day each way was reinstated: 7.37 am Tonbridge to London Bridge, returning at 2.18 pm (Saturdays), 5.33 pm (not Saturdays) to Penshurst via the Crowhurst spur. On 16th June, 1919, another service was restored: 7.10 am Tonbridge to London Bridge and 1.30 pm (Saturdays), 6.27 pm (not Saturdays) return. Selsdon Road had re-opened on 1st March, 1919. Two trains each way was the maximum service provided; it was soon reduced to one each way and from 11th June, 1922, the timings were 7.33 am Tonbridge to London Bridge and 1.34 pm (Saturdays), 6.27 pm (not Saturdays) return. There was also one very odd up morning train that started at Woldingham at 7.46 am for London Bridge; it was formed of a single SECR three-coach set which came down empty from Rotherhithe Road carriage shed on Mondays and empty from London Bridge on other days. This 7.46 seems to have been the only train ever to start its journey at Woldingham station.

The inadequacy of the SECR service was discovered the hard way one Saturday afternoon by the editor of the *East Grinstead Observer*, W.H. Hills. In February 1922 he told his readers :

Leaving East Grinstead by the 1.50 train I went to Oxted, and from thence travelled by the South Eastern line to Edenbridge, where I arrived by 2.40 pm. 'What is the next train back?' I asked the ticket collector. 'No more trains stopping here until 7.51 on Monday morning' was the astonishing reply.

Hills managed to catch a train at Edenbridge Town station 'and shake the dust of that miserable little town from my feet'.

Southern Railway

No very startling changes were made to the Oxted line timetable by the Southern Railway, although some attempt was made to integrate services with those on the former SECR, with more through running between Tunbridge Wells West and Central stations. In July 1923 a new train was put on: 6.50 am

Class 'D3' 0-4-4 tank No. 2383 of Tunbridge Wells enters Oxted with a push-and-pull train from Tunbridge Wells via East Grinstead in the late 1930s. It is displaying the duty number 635.

Lens of Sutton

Another light load for Tunbridge Wells-based Class 'I1x' No. 2006 (displaying duty number 621) as it enters Oxted with an afternoon train from Victoria formed of an ex-LBSCR three-coach set.

Tonbridge to Cannon Street (due 9.04) via Tunbridge Wells West, East Grinstead, Lingfield and Oxted. It was balanced by the 12.16 pm (Saturdays), 4.16 pm (not Saturdays) Cannon Street to Tonbridge via Oxted, Edenbridge Town and Tunbridge Wells. By 1928 they had ceased to run between London Bridge and Cannon Street. The up train, later retimed as the 7.08 am from Tunbridge Wells West and due into London Bridge at 9.00, was taken off during World War II but restored again in 1946.

The summer 1925 business service of trains between Oxted and London was now:

Up

am		Due
6.36	Tunbridge Wells West-Victoria	8.12
6.50	Tunbridge Wells West-Tonbridge-Crowhurst spur-London Bridge	8.27
7.10	Tunbridge Wells West-Victoria	8.40
7.35	Tonbridge-Crowhurst spur-Charing Cross	8.58
6.50	Tonbridge-Tunbridge Wells West-East Grinstead-Cannon Street	9.04
7.45	Tunbridge Wells West-London Bridge	9.12
6.52	Brighton-Eridge-London Bridge	9.32
8.38	Forest Row-London Bridge (9.56) and Victoria	9.59
8.32	Uckfield-London Bridge	10.04
8.38	Tunbridge Wells West-East Grinstead-London Bridge	10.07
7.51	Eastbourne/ 8.05 Brighton-Eridge-Victoria	10.20
8.10	Lewes-East Grinstead-London Bridge	10.38
9.28	Tunbridge Wells West-Victoria	10.47

Down

pm	
3.45	Victoria-Brighton/Tunbridge Wells West-Eastbourne
4.10	London Bridge-East Grinstead-Brighton
4.16	(not Saturdays) Cannon Street-Tunbridge Wells West
4.37	(not Saturdays) London Bridge-Uckfield
4.50	Victoria-Brighton and Tunbridge Wells West
5.03	Victoria-East Grinstead-Lewes
5.21	London Bridge-Tunbridge Wells West
5.36	(not Saturdays) London Bridge-Oxted
5.48	Victoria-East Grinstead-Tunbridge Wells West
6.10	(not Saturdays) Victoria-Uckfield, Heathfield, Tunbridge Wells West
6.27	(not Saturdays) London Bridge-Crowhurst spur-Tonbridge
7.22	East Croydon-East Grinstead

There were now two up trains over the Crowhurst spur but only one down. In autumn 1927 even this one service was withdrawn, and later the up trains were both arranged to start at Tunbridge Wells West (6.46 and 7.16 am) and run to London Bridge, where they were due at 8.20 and 8.47 respectively. In summer 1931 the first was cut back to Penshurst and the same autumn arranged to start at Edenbridge at 7.25 am, the stock running empty from Tonbridge. This 7.25 continued running until September 1939, when it was discontinued for the duration of the war. Surprisingly it was restored in October 1946, still with no balancing down working. The other up train was withdrawn about 1935, although its timings between Hurst Green and London Bridge were taken up by

OXTED (Surrey) from *Victoria, London Bridge,* or *Charing Cross.* 20¼ miles. *Map Square* 23. Pop. 3,799.
Ordinary Single.
Vic. or Lon. Bdg., 4/4a, 2/7o.
Charing Cross, 4/6a, 2/8c.
Week-End Return, 9/0a, 3/9o.
Summer Return, 8/6a, 5/0c.
Cheap Day (Note 6), 4/6a, 2/9o.
TICKET CONDITIONS, see page 1.

Leave VICT.	LON. B.	Arrive at OXTED
A 5.20	5.25	6.18
6.30	6.35	7.25
8. 0	8. 3	8.58
9. 5	9. 0	9.54
10.46	10.45	11.37
11.15	11.11e	11.52
P 12. 3 M	12. 0	12.54
	12.20d	1.10
12.46d	12.47d	1.37
1.25d	1.16d	2. 0
1.28e	1.33e	2.28
1.28d	1.38d	2.28
1.51d	2. 6d	2.53
2.30d	2.18d	3. 9
2.30e	2.31e	3.24
2.30d	2.36d	3.28
2.46e	2.50e	3.43
3.45	—	4.18
4. 5e	4. 9e	4.54
4. 5d	4.14e	5. 3
4.18e	4.23e	5.14
4.30e	4.40e	5.22
4.50	4.55e	5.38
—	5. 0d	5.57
5.10	5.12e	5.58
	5.20	6. 9
5.31e	5.40e	6.28
5.50	5.50e	6.37
6.10e	6. 9e	6.47
6.10d	6.11d	7. 4
—	6.30e	7.19
6.48e	6.55e	7.45
6.53d	6.51d	7.45
7.28	7.40	8.31
8. 2e	8. 0e	8.38
8. 2d	8. 0d	8.52
—	8. 4e	8.54
9.14	9.16	10. 6
10.30	10.31	11.25
11.50h	11.41h	12.38
—	—	—
—	—	—
—	—	—
—	—	—
—	—	—

Sunday Trains.

Leave		Arrive at
A 8.28 M	8.35	9.25
8.50	—	9.38
9.35	9.30	10.31
10.15	10.16	11.10
P 12. 4 M	12.16	1. 6
1.15	1.16	2.10
2.10	2. 0	3. 2
2.30	2.30	3.31
3.28	3.30	4.21
5. 5	5. 0	5.58
5.28	5.30	6.19
6.30	6.40	7.37
7. 8	7. 0	7.57
9.15	9.16	10. 9
—	—	—
—	—	—
—	—	—

OXTED—*continued.*
Trains from Oxted.

Leave OXTED	LON. B.	Arrive at VICT.
A 6.58 M	7.43	—
7.18	8.10	8. 7
7.36	8.20	8.27
7.52	8.44	8.43
8. 2	8.47	8.57e
8.16	9. 0	—
8.27	9.14	9.16
8.43	9.28	9.33
8.53	9.39	9.37
9.11e	9.55	9.46
9.26	10. 8	10.10
9.47	—	10.21
9.54	10.40	—
10. 8	10.52	10.48
10.51	11.51	11.41
11.32	12.28	12.23
11.52	12.31	12.33
P 12.42 M	1.31	1.37
2.14	3. 4	3. 8
2.53	3.51	3.42
3.59d	4.50	4.47
3.59e	4.45	4.57
4.31	5.19	5.23
5.18e	6. 7	6.15
5.53	6.47	6.40
7.12	8. 6	8. 4
7.27	8.31	8.17
8.30e	9.22	9.23
9.35	10.23	10.23
9.43	10.32	10.33
11. 7	11.55	12. 7
—	—	—

Sunday Trains.

Leave	LON. B.	VICT.
A 9.19 M	10. 9	10.10
10.20	11.10	11. 9
11.16	12.10	12. 5
P 12. 8 M	1.10	12.57
12.41	1.35	1.38
2.10	3.10	3. 5
3.20	4.10	4.14
4.40	5.35	5.56
5.29	6.35	6.19
6.28	7.24	7.22
7.28	8.35	8.18
8.22	9.10	9. 4
8.35	9.28	9.45
9. 6	10. 2	9.50
10.22	11. 9	11.10
—	—	—

d Saturdays only.
e Saturdays excepted.
h Wednesdays and Saturdays only.

EAST GRINSTEAD (Sussex) from *Victoria* or *London Bridge,* via *Dormans,* 30 miles.
Map Square 23. Pop. 7,901.
Ordinary Single.
Victoria or London Bridge,
Via Dormans, 6/3a, 3/9c.
Via Three Bridges, 6/7a, 3/11c.
Summer Return,
Via Dormans, 8/6a, 5/0c.
Via Three Bridges, 9/0a, 5/3c.
Cheap Day (Note 6),
Via Dormans, 6/6a, 4/0c.
Via Three Bridges, 6/9a, 4/0c.
TICKET CONDITIONS, see page 1.

Leave VICT.	LON. B.	Arr. at E. GRIN.
A 5.51h M	6.10h	7.27
	6.18h	7.48
6.30	6.35	7.51
7.11h	7.20h	8.45
8. 0	8. 3	9.23
9. 5	9. 0	10.25
10.19h	10.15h	11.41
10.46	10.45	12. 2
P 12. 3 M	12. 0	1.17
—	12. 5eh	1.22
—	12.16eh	1.47
—	12.30dh	1.47
12.46d	12.47d	1.59
1.25d	1.16d	2.23
1.28e	1.33e	2.55
1.32dh	—	2.55
—	1.38d	2.56
2.46h	3. 0h	4. 1
4. 5e	4. 9e	5.19
4. 5dh	4. 5dh	5.25
—	4.14d	5.25
4.50	4.55e	6. 4
—	5. 0dh	6. 9
—	5. 9eh	6. 9
5.10	5.12e	6.23
5.31e	5.40e	6.50
5.50	5.50e	7. 0
6.10dh	6.16dh	7.58
6.10e	6.30e	7.44
6.25eh	6.40eh	7.58
6.48e	6.55e	8. 8
6.53d	6.51d	8. 8
7.28	7.40	8.55
7.46h	8. 0h	9. 7
9.14	9.16	10.30
10.30v	10.31v	11.47
11.50z	11.41z	1. 0

Sunday Trains.

A 8.28 M	8.35	9.48
10.15	10.16	11.33
P 6.28h M	6.16h	7.37
6.30	6.40	8. 3
7.46h	7.30h	9. 4

Trains from East Grinstead.

Leave E. GRIN.	LON. B.	Arrive at VICT.
A 6.36h M	—	8. 7
6.39	7.43	—
7. 9	8.21	8.27
7.54	9. 0	—
7.58h	9. 8	9.15
8.12	9.28	9.33
8.32	9.39	9.37
9. 7	10. 8	10. 9
9.24	10.20	—
9.32	10.39	10.48
10.30	11.51	11.41
10.33h	11.58	11.57
P 12. 6h M	—	1.17
12.22	1.30	1.37
1.52	3. 4	3. 8
1.55h	2.56	2.57
3.16h	4.34	—
3.38d	4.50	4.46
4.10	5.19	5.23

EAST GRINSTEAD—*continued.*

Leave	Arrive at	
	LON. B.	VICT.
P 4.15h M	5.38	—
5. 7	6.47	6.40
5.28h	6.56	6.57
6.22	8. 6	8. 4
7. 5	8.31	8.15
8. 9e	9.22	9.23
9.15	10.23	10.23
10.46	11.55	12. 5

Sunday Trains.

A 8. 2h M	9.35	9.12
9.56	11.10	11. 9
11.49	1.10	12.57
P 6.19h M	7.35	7.56
8.11	9.28	9.45

d Saturdays only.
e Saturdays excepted.
h Via Three Bridges.
v 2nd and 4th Wednesdays only.
z 1st and 3rd Wednesdays only.

Taxi Cabs can be hired to meet any train at this station by telegram, or telephone No. 12, to NUTT, Station Road, East Grinstead.

Ye Felbridge Hotel. An Ideal old-world Residential and Motorists' Hotel. *See advt. p. 156.*

Ye Dorset Arms Hotel. Established over 300 years. First class for Military, Families and Motorists. Main Eastbourne and Brighton roads. Hot Luncheons and Table d'Hôte daily. Officially appointed A.A. and R.A.C. Best centre for beauty spots of Sussex and Surrey. Telephone No. 24.

Crown Hotel. Family and Commercial. Most centrally situated. Comfortable Commercial Dining and Sitting Rooms. Ordinary daily, 1 o'clock. Motors. Posting. Garage. Good Stabling. Billiards. Telephone 117. Prop., STANLEY C. BALL.

Extracts from the *ABC Guide*, July 1934.

a much-needed new train from East Grinstead at 7.45 am (itself put on by extending the 6.20 am Brighton to East Grinstead through to London Bridge, where it was due at 8.47).

The 7.30 am from Tonbridge, meanwhile, ran as far as Oxted between 1935 and 1939, providing a connection into the 7.45 from East Grinstead, then formed a new 8.10 am Oxted to Eastbourne via Crowhurst Junction, Tonbridge and Tunbridge Wells. Until then the only down train regularly to run over the spur was the empty stock off the 1.58 pm (Saturdays) London Bridge to Oxted.

A new train that started running in about 1926 was the 6.50 pm Victoria to East Grinstead, replacing the 7.22 pm from East Croydon. After 1941 the Saturday version of this train was extended from East Grinstead to Tunbridge Wells.

Several improvements to the timetable were made in June 1928. At long last the 5.03 pm from Victoria, which every evening since 1891 had waited about 15 minutes at Oxted to allow the train behind to overtake it, was accelerated. It now left Victoria at 5.08 pm and was due in East Grinstead at 6.23, an acceleration of 19 minutes. A new train at 5.40 pm (not Saturdays) from London Bridge to East Grinstead was inaugurated, and a service withdrawn in the war was reinstated: the 6.32 pm (not Saturdays) from London Bridge to East Grinstead. However, City-bound travellers were annoyed by the withdrawal of the London Bridge portion of the 8.38 am from Forest Row; the train was retimed to leave at 8.27 and arrive at Victoria at 9.47. Finally, the 9.15 pm from Victoria to East Grinstead, previously Wednesdays and Saturdays only, now ran every weekday.

Two main goods trains ran each way during the 1920s and 1930s, each shunting at stations along the line. The 5.20 am Norwood Junction to Groombridge via Edenbridge Town was balanced by the 5.20 pm Tunbridge Wells West to Norwood Junction. The 7.00 am Norwood Junction to East Grinstead returned at 12.30 pm (Saturdays), 2.25 pm (not Saturdays), calling at Dormans Park Siding if required, and Lingfield Brick Siding; leaving here the load was restricted to 24 wagons. In addition a short goods train ran from Upper Warlingham to Oxted each afternoon and shunted at Oxted Lime Siding.

The timetable was now more-or-less settled, no changes of note being made in 1930 or 1931. To the passenger there was no logical pattern to the train service; in the morning there were more trains to London Bridge than returned in the evening; some trains missed out stations in one direction and not the other; in short, every train was an individual animal and ran thus because it was ever so. Two trains each way ran between Victoria and Brighton via Eridge conveying through carriages to or from Eastbourne. (During World War II only the 3.55 pm down and the 8.00 am up continued as semi-fast Brighton/Eastbourne through services.)

The fastest train on the line was the 3.45 pm from Victoria to Brighton, which ran non-stop to Eridge in 56 minutes, shedding there a portion for Eastbourne. The 3.45 was often worked by a 'B1' class 0-4-2, No. B172 being the last such, in June 1933; by 1937, when the train was retimed to leave Victoria at 3.55 and make an additional call at Oxted, a 'B4', 'B4X' or even an 'H1' Atlantic was usually seen. By 1941 an extra stop at East Croydon had been inserted. After the war the 3.55 was usually worked by a class 'N' 2-6-0, Nos. 1817 and 1854 being recalled.

SELSDON ROAD.

Blackwells and National Roofings, siding.—Inwards wagons for this siding must be detached in Selsdon Road Goods yard and propelled thence on the down line to a point clear of the crossover road at Selsdon Road Junction, after which they must be drawn to the up line and propelled into the private siding, being detached in the shunting neck, the engine returning light to Selsdon Road goods yard.

Wagons to be forwarded from the siding will be placed by Messrs. Blackwells and National Roofings, in the shunting neck at the southern end of the siding and must be taken from there by a special trip to Selsdon Road goods yard.

No attempt must be made to combine the operations of placing wagons in the siding and removing outgoing wagons but two separate trips must be made. The maximum number of wagons to be taken on any one trip is five.

Wagons will be worked to and from the northern end of the private siding by Messrs. Blackwells and National Roofings.

All movements between Selsdon Road North and Selsdon Road Junction boxes must be signalled on the block instruments.

OXTED.

Nos. 5, 6, 7 and 8 sidings.—Whilst shunting operations are being performed on these sidings a man must be in attendance at the sleeper crossing in the goods yard adjoining Messrs. Hall and Co.'s depot to prevent road vehicles passing over the crossing. Wagons for these sidings must remain attached to the engine and must not be loose shunted.

LINGFIELD.

Sussex Brick Co.'s sidings.—Scotch blocks exist on both sidings 44 yards inside the gates. Wagons are exchanged immediately inside the scotches. Loose shunting in these sidings is prohibited.

EAST GRINSTEAD HIGH LEVEL.

Level crossing.—When the Signalman in the East Box rings the hand bell the Goods Porter must take up a position at the level crossing in order to protect users of the crossing and prevent any vehicle passing over until the shunt movement has proceeded clear.

Stenning and Son's siding.—Care must be exercised in shunting this siding as the gradient of the single line is a sharply falling one towards Forest Row, and a goods brake van must be provided on the single line on to which wagons from the siding are to be shunted. The person in charge of the shunting will be responsible for seeing that the hand brake in this van is fully applied before shunting operations are commenced.

Extract from Appendices to the Working Timetable, 26th March, 1934.

The evening train service of 1930-2 had some similarities to that provided up to May 1978. There were the 4.09 (not Saturdays), 4.15 pm (Saturdays), from London Bridge to Brighton via East Grinstead; the 4.43 (not Saturdays) East Croydon to Redhill via Edenbridge Town, Tunbridge Wells and Tonbridge, detached from the 4.20 pm London Bridge to Redhill direct; the 4.40 (not Saturdays) London Bridge to Uckfield; and the 4.50 Victoria to Brighton and Tonbridge, the rear portion being detached at Ashurst.

Then came, thick and fast, the 5.08 Victoria to East Grinstead, continuing after a ¾-hour wait as the 7.07 to Lewes; the 5.20 London Bridge to Tunbridge Wells; 5.40 (not Saturdays) London Bridge to East Grinstead; 5.50 Victoria to Tunbridge Wells via East Grinstead, where connection was made for Lewes at 7.07; and the 6.10 from Victoria. On Saturdays this was simply a train to Tunbridge Wells, but on other days it was more complicated. In *Bradshaw's Railway Guide* it appeared as four separate trains, but actually comprised three portions, with a connecting service from Oxted. The front part was for Uckfield, fast from East Croydon to Oxted. A push-and-pull train provided a connection from Oxted to Cowden, and at Eridge through carriages off the 6.10 were attached to the 6.58 pm from Tunbridge Wells to Heathfield. Meanwhile the slow portion of the 6.10, detached at East Croydon, ran via Edenbridge Town to Tunbridge Wells West and Tonbridge.

The evening business service was wrapped up with the 6.30 (not Saturdays) London Bridge to Forest Row and the 6.50 (3 min. later on Saturdays) Victoria to East Grinstead, extended to Lewes on Wednesdays and Saturdays only. In the best tradition of LBSC timetables, the 6.30 stopped at Hurst Green Halt 'to set down London passengers only'.

To cater for business people who worked on Saturday mornings there was quite a respectable lunchtime service of down trains for many years. This had the unfortunate side-effect of complicating the timetable as more trains than before started to run at different times on Saturdays, and some of the evening trains became 'Saturdays excepted'. On Saturdays extra trains left London Bridge at 12.20 for Tunbridge Wells via Edenbridge Town, 12.48 for Tunbridge Wells via East Grinstead, 1.38 for Tonbridge via Edenbridge Town and Tunbridge Wells, and 1.58 for Oxted, thence empty for Tonbridge via Crowhurst Junctions. There was an extra train from Victoria on Saturdays at 1.26 pm for Forest Row via East Grinstead.

The service of up trains was similar to that provided in 1925. The 6.37 am from Tunbridge Wells to Victoria now started at Tonbridge at 6.10, and was due to leave Oxted at 7.17. This was the first train of the day to London. Other trains for Victoria left Oxted at 7.51, 8.59 and 10.08 am. Oxted's London Bridge service for business people was 7.36, 8.03, 8.18, 8.27, 8.50, 9.24 (4 min. later on Saturdays), and 9.52 am. The 8.32 am Uckfield to London Bridge no longer ran on Saturdays. The 8.40 (not Saturdays) Tunbridge Wells to London Bridge via East Grinstead still ran non-stop from Lingfield, being due in London at 10.08. The only other up train not calling at Oxted was the 7.51 Eastbourne/8.05 am Brighton which, running non-stop from Eridge, was due into Victoria at 10.18.

There was an appreciable amount of milk traffic too. The 8.10 am Lewes-London Bridge conveyed a van of empty churns which was detached at East

A through train from Hastings to London via Crowhurst Junction, Oxted and the Mid-Kent line passes through Oxted. The class 'E' 4-4-0, No. 1036, carries Bricklayers Arms duty No. 97 and a Bank Holiday train number board; stock comprises an ex-SECR three-coach set and a Maunsell seven-corridor set, all coaches of which are roofboarded.   *Lens of Sutton*

A morning London Bridge to Tunbridge Wells Bank Holiday train arrives at Oxted in charge of 'B1' 4-4-0 No. 1454. Maunsell three-corridor set No. 225 makes a light load.   *Lens of Sutton*

Croydon. A separate milk train left Lewes at 8.34 am for Tulse Hill via Eridge and Oxted, and the 10.35 am Brighton to Victoria conveyed two vans of milk from Sheffield Park to East Croydon.

The 1933 table showed some changes. A new early train for London Bridge left East Grinstead at 6.39 am (Oxted 6.58, London Bridge due 7.43). The stock was used to form the long-standing 8.03 from London Bridge to Brighton via East Grinstead. The 8.32 am Uckfield to London Bridge was replaced by an 8.18 am (not Saturdays) Uckfield to Victoria, which ran fast from Oxted (9.11) to East Croydon. The 8.30 am from Tunbridge Wells to London Bridge via East Grinstead was slowed down and now called at Oxted, Woldingham and Upper Warlingham; and the 7.51 Eastbourne/8.05 am Brighton to Victoria also called at Oxted. This village was expanding and was now regarded as too important a place to miss. The 3.45 pm down was the only remaining train not to call, but in 1934 this too succumbed to Oxted's charms and made a call there.

Some minor changes were made in about 1935: as mentioned earlier the 6.20 am Brighton-East Grinstead was extended to London Bridge, taking the path of the former 7.32 am Tonbridge to London Bridge from Crowhurst Junction. A new train left East Croydon at 7.24 pm for Tunbridge Wells and the mid-afternoon London Bridge-East Grinstead-Brighton train now left at 4.20 pm (4.18 on Saturdays). Except on Saturdays, the 4.20 pm divided at East Croydon, the front part running fast to Oxted - becoming East Grinstead's fastest service - and the rear portion was slow to Tonbridge via Edenbridge Town. Formerly this train had been detached from a Redhill service.

On 8th September, 1939, staff were informed that an emergency train service would operate from 11th September. As no revised tables were available to the public, Oxted's booking clerk, C.J. Leigh, took the initiative and had service cards printed locally within 12 hours.

Within a month or so the service was restored almost to normal. Several off-peak trains were withdrawn, but in the peak period the only trains to be discontinued were the 7.25 am Edenbridge to London Bridge, 7.08 Tunbridge Wells to London Bridge, 8.18 am Uckfield to Victoria, the 6.10 pm Victoria to Uckfield and the 6.30 pm London Bridge to Forest Row. The 6.10 was replaced by a slow train to Tunbridge Wells. The 3.55 from Victoria now called at East Croydon; the 5.20 pm from London Bridge and 7.24 pm from East Croydon no longer ran on Saturdays. All the discontinued trains were restored after the war. By 1944 the 5.09 pm Victoria to East Grinstead was extended to Forest Row except on Saturdays, when it continued as the 7.07 pm East Grinstead to Lewes. The 5.40 pm from London Bridge now continued as the 7.07 pm from Mondays to Fridays. Also on Saturdays, the 6.53 pm from Victoria continued from East Grinstead to Tunbridge Wells.

The 6.10 pm from Victoria regained its pre-war timings on 1st January, 1945, the main portion running semi-fast to Uckfield and the rear portion being detached at East Croydon as before. A Stewarts Lane-based 'J' class 4-6-2 tank worked the 6.10, returning on the 9.00 pm from Tunbridge Wells; and a Tunbridge Wells 'I3' 4-4-2 tank worked the rear portion from East Croydon. Later the 6.10 pm was worked by a Newhaven-based Marsh Atlantic.

Class 'I3' 4-4-2 tank locomotive No. 2076 of Bricklayers Arms works the 3.35 pm Oxted to Brighton past Chellows Farm, near Lingfield Brick Siding, in June 1948. This working was part of Bricklayers Arms duty No. 533.   *R.W. Kidner*

On 1st September, 1949, the magnificent 'J1' class 4-6-2 tank locomotive No. 32325 worked the 11.08 am Victoria to Eastbourne, as it often did at this period. Here the train is shown entering Oxted. The LBSCR co-acting up starting signal was still in use, but the down home had been replaced by a Southern upper quadrant.   *D. Cullum*

1948 to 1963

One or two off-peak trains withdrawn in the war had still not been restored at the time of Nationalisation. They had to wait until 23rd May, 1949, when the 10.45 am London Bridge to Tunbridge Wells via East Grinstead reappeared, as did the 11.08 am Victoria to Brighton and Eastbourne via Edenbridge Town. This, like the 6.10 pm down, had been replaced by a slow train to Tunbridge Wells. Through Eastbourne portions were now run in the 11.08 am and 3.52 pm down and the 7.52 am up; the planners never got round to restoring the through carriages to the 9.55 am from Eastbourne and so the 10.18 am from Brighton to Victoria had only a connection at Eridge. Another new train was the 3.39 pm (Saturdays excepted) East Grinstead to East Croydon, worked by an 'H' class locomotive which ran bunker first and returned with the 6.36 pm East Croydon to Tunbridge Wells; and the 6.30 pm Tunbridge Wells-Oxted was extended to Victoria.

Freight services at this time also were little changed. They were the 5.10 am Norwood to Groombridge and 7.10 am Norwood to East Grinstead, as well as the wartime 7.25 pm Norwood to Polegate via East Grinstead and Lewes, which by 1948 ran only when required and was discontinued shortly afterwards. The up freight services ran to different timings on Saturdays, the service from East Grinstead calling at Lingfield Brick Siding every day. Oxted Lime Siding was now served only when required by a short working, the 2.35 pm (Saturdays excepted) Upper Warlingham to Oxted.

A minor change from 30th June, 1952, was that the 8.22 am Lewes to London Bridge via East Grinstead was arranged to start at Brighton at 8.00. In consequence the 5.40 pm London Bridge to East Grinstead and Lewes was extended to Brighton. This change saw the end of Newhaven-based Marsh Atlantics on these services as the trains were now worked by Brighton-based locomotives.

Snow was not unknown on the Oxted line! Here, on 14th February, 1953, class '4PT/FT' No. 42102 is seen working the 10.52 am Tunbridge Wells to London Bridge under a heavy sky. Upper Warlingham's footbridge still had full protection against the weather.   *D. Cullum*

On Wednesday, 15th June, 1955, the timetable was recast to provide regular-interval services in the off-peak period. Peak trains remained much the same, as they could not be altered without serious disruption to other train services passing between South Croydon and Windmill Bridge Junction. Trains now left Victoria for East Grinstead and Tunbridge Wells at eight minutes past each hour, and the service via Edenbridge Town was provided by a push-and-pull train leaving Oxted at four minutes past. In the other direction the standard departure time from Tunbridge Wells was 47 minutes past each hour, East Grinstead 26 minutes past and Oxted 47 minutes past the hour. There were several exceptions: for example the 11.08 remained as a fast Brighton/Eastbourne train but now had a slow portion for Tunbridge Wells detached at East Croydon, and the 2.08 and 3.08 pm terminated at East Grinstead Mondays to Fridays. Although it was in the main an excellently planned timetable, with good connections at various key points, the two main disadvantages were that London Bridge ceased to have any through services except in the peak period, and that passengers from London to Eridge and points south usually had to make two changes - at Oxted and Groombridge. However, the semi-fast through services between London and Brighton/Eastbourne were retained, and added interest to the timetable.

One casualty of the old service was the 7.26 am Edenbridge to London Bridge, for many years the only regular train over the Crowhurst spur. To replace it a new train left Forest Row at 7.04 am for London Bridge, running in the timings of the old 7.26 as between Hurst Green Junction and London. The 7.09 am push-and-pull train from East Grinstead to Oxted was discontinued; it had for some time been the subject of many complaints about overcrowding, and the new through train that replaced it was a great improvement.

Another new service was a push-and-pull connection off the 6.10 pm Victoria-Uckfield leaving Oxted at 6.54 pm for East Grinstead and Tunbridge Wells; this filled quite a large gap between the 5.50 from Victoria and the 6.30 pm from London Bridge. The 6.30 pm, which formerly ran to Tunbridge Wells, now terminated at Forest Row where the stock was berthed overnight to form the 7.04 am up next morning.

The timetable took some weeks to settle down, as the drivers had been on strike and were completely unfamiliar with it. The biggest problem was the push-and-pull trains, booked to be worked by 'M7' class 0-4-4 tank engines, few of which had been transferred to Tunbridge Wells depot before the service started. When they were, the crews could not get on with them at first and often an 'H' class 0-4-4T had to be substituted.

Various holes in the timetable were plugged in summer 1956. Interval services were inaugurated on the Crowborough and Heathfield lines. The 11.08 am from Victoria became a standard-interval train for Tunbridge Wells, the semi-fast Brighton and Eastbourne train being retimed to 10.38. The 3.50 pm Victoria to Brighton and Eastbourne ran at 3.38 pm on Saturdays. The 4.40 pm London Bridge-Uckfield and 6.10 pm Victoria-Uckfield were both extended to Brighton. On Saturdays a new train at 6.38 pm from Victoria to Brighton replaced a through portion off the 5.08 pm.

The 7.06 am Brighton to London Bridge was accelerated and now started at 7.20. The 8.23 am Uckfield-Victoria now started at Brighton at 7.35 am. Other through trains between Brighton and Victoria left at 9.55 am, 1.55 and 6.55 pm, replacing the 10.56 am from Brighton and 4.14 pm from Lewes to Victoria. The 2.08 and 3.08 pm from Victoria now ran through to Tunbridge Wells and the 4.09 pm East Grinstead to London Bridge started at Tunbridge Wells at 3.47 pm. Most of the Oxted to Tunbridge Wells push-and-pull services, now worked by class 'H' after the disastrous failure of the 'M7s', were extended to Tonbridge; from 13th June, 1960, they were cut back to Tunbridge Wells West again. Finally, the Saturday business service was reduced; although there were still quite a few trains up in the morning the only lunchtime extra train back was the 12.47 pm from London Bridge.

The improved services could not quite keep up with the increase in passenger travel, and certain business trains, particularly the 5.40, 5.50 and 6.10 pm, were always overloaded and in consequence often ran late. It was decided to increase capacity on the 6.10 pm. From 9th June, 1958, this ran as a complete 9-coach train from Victoria to Oxted, not splitting at East Croydon. From Oxted the front six coaches continued to Brighton; the rear three continued as the 6.54 pm Oxted to Tunbridge Wells via East Grinstead, replacing the push-and-pull connection. What used to be the slow portion of the 6.10 was taken over by a new 6-coach train that started at London Bridge at 6.15 pm, running to Tunbridge Wells via Edenbridge Town.

This close timing had the disadvantage that if the 6.10 was delayed (as it often was) it would get behind the 6.15 and would then stop for signals all the way to Oxted. The 6.15 was often held on the relief line at Windmill Bridge Junction waiting for the 6.10 to appear and pass in front of it, but there was a limit to the signalman's patience.

After this change the timetable was more or less fixed until June 1962. From 15th September, 1958, the 5.20 am Victoria to Tunbridge Wells was diverted to Eastbourne in the timings of the former 7.01 am Groombridge to Eastbourne, but it is not thought that any passengers actually used the train from end to end. From 15th June, 1959, the last train from Victoria, the 11.08 pm (10.08 pm on Sundays) was altered to leave half-an-hour later in response to public demand; two years later the trains were put back to their original departure times in response, it was said, to public demand!

From 18th June, 1962, diesel-electric units began operating many of the trains in 'steam' timings, and several alterations were made. All off-peak departures from Victoria were at nine minutes past the hour. The 10.38 am Victoria to Brighton no longer included an Eastbourne portion, and on Saturdays Eastbourne portions were not run in the 8.20 am Brighton to Victoria and 3.38 pm return. The 4.48 pm from Victoria no longer ran to Brighton; it was purely a Tunbridge Wells train. That did away with the detaching at Ashurst and the working thence to Tunbridge Wells of the rear portion by a locomotive off the Norwood goods. The 5.09 pm Victoria to Tunbridge Wells via East Grinstead (diesel) now included a portion for Brighton at rear, detached at Oxted. In the morning a new diesel train left Lewes at 6.38 am for Victoria, replacing the 7.12 am Tunbridge Wells to Victoria; to connect with it a push-and-pull train ran from Tunbridge Wells to Ashurst. More changes came in June 1963.

Freight traffic was declining in the early 1960s. Most of the trains were 'Saturdays excepted' and loaded to only a handful of wagons, which were ritually shunted at most of the yards down the line. In 1961/62 Norwood depot provided a 'C2X' or 'Q' 0-6-0 (later 'U1' 2-6-0) for the 5.20 am Norwood Yard to Groombridge and 7.05 am Norwood Yard to East Grinstead. The first train still called at Selsdon, Upper Warlingham, Oxted and Edenbridge Town; the second called only at Oxted and Lingfield, although no traffic for Oxted was conveyed. The return goods services were at 12.40 pm East Grinstead to Oxted (calling at Lingfield and Lingfield Brick Siding); 6.05 pm Oxted to Norwood Yard (calling at Upper Warlingham and Selsdon); and 7.55 pm Crowborough to Norwood Yard, calling at Oxted. Oxted Lime Siding was no longer served. On Saturdays, only the down Norwood-Lingfield freight ran, the engine returning light or working a freight if required.

However, one traffic seemed secure, and that was the bananas that were railborne to a ripening shed that Geest had set up at Lingfield in 1958. A daily train of refrigerated vans, sometimes as many as 30, brought in green bananas; hauled by a 'Q' class locomotive, it used to arrive at Lingfield at about 8.40 am. Later this train became diesel-hauled and continued running until 1st October, 1971. By then, BR had decided that the service was uneconomical and so Geest was forced to bring in the fruit by heavy lorries direct from Southampton. It was particularly regrettable as Geest had chosen the Lingfield site after much hunting, the decision being taken to build a depot there because of Lingfield's central location, the availability of a workforce, and the fact that it was the only place in south-east England with land for building adjacent to a siding. A regular railway service was then considered essential, although the ripened fruit was distributed by road to the various customers in Surrey, Kent, Sussex and South London. In the mid-1990s Geest PLC ceased operations at Lingfield.

1963 to 1987

Steam trains were progressively reduced in number during 1963 as the full diesel service was introduced. In May of that year the following trains were now booked to be diesel-hauled by type '3' locomotives: 6.29 am Victoria to Tunbridge Wells and 9.47 am return; 3.44 pm East Croydon to East Grinstead and 5.25 pm return to Victoria; 8.01 am London Bridge to Tunbridge Wells and 10.47 am return to Victoria; 3.54 pm Victoria to Brighton and 6.55 pm return; 4.48 pm Victoria to Groombridge and 9.20 pm Tunbridge Wells to Victoria.

On 17th June, 1963, a new accelerated service was introduced, with diesel trains scheduled to take 64 minutes from Victoria to East Grinstead, where some of them now terminated instead of running on to Tunbridge Wells. This was 11 minutes quicker than the steam schedule. The 8.01 am London Bridge to Tunbridge Wells was replaced by a train leaving Victoria at 8.09; the 4.48 pm Victoria to Groombridge now ran via East Grinstead instead of Edenbridge Town; and the 5.38 pm London Bridge to East Grinstead included a Brighton portion detached at Oxted.

Many more changes came with the introduction of the winter timetable on 9th September, 1963. The 5.20 am Victoria to Eastbourne was diverted to Brighton; a new train left London Bridge for East Grinstead at 7.55 am; and the 9.09 am Victoria to Tunbridge Wells via East Grinstead included a through portion to Tunbridge Wells via Edenbridge Town, detached at Oxted. The 8.34 am Brighton to Victoria and 3.54 pm return no longer conveyed through carriages between Eastbourne and London. Division of trains at East Croydon ceased when the 4.20 pm London Bridge to East Grinstead, which had for many years detached a Tunbridge Wells portion at East Croydon, no longer did so. Instead, a separate train for Tunbridge Wells now left London Bridge at 4.25 pm. The 5.06 pm Tunbridge Wells to London Bridge, always a slightly odd train, was replaced by a 5.49 pm East Grinstead to Victoria train. Finally, on Saturdays the 8.26 am Tunbridge Wells to London Bridge was discontinued - all part of the gradual reduction of London Bridge through trains.

BR took one look at Tunbridge Wells, noted that there were two routes to London (the main line via Tonbridge and Sevenoaks, and the Oxted line) and decided that this situation could not be allowed to continue. So, without even waiting until the normal date for timetable changes, the planners implemented big changes on 6th January, 1964, with the object of almost totally isolating Tunbridge Wells from Ashurst and Edenbridge Town. The Oxted-Tunbridge Wells service, with one exception, was diverted to Lewes, and most of the off-peak Victoria-Tunbridge Wells via East Grinstead now terminated at East Grinstead (Low Level). A few Tunbridge Wells-East Grinstead-London trains were retained in the peak hours, but that was all. Other alterations made on 6th January, 1964, included the diversion of the 6.25 am Victoria-East Grinstead-Tunbridge Wells to Brighton via Edenbridge Town; the diversion of the 5.20 pm London Bridge-Tunbridge Wells to Crowborough, balanced by a new 7.46 am Crowborough to London Bridge replacing the 7.55 am from Tunbridge Wells; and the introduction of a new train, 5.57 am Brighton to Victoria, replacing the 6.43 am from Tunbridge Wells to Victoria. The 9.38 am East Grinstead to London Bridge became the 9.45 East Grinstead to Victoria.

The freight service also was recast when booked to be diesel-worked in 1964. The 'Saturdays excepted' service now included a train at 4.15 am from Norwood Junction to East Grinstead, calling only at Lingfield. It returned at 10.18 am, calling at Lingfield, Lingfield Brick Siding when required, and Selsdon. A second train left Norwood Junction at 5.05 am for Selsdon and Oxted, the locomotive continuing light to East Grinstead to work an up passenger train. In the afternoon there was a train from Norwood Junction to Selsdon at 12.26, continuing to Oxted at 1.20 pm, and thence to Edenbridge Town at 2.25 pm. This returned to Oxted at 3.10, from where after two hours there was a further train to Selsdon and Norwood Junction due to leave at 5.25 pm. On Saturdays only one train ran each way: 5.55 am Norwood Junction to Selsdon, Oxted and Lingfield, returning at 9.00 am non-stop to Norwood Junction.

The last steam locomotives normally seen at Oxted had been the class 'H' on the push-and-pull services, but these were now replaced by the new Oxted-Lewes diesel service. Only very rarely did steam engines appear, and not at all after June 1965 except for the occasional enthusiasts' special.

The Sussex and Dorking Brickworks at Crowhurst, still rail-served on 18th July, 1966.
Author

By April 1966 there had been some further accelerations and East Grinstead was now reached from Victoria in exactly one hour. The 5.38 pm London Bridge to East Grinstead no longer had a Brighton portion; on Saturdays London Bridge lost yet another service, the 7.58 from Eridge; also on Saturdays the 7.23 am Eridge to Victoria started from Brighton at 6.25. During the currency of this timetable (which was now issued annually instead of twice a year) the Three Bridges-Groombridge line closed and the few remaining trains running between Tunbridge Wells and London via East Grinstead now started and finished at East Grinstead Low Level, the High Level and St Margaret's Loop falling into disuse.

Because the Southern Region did not really like running locomotive-hauled trains, it sought to reduce their number wherever possible. In 1965 the first of the 'Hampshire' diesel units of 1957 were brought in and took over some former diesel-hauled services. During November 1965 there was a great number of train failures, following which a type '3' locomotive was provided at Oxted as standby during the morning and evening business periods.

There had been a great deal of trumpeting about the 'entirely recast' timetable that was introduced on 10th July, 1967. It had been three years in the planning, and there had been questionnaires handed out about 'what sort of train service you want'. Actually the mountain became a molehill, for very few changes were made; it was basically the same service as before. One new train each way had been squeezed in, however: the 6.58 am Brighton-Oxted was extended to Victoria, due 8.50, and it was balanced by a new 5.37 pm Victoria to Brighton. The 4.25 pm London Bridge to Lewes now terminated at Hurst Green and the train later formed the 5.34 pm Oxted to Tunbridge Wells - the only remaining down train to use the Ashurst-Groombridge connection. The 5.34 pm from

London Bridge was now East Grinstead's best train, calling only at East Croydon and Oxted; moreover, it was locomotive-hauled where the old 5.38 had been a nine-car diesel! The train was accelerated by nine minutes, although unfortunately it never ran to time until about February 1968. Only two months before East Grinstead was given this semi-fast train the divisional manager, George Weeden, had said: 'East Grinstead, as a town, cannot demand a semi-fast train. Everybody wants a non-stop train from their station. The population of East Grinstead does not justify causing inconvenience to other people's services.' Well, he was half-right, because there was no semi-fast train up in the morning to balance the 5.34 down.

The Saturday service was almost entirely provided by three-car trains, most of which were very crowded. It took several years for this fact to sink in, and from May 1970 through portions to and from Uckfield were run in most Saturday trains, making six-car trains over the busiest section of the line.

Once again, it was during the currency of a timetable that big changes were made; on this occasion because of the closure of the Uckfield-Lewes section and Ashurst-Groombridge. There was a further reduction in the number of locomotive-hauled trains (there were now only four each way) and the service between Hurst Green and Uckfield was reduced so that the line could be singled without further disruption to the timetable, although the line actually remained double track. From 6th January, 1969, Uckfield became the terminus of most of the trains that had previously run to Lewes or Brighton. The 5.23 am from Victoria terminated at Oxted; the 5.20 pm London Bridge to Crowborough was extended to Uckfield; the 5.36 pm from Victoria terminated at Crowborough and also included an East Grinstead portion, detached at Oxted; the 5.34 pm London Bridge to East Grinstead now called at Hurst Green, Lingfield and Dormans; and the 6.15 pm from London Bridge now terminated at Hurst Green, continuing empty to East Grinstead to berth the 8-corridor set. Coming up, the 7.57 Crowborough to London Bridge was discontinued, but its timings from Hurst Green (depart 8.30) were taken up by a train that ran empty from East Grinstead. Running empty trains in the direction of the peak-hour flow was a new idea; presumably the planners didn't see why East Grinstead should benefit by the withdrawal of certain trains from Uckfield! Regular passengers soon got wise, and began to 'sit-in' at Hurst Green on the 6.15 pm down; from May 1969 the staff were informed that the 6.15 pm would convey East Grinstead passengers if required, but it was not to be advertised to do so. From 3rd May, 1971, the 8.30 am from Hurst Green started as a passenger train from East Grinstead at 8.11, but it was not until May 1974 that the 6.15 pm down was 'officially' extended to East Grinstead.

The number of off-peak semi-fast trains was reduced in January 1969, though there was still one starting from Hurst Green at 9.45 (all that remained of the former 8.27 am from Brighton). The 3.54 pm from Victoria still ran as far as Uckfield; a continuing reminder of the old 3.45 that had run ever since 1888. But the Saturday service was very much reduced, there being no fast trains at all and only two trains to London Bridge in the morning and nothing from there. Later in 1969 one of the semi-fast trains was restored on Mondays to Fridays when the 10.10 am Uckfield to Oxted was extended to Victoria, calling only at East Croydon.

From 6th May, 1972, only one train ran to London Bridge on Saturdays but in May 1977 even this sole survivor was diverted to Victoria. Through London Bridge services were now Mondays to Fridays only. From October 1972 the 4.25 pm London Bridge-Hurst Green was extended to Uckfield and a new train left East Grinstead for Victoria at 5.00 pm, Saturdays excepted. Further improvements came in May 1974 as the authorities realised that the 1969 cuts had perhaps been a little severe. The 5.36 pm Victoria-Crowborough was extended to Uckfield, and a new morning train left Uckfield for Victoria at 9.00 am, taking up the timings of the 9.45 from Hurst Green. Sunday services to East Grinstead, which had been two-hourly ever since 1955, were stepped up to hourly.

In May 1975 through portions to the Uckfield line were formed in all off-peak Monday-to-Friday East Grinstead trains except the 9.09 am, 1.09, 2.09 and 11.09 pm from Victoria. A new train left Victoria for East Grinstead at 3.40 pm, Saturdays excepted, taking up the timings of the 3.55 from East Croydon. The 8.22 am East Grinstead to Oxted, which had connected with the 7.55 from Uckfield to London Bridge, was now run as a through portion from Oxted to London.

Really big changes were brought in from 8th May, 1978, when the whole Central Division timetable was revised. Off-peak Victoria to East Grinstead and Uckfield trains now left at 13 minutes past each hour, and the peak service no longer bore much resemblance to that which had been in use for so many years. In the evenings, the principle appeared to be to provide two trains per hour from Victoria and four trains per hour from London Bridge. Once again, there was an afternoon train starting at 3.53 pm from East Croydon for East Grinstead and, what is more, it was locomotive-hauled, the 8-coach set used providing a superabundance of capacity, especially during school holidays.

The peak service of trains was now:

Up

am		Due
6.31	East Grinstead-Victoria	7.27
6.50	East Grinstead/6.27 Uckfield-London Bridge (semi-fast)	7.48
7.01	East Grinstead-Victoria	7.58
6.43	Uckfield-Victoria	8.13
7.25	East Grinstead-London Bridge (semi-fast)	8.18
6.58	Uckfield-London Bridge	8.28
7.21	Uckfield-Victoria (semi-fast)	8.43
7.53	East Grinstead-London Bridge	8.48
8.01	East Grinstead-London Bridge	8.58
7.43	Uckfield-Victoria	9.13
8.25	East Grinstead-London Bridge (semi-fast)	9.19
8.45	Hurst Green-London Bridge	9.28
8.49	East Grinstead/8.25 Uckfield-Victoria	9.51
9 09	East Grinstead-London Bridge	10.05
9.00	Uckfield-Victoria (semi-fast)	10.23

Down

pm
3.47   Victoria-Uckfield (semi-fast)
4.17   London Bridge-East Grinstead
4.35   London Bridge-Uckfield/East Grinstead (semi-fast)
4.38   Victoria-Uckfield
4.50   London Bridge-East Grinstead
5.05   London Bridge-East Grinstead/Uckfield (semi-fast)
5.08   Victoria-East Grinstead
5.20   London Bridge-Uckfield
5.35   London Bridge-East Grinstead (semi-fast)
5.38   Victoria-Uckfield/East Grinstead
5.50   London Bridge-East Grinstead
6.08   Victoria-East Grinstead/Uckfield
6.21   London Bridge-East Grinstead
6.35   London Bridge-East Grinstead (semi-fast)
6.42   Victoria-East Grinstead

It will be seen that some of the down trains ran in approximately their old timings, such as the 3.47, 5.08, 5.20, 5.35 and 6.08. Trains marked 'semi-fast' did not stop between East Croydon and Oxted, except that the 5.05 pm called at Sanderstead. This peak service was the most lavish ever offered to Oxted line passengers, but it lasted only three years before retrenchment came in.

However, before that, East Grinstead was given a new off-peak train at 9.24 am, which attached at Oxted to the 9.00 semi-fast train from Uckfield to Victoria, starting on 12th May, 1980. Unfortunately this new train tended to rob the 9.09 up of passengers, especially as off-peak tickets were not available, despite the fact that very few season ticket holders used it; and so the 9.09 was withdrawn from 1st June, 1981, and London Bridge lost yet another through train. Far worse than this was the placing of Uckfield portions at the front and East Grinstead at the rear of all down off-peak trains, so that the overall journey time was now 63 minutes, because of the increased waiting time at Oxted.

Because of the state of the track on the Uckfield line there was some deceleration, and perhaps it was felt that by sending the Uckfield portion from Oxted first the overall journey time would not be unduly increased. As it was, this branch already ranked among Britain's slowest. The East Grinstead portion of the 5.04 pm London Bridge to Uckfield was discontinued; the time spent detaching this at Oxted had tended the to delay the closely-following 5.06 from Victoria to East Grinstead, which was accelerated by five minutes from 1st June, 1981.

In August 1981 work on rebuilding Victoria station was begun, and in consequence there was a shortage of platform capacity. It was decided to divert the entire Oxted line service to and from London Bridge, with the exception of the 5.25 am Victoria-Oxted and 10.49 pm East Grinstead-Victoria. Very little notice was given, and Victoria passengers were duly disgruntled when these changes came into force on 5th October, 1981; they lasted until Sunday, 13th May, 1984. On the other hand, London Bridge passengers were delighted, especially as the journey time was reduced to 60 minutes from there to East Grinstead. The 8.25 semi-fast train from East Grinstead to London Bridge was replaced by an 8.27 slow train, taking up the timings of the 8.45 from Hurst Green to London Bridge.

Strange sight at Hurst Green on 22nd August, 1975, when the 4.20 pm London Bridge to East Grinstead finds itself only a few yards behind another train, which is fouling Hurst Green Junction.   *Author*

The 4.59 pm East Grinstead to London Bridge train passing Merle Common, between Crowhurst Junction and Hurst Green, on 12th April, 1979.   *Author*

Class '33' locomotive No. 33 058 with the 5.04 pm East Grinstead to London Bridge train on Cook's Pond viaduct, 12th May, 1980.   *Author*

No. 33047 enters East Grinstead with a ballast and ash train on 15th August, 1980. To keep the platform clear the demu working the 10.49 am up had to wait in the dock siding.   *Author*

From 14th May, 1984, the Victoria service was restored, but not at its previous timings. Off-peak trains now left at 36 minutes past the hour, with the East Grinstead portion at the front and Uckfield at rear once more. Peak services to Uckfield were savagely cut, as the intention was now to single the line; there were no separate Uckfield trains at all, only portions detached from East Grinstead trains. The popular 5.20 pm London Bridge-Uckfield, the only locomotive-hauled train down this line, made its last journey on 11th May. The 7.52 am East Grinstead to London Bridge was replaced by a 7.48 to Victoria (due 8.39) and the 6.35 pm semi-fast from London Bridge to East Grinstead was replaced by a 6.36 from Victoria. The full peak service from 14th May, 1984, was as follows:

am	Up	Due
6.17	East Grinstead-Victoria	7.13
6.09	Uckfield/6.48 East Grinstead-London Bridge (semi-fast)	7.37
7.01	East Grinstead-London Bridge	7.57
6.32	Uckfield-Victoria	8.05
7.26	East Grinstead-London Bridge (semi-fast)	8.15
7.50	Oxted-London Bridge	8.27
7.08	Uckfield-London Bridge (semi-fast)	8.30
7.48	East Grinstead-Victoria (semi-fast)	8.39
8.12	Oxted-London Bridge	8.51
8.03	East Grinstead-London Bridge	9.01
7.38	Uckfield-Victoria	9.11
8.26	East Grinstead-London Bridge	9.23
8.53	East Grinstead-Victoria	9.49
8.37	Uckfield/9.25 East Grinstead-Victoria (semi-fast)	10.15

pm	Down
4.10	London Bridge-East Grinstead
4.36	Victoria-Uckfield/East Grinstead (semi-fast)
4.40	London Bridge-Oxted
5.02	Victoria-East Grinstead/Uckfield (semi-fast)
5.08	London Bridge-East Grinstead
5.25	London Bridge-East Grinstead/Uckfield (semi-fast)
5.32	Victoria-East Grinstead
5.38	London Bridge-Oxted
5.50	London Bridge-East Grinstead
6.02	Victoria-East Grinstead/Uckfield (semi-fast)
6.18	London Bridge-East Grinstead
6.36	Victoria-East Grinstead/Uckfield
7.08	London Bridge-East Grinstead

Remarkably, some extra trains began to run on Saturdays, in belated recognition of the often-heavy traffic (especially shoppers) on that day. Additional trains from East Grinstead to East Croydon left at 6.52, 7.52, 8.52 and 9.52 am, returning at 2.21, 3.21, 4.21 and 5.21 pm. From October 1984 the 5.38 pm London Bridge to Oxted was extended to Eridge.

In contrast to the 1970s timetables those of the 1980s showed little stability. In May 1985 the off-peak departures from Victoria were altered from 36 past to 24 past; a year later, believe it or not, they were back to 36 past the hour again! Such alterations served only to irritate the travelling public. These were the dying days of the diesel-operated train service, for the line was now being electrified.

Chapter Six

Steam Locomotives

The Croydon, Oxted & East Grinstead Railway was not really a branch line but part of a series of alternative routes to various places quite far afield, and for this reason throughout its life it saw a larger proportion of tender engines than might be expected. Many different engine sheds supplied the motive power: Tunbridge Wells, Three Bridges, Newhaven, Brighton, Eastbourne and, in London, Battersea and New Cross. In Southern Railway days Battersea was closed and the allocation was transferred to nearby Longhedge (ex-London, Chatham & Dover Railway) which was renamed Stewarts Lane; New Cross was closed in 1947, being replaced by the nearby Bricklayers Arms depot (ex-SER); and at Norwood Junction a new shed was opened, this supplying the locomotives for the Oxted line goods services as well as some additional passenger trains at Bank Holidays.

The line had its fair share of new locomotives of Stroudley's design, although there may well have been odd survivors from the Craven regime; in particular Craven 2-2-2 locomotives Nos. 164/5 were at Tunbridge Wells from 1888 to 1890. But Tunbridge Wells also had Stroudley's 'G' class 2-2-2 No. 325 *Abergavenny* from October 1888 for working the 11.10 am to Victoria and 3.45 pm return trains. Battersea supplied Stroudley 'singles' for the 11.15 am and 5.00 pm Victoria to Tunbridge Wells trains, and New Cross 'singles' were on the 1.40 and 4.25 pm London Bridge to Tunbridge Wells. In the mid-1890s there were four of these engines at Tunbridge Wells, two still remaining in 1909.

In 1888 the 'Lyons' class 0-4-2, five of which were at New Cross, appeared on the 4.35 am goods to Tunbridge Wells and on some Oxted line passenger trains; and in the 1890s Brighton had four 'Belgravia' class 2-4-0 engines which were used on London via East Grinstead services. Stroudley's famous 'Gladstone' class 0-4-2 began putting in an appearance in the early 1890s, one occasionally working the 5.50 pm Victoria to Tunbridge Wells via East Grinstead and 8.40 pm return if a 'single' was not used. Later, the 'Gladstones' became more common, especially during and after the Great War: in 1917 there were five 'Gladstones' allocated to Tunbridge Wells and eight at Brighton; there would usually be one on the 6.57 am Brighton to Victoria via Eridge and 3.45 pm return. In spring 1920 Nos. 174/5/87 of Tunbridge Wells and 193 and 214 of Brighton were noted on Oxted line trains by H.C. Casserley at Clapham Junction; and by 1923 there were six shedded at Tunbridge Wells and 11 at Brighton.

These tender engines were supplemented by a great many tank locomotives, and the proportion of tank to tender engines increased over the years. Stroudley's 'D' class 0-4-2 tank engines proliferated and the first of the long line of 0-6-2 tank types, the 'E3', came out in 1894 under his successor, Robert Billinton. 'E3' class No. 453 was at New Cross in the mid-1890s to work the 6.00 am Norwood to East Grinstead goods train. There were also the very useful 'D3' class 0-4-4 tank engines, built between 1892 and 1896, four of them being allocated to Tunbridge Wells. Between December 1902 and May 1903 No. 387 of

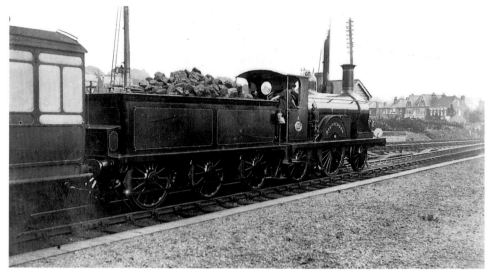

Selsdon Road with a down Oxted line train headed by Stroudley 'single' No. 329A *Stephenson*, built in 1881. Originally No. 329, it received the suffix in 1909 and was withdrawn five years later.
Lens of Sutton

Class 'E4' 0-6-2 tank, fitted with an Ashford pattern flush-fitting smokebox door, at Oxted about 1936 with a Victoria to Tunbridge Wells train, formed of four-corridor set No. 471. The train is a Bank Holiday working ; the engine was shedded at Norwood Junction, which did not normally have any passenger duties.

this class ran as an oil-burner on London Bridge-Tunbridge Wells trains, as did 'E4' class No. 565. Marsh began his 4-4-2 tank locomotive series with the 'I1' class in 1906 ; with their 5 ft 6 in. wheels these were more suited to the Oxted line gradients than the later version, the 'I3' class, which had 6 ft 9 in. driving wheels. Given larger boilers by the Southern Railway and reclassed 'I1x', they were even better, and most were still at work on the line until 1947/48. In 1908 two of the 'I2' class were at Tunbridge Wells, and four 'I4' engines, Nos. 31-4, were at Battersea for the Oxted line trains. The 'I3', being a main line engine, did not appear on the Oxted line until later; on Saturdays in 1916 the 6.57 am Brighton to Victoria via Eridge and 3.45 pm return were in their charge.

The South Eastern used tender engines on its service via Oxted, the 'E1' class 2-4-0 in the early days and the 'F' class 4-4-0 later, although trains reversing at Edenbridge were often hauled by a 'Q' class 0-4-4 tank. After Grouping more ex-SECR types did show up, both regularly and at Bank Holiday times, being sent out in the main from Stewarts Lane and Bricklayers Arms: classes 'B1', 'D', 'E' and 'E1' 4-4-0, and the ever-reliable 'H' class 0-4-4 tank engines.

Meanwhile the Brighton was introducing more tender locomotives, primarily for the main line but some did filter through to the Oxted route. The 'B4' class 4-4-0 was certainly seen, particularly on race days, as were the smaller 'B2' and 'B2x' 4-4-0 ; but the 'H1' and 'H2' class Atlantics did not work regularly until about 1916, except on 'running-in' when fresh from Kitson & Co. (Nos. 37-41) or Brighton works (Nos. 421-6). From 1916 an Atlantic was often on the 6.57 am Brighton to London Bridge via Ashurst, the 8.05 am Brighton to Victoria via Ashurst, and 3.45 pm return. As for goods tender locomotives, the 'C2' class 0-6-0 was very popular but the 'C3' class 0-6-0 less so; in 1911 No. 300 was at New Cross and No. 305 at Tunbridge Wells for Oxted line goods trains.

In the last couple of years of the LBSCR the following locomotives were noted at East Grinstead Low Level: 'D1' class No. 248 of Tunbridge Wells (rebuilt after an accident with square-topped tanks); 'E5' class No. 403 of Brighton; 'E5' class Nos. 567/74 of Battersea; 'D3' No. 390 of Tunbridge Wells; 'I1' Nos. 3 and 7 (New Cross and Battersea respectively); 'I2' Nos. 14 and 19; and 'I3' No. 85 of Battersea. At the end of 1922 there were seven 'D1', three 'D3', one 'E3', four 'E4' and two 'I1' shedded at Tunbridge Wells. Also noted at East Grinstead in 1922/23 (by local resident Kenneth Nutt) were 'A1x' 0-6-0 tank No. 663, 'D1' 0-4-2 tanks Nos. 214, 244 and 252; 'E5' 0-6-2 tank No. 585; 'I1' No. 1 of Tunbridge Wells; 'I2' Nos. 11, 12 and 16; and 'I3' No. 30 of New Cross. On race days 'B4' class 4-4-0 locomotives Nos. 46 and 74 were visitors to East Grinstead.

During the 1920s the Oxted line continued to be worked by ex-LBSCR and ex-SECR locomotives, now appearing in Southern Railway livery with their numbers prefixed by the letter 'B' or 'A'. The 'Gladstone' 'B1' class was still often seen on the 3.45 pm Victoria to Brighton via Eridge, Nos. B176/83/93/98 being noted at various times. The number of 'D3' 0-4-4 tanks in the area increased, many of the machines being fitted for working push-and-pull trains, although many of these continued to be worked by the tiny 'D1' class 0-4-2 tanks. In 1924 the 4.44 pm London Bridge-Uckfield was 'D3'-worked, and there was a Tunbridge Wells 'D3' on the 8.10 pm London Bridge to Tunbridge Wells; in June 1931 there were 11 'D3' locomotives allocated to that depot.

Marsh 4-4-2 tank engine class 'I2' No. 14 at East Grinstead Low Level; the driver is taking advantage of some time in hand to go round with his oil can. *C.E.K. Nutt*

Marsh class 'I3' 4-4-2 tank No. 85 runs round its train by using the north crossover at East Grinstead Low Level. On the balcony of the North signal cabin stands porter-signalman George 'Juggy' Wren, *c.*1921. *C.E.K. Nutt*

One afternoon in 1926 Patrick Ransome-Wallis took his camera to Oxted and Hurst Green Junction and photographed a procession of trains which have been identified with a fair degree of certainty as:

2.12 pm Tunbridge Wells West to Victoria, with 'D3'No. B373 (Tunbridge Wells West). Two 3-sets; one of which was attached at Ashurst (1.42 pm from Uckfield).
1.25 pm Brighton to Oxted push-and-pull, with 'D1' No. B215 (Brighton).
2.25 pm East Grinstead to Oxted goods, with 'E6' No. B410 (New Cross).
3.45 pm Victoria to Brighton/Eastbourne, with 'B2x' No. B206 (Battersea). Van, two bogies for Brighton; 2 bogies and van for Eastbourne.
3.43 pm Haywards Heath to London Bridge, with 'B1' No. B193 (Brighton).

Illustrations of all five appeared in *Southern Album* (Ian Allan, 1968), some with inaccurate captions. It is recorded that a 'B2x' was the regular power for the 4.10 pm London Bridge to Brighton via East Grinstead during 1928.

Tunbridge Wells West depot had class 'I1x' Nos. B1-10 (later renumbered 2001-10) throughout most of the 1930s, and 'I4' Nos. B31-35 (later 2031-35) until they were withdrawn. By 1933 the 'I3' 4-4-2 tanks were distributed among Stewarts Lane, New Cross, Brighton and Three Bridges, but by 1939 Tunbridge Wells had Nos. 2021/2/4 and Three Bridges' share had been replaced by 'I1x' Nos. 2602-4. Brighton also had lost all its 'I3' engines, being left with two 'I1x' (Nos. 2595 and 2600).

On Saturday, 3rd October, 1936, H.C. Casserley photographed some early afternoon trains near Hever; the list shows that the motive power had changed little since 'Brighton' days:

12.20 pm London Bridge to Tunbridge Wells, with 'I3' No. 2084. 6-corridor set 465 or 466.
1.20 pm Tunbridge Wells to Oxted motor train, with 'D1/M' No. 2224. Push-and-pull set 720.
2.12 pm Tunbridge Wells to Victoria, with 'I1x' No. 2007. Duty 626. Two 3-sets (ex-SECR) and van.
1.38 pm London Bridge to Tunbridge Wells, with 'B4' No. 2062. Duty 701. 7-set 686 (ex-SECR stock).

At holiday times one could see some unusual engines, particularly ex-SECR types, such as the 'B1', 'E' or 'E1' 4-4-0. A Lingfield race special was worked by a Stewarts Lane 'H' 0-4-4 tank, No. 1533, on 22nd May, 1937. In spring 1937 Eastern Section 'L', 'L1' and sometimes 'E' class locomotives began working the 5.20 pm London Bridge to Tunbridge Wells, all from Bricklayers Arms Shed (no doubt New Cross men were sorely displeased with this state of affairs). An Eastern 'E1' of Bricklayers Arms was also on the 6.22 am Brighton to London Bridge via East Grinstead and the 5.40 pm London Bridge to East Grinstead. A Tonbridge 'L1' worked the 7.25 am Edenbridge to London Bridge via the Crowhurst spur. Examples of the SER 'F1' 4-4-0 (which had outside springs on the tender) were seen on the 11.08 am Victoria to Eastbourne and 8.03 am London Bridge to Brighton about 1932. Oliver Potter, of Edenbridge, recalled that the SECR 'J' class 0-6-4 tank locomotives were regular performers on Tonbridge to London Bridge trains and did well between Crowhurst Junction and Hurst Green - always very heavy going - when in charge of the 7.26 am Edenbridge to London Bridge.

Two of the ex-LBSC 'D3' 0-4-4 tanks had been rebuilt by Marsh as 'D3x' with larger boilers, and between 1935 and 1937 both these rarities were allocated to Tunbridge Wells (SR Nos. 2396/7). The first was withdrawn in May 1937, but the other was transferred to Eastbourne by 1939. Another rare rebuild, 'E4x' No. 2477, was at Norwood Shed in the late 1930s, and turned up at Oxted on a Bank Holiday train in 1939. Norwood also sent out 'E4' 0-6-2 tank No. 2498 to work an extra train to Oxted composed of 4-corridor set No. 471 and two loose corridor coaches.

During late August/early September 1938 A.C.E. Notley made some observations of Oxted line motive power on trains running via East Grinstead. The following were noted:

8.21 am Lewes to London Bridge: 'B4' 4-4-0 2042, 2044, 2062, 2063.
8.03 am London Bridge to Brighton: 'B1' 4-4-0 1013, 1101, 1440, 1459.
10.48 am Brighton to Victoria: 'E4' 0-6-2T 2465, 2484; or 'E5' 0-6-2T 2405, 2594.
12.03 pm Victoria to Brighton: 'E1' 4-4-0 1019, 1165, 1511
3.35 pm Haywards Heath to London Bridge: 'I1X' 4-4-2T 2006, 2602 or 'E4' 0-6-2T 2498, 2512. On 7th September: 'D3' 0-4-4T 2370.
4.20 pm London Bridge to Brighton: 'B4' 4-4-0.
5.18 pm Brighton to Victoria: 'E1' 4-4-0 1019, 1165, 1511.
5.40 pm London Bridge to Lewes: 'B4' 4-4-0 2044, 2063, or 'I1x' 2599, or 'E5' 0-6-2T 2567.

On Sunday, 21st August, 1938, the 8.36 am London Bridge to Brighton and 6.48 pm return were worked by Stirling 'B1' class 4-4-0 No. 1013, and 'B4' 4-4-0 No. 2063 was on the 6.40 pm London Bridge to Brighton. There were only two trains each way via East Grinstead Low Level on Sundays. These observations originally appeared in *Bluebell News* Vol. 2 No. 10 (December 1960).

During winter 1937/8 New Cross Gate Duty No. 544 was booked for a 'B4x' 4-4-0 or 'I3' 4-4-2 tank, and the following trains were worked: 6.10 am vans London Bridge to Brighton via main line, 10.18 am Brighton to Victoria via Ashurst and 3.55 pm return; light to Haywards Heath thence 8.35 pm passenger to London Bridge via East Grinstead. It is recorded that No. 2045 of New Cross ran at up to 70 mph on the 3.55 pm.

Also during 1937/38 a Brighton-based 'B4' 4-4-0 had a duty on the 6.22 am to London Bridge via East Grinstead; except Saturdays it returned on the 5.40 pm to East Grinstead, continuing as the 7.07 pm to Lewes and 9.18 pm freight to Brighton. On Saturdays it took the 1.38 pm London Bridge to Tonbridge via Ashurst, and 5.11 pm Tonbridge to Brighton. Another Brighton 'B4' worked (Saturdays excepted) the 6.58 am Brighton to London Bridge via Ashurst, 1.33 pm London Bridge to Tonbridge via Ashurst, and 5.15 pm Tonbridge to Brighton.

The workings were altered for the winter 1938/9 timetable. New Cross Gate was still sending out 'B1' 4-4-0 Nos. 1013, 1101 and 1440 on the 8.03 am London Bridge to Brighton via East Grinstead, but the return working was the 3.35 pm Haywards Heath to London Bridge. Another 'B1' was in charge of the 1.33 pm London Bridge to Tonbridge via Ashurst, 5.16 pm Tonbridge to Brighton and 11.18 pm vans Brighton to London Bridge via the main line.

By 1939 the allocation of 'D3' 0-4-4 tanks at Tunbridge Wells had been reduced from 13 in 1933 to five, and the four 'D1' 0-4-2 tanks of 1933 had been replaced by three (Nos. 2244, 2275 and 2358). In addition, No. 2224 of Tonbridge Shed was often seen on Oxted push-and-pull trains in the late 1930s.

Duty numbers began to be displayed on one of the headcode discs of each locomotive from about 1936. As blocks of these numbers (beginning at 501 for Stewarts Lane in the case of the Central Section) were used for each depot, it helped the observer to identify to which shed a particular locomotive was allocated. Tunbridge Wells numbers originally began at 620, though in later years the commencing number became 655. Similarly, Brighton numbers, which had begun at about 675, later started at 730. Some sheds were more conscientious about displaying duty numbers than others; Tunbridge Wells, Eastbourne and New Cross Gate were usually very good, but Brighton and Three Bridges seldom displayed their numbers.

Gradually the 'I3' 4-4-2 tank engines became the mainstay of the Oxted line. The 1939 allocation of three at Tunbridge Wells (2021/2/4) was augmented in 1940 by Nos. 2076 and 2084; by about 1943 that depot had Nos. 2021-30 and New Cross Nos. 2075-7/9/85/7. These locomotives were not ideal for the line but performed well, according to Norman Harvey (writing in *Railway World*, September 1960).

Goods trains seem to have been in the hands of the 'C3' 0-6-0, No. 2302 of Norwood Junction being noted on the Tunbridge Wells to Norwood freight. On rare occasions they were seen on passenger trains: on 21st June, 1937, No. 2300 of Horsham worked the 6.48 pm Victoria to East Grinstead.

Push-and-pull trains, previously worked almost entirely by 'D1/M' 0-4-2 tank engines, were now worked by 'D3' 0-4-4 tanks, which had been fitted with motor gear. Sometimes an 'E4' 0-6-2 tank would appear, but as none of these was fitted for auto-train working they had to 'run round' the train at each end of the working. An 'E5' 0-6-2 tank, No. 2594, was fitted for auto-train working in July 1938 and used on the Oxted lines, but by summer 1939 it had been transferred to Horsham.

The 'H1' and 'H2' class Atlantics, displaced by electrification of the main lines, went briefly to the 'Chatham' line, but returned to their home area and, from about the summer of 1938, began working some Oxted line trains such as the 3.55 pm Victoria to Brighton semi-fast. In 1940 one was regularly on the 10.18 am Brighton to Victoria and 4.50 pm return. Then in February 1944 an 'H1' was seen on the 10.50 am Brighton to Victoria via East Grinstead; the 5.18 pm Brighton to Victoria via East Grinstead was also regularly worked by an 'H2'.

In January 1946 Nos. 2421/2 were transferred from Brighton to Newhaven Shed, and the 8.18 am Uckfield to Victoria and 6.10 pm return trains began to be worked by an Atlantic (Newhaven Duty No. 786). Two Atlantics, Nos. 2424/5, were at New Cross for the 3.25 am London Bridge to Brighton via the main line and 6.58 am return via Ashurst, but in December 1947 all the surviving Atlantics were concentrated at Newhaven. Here, their Oxted line duties were: No. 782 - 8.22 am Lewes to London Bridge and 5.40 pm (Saturdays excepted) return or 5.09 pm (Saturdays only) Victoria to Lewes. No. 783 (Saturdays excepted) - 8.18 am Uckfield to Victoria and 6.10 pm return. These workings were maintained until 1952, after which Atlantics appeared only occasionally.

The Maunsell 'N' class Moguls were unusual on passenger workings during the war, but from January 1946 the 10.50 am Brighton to Victoria and 3.55 pm

During 1952 the 1.42 pm (Saturdays-only) London Bridge to Tunbridge Wells was booked to be worked by a class 'N' 2-6-0 of Bricklayers Arms (duty No. 532). Here No. 31855, which was allocated to that depot then, stands at Oxted with this train, while passengers head for the connecting service which is waiting in the down bay.   *Lens of Sutton*

Oxted to Norwood Junction freight train at Selsdon, headed by class 'Q' 0-6-0 No. 30537 of Norwood depot about 1955.   *Lens of Sutton*

return were regularly worked by No. 1851 or 1854, which had been transferred from Exmouth Junction to Brighton. From mid-1946 an 'N' worked the 8.00 am Brighton to Victoria and 12.03 pm return, and the 10.50 am up became the preserve of No. 1817, the first 'N' to be painted malachite green and lined out (by Ashford works). 'N' class Oxted line duties until July 1947 were:

Bricklayers Arms Duty No. 532: 10.18 am Brighton-Victoria and 5.09 pm Victoria-Forest Row or East Grinstead.
Norwood Junction Duty No. 581: 7.25 pm freight Norwood-Lewes via East Grinstead.
Brighton Duty No. 735: 6.15 am Brighton-London Bridge.
Brighton Duty No. 737: 8.00 am Brighton-Victoria, 12.03 pm Victoria-Brighton and 5.18 pm return.
Brighton Duty No. 738: 10.50 am Brighton-Victoria and 3.55 pm return.
Brighton Duty No. 740: 8.21 am Lewes-London Bridge and 5.40 pm (Saturdays excepted), 4.18 pm (Saturdays only) return.

In July 1947 the 'N' class locomotives were largely replaced by three-cylinder 'U1' 2-6-0 machines, Nos. 1890-4. These now worked Brighton duties Nos. 735, 737 and 738; duty No. 740 was altered to take in the 6.58 am Brighton to London Bridge and 4.20 pm return (Saturdays excepted); Bricklayers Arms duty No. 532 remained the same but booked for a 'U1'. Between 1947 and 1952 Stewarts Lane rostered a 'U1' for the 4.50 pm Victoria to Brighton (Duty 501); and between 1947 and 1950 a Redhill-based 'U1' worked the 9.28 am Tunbridge Wells West to Victoria and 5.50 pm return (Duty No. 620). This seems to have been the only period that a Redhill engine was regularly seen on the Oxted line. The 'U1' class largely disappeared when the LM and BR 2-6-4 tanks took over most trains in 1951, but was usually seen on race specials.

Two well-loved locomotives were the Marsh 4-6-2 tanks, class 'J1' No. 2325 and class 'J2' No. 2326. Based at Stewarts Lane in the later years of the war, about January 1946 both locomotives were transferred to Tunbridge Wells. No. 2325 had only recently been repainted black, but in June 1946 it received a coat of malachite green; the 'J2' had also been painted green a month earlier. Withdrawal of both engines came in 1951. On 22nd May, 1951, the LM 2-6-4 tank working the 4.40 pm London Bridge to Uckfield failed at Eridge, and 'J2' No. 32326 hauled the empty train and its defective engine back to Tunbridge Wells. As its reward for assisting a failed modern locomotive it was withdrawn a week later! Still, as both the 'J1' and 'J2' had lasted longer than many people expected and had needed frequent repairs to keep them going, it was not too surprising that BR should wish to eliminate them.

Because the 'I3' class was proving somewhat inadequate, the Southern in 1947 decided to try its own design of 0-6-0 goods locomotive on Oxted line passenger trains: class 'Q', of 1938. No. 543 was loaned by Horsham to Tunbridge Wells, and on 3rd April it worked the 4.02 pm relief service from Victoria to Eastbourne. The 'Q' was one of the few tender engines that could use the small turntable at Tunbridge Wells; however, it was not until the following year that four of the 'Q' class, Nos. 30534, 30542/3 and S544, were allocated to Tunbridge Wells, where they remained until August 1950 when they were displaced by new 2-6-4 tank engines. Three Bridges also had three from 1948:

Nos. 540/1 and 547. One of these was rostered to work the 8.21 am Forest Row to Victoria and 6.48 pm Victoria to East Grinstead (Saturdays excepted) or 7.42 pm London Bridge to Haywards Heath (Saturdays only); and another, on Duty 676, was on the 10.52 am Tunbridge Wells to London Bridge and 4.44 pm East Croydon to Tunbridge Wells. After 1950 the 'Q' did not normally appear on passenger trains except on odd occasions, although for a time during 1958/9 the 8.24 am Forest Row to Victoria regularly had one provided by Three Bridges, and in the early 1960s the 'Q' used on the Norwood to Groombridge freight regularly took the rear portion of the 4.50 pm Victoria-Brighton from Ashurst to Tunbridge Wells before returning on the up freight.

The former South Eastern depot at Tonbridge was responsible for some of the Oxted line workings. During the 1947-52 period an 'L' class 4-4-0 was provided for the 7.26 am Edenbridge to London Bridge via Oxted, returning to Tonbridge via Orpington; and from 1948 to 1950 a Tonbridge 'D1' 4-4-0 was booked to work the 10.06 am Tunbridge Wells to Victoria and 2.30 pm (Saturdays excepted) or 1.25 pm (Saturdays only) return, on Duty No. 294.

When the allocation of 'I3' engines at Bricklayers Arms was reduced to one (No. 2075) in December 1948, Duty No. 533 began to be worked by an ex-SECR class 'E' 4-4-0 (8.03 am London Bridge to Brighton and 8.35 pm Haywards Heath to London Bridge), until the arrival at Bricklayers Arms of new 2-6-4 tank locomotives. The other major ex-SECR locomotive to figure largely on the Oxted line was the 'H' class, fitted for push-and-pull working; these rapidly replaced the ex-LBSCR 'D3' 0-4-4 tanks. Three 'H' class were on loan to Tunbridge Wells from Stewarts Lane in November and December 1948; then in February 1949 Nos. 31177, S1184 and 1295 were transferred there from Stewarts Lane. No. 31016 followed in July. After that, the allocation changed frequently, but these engines were always popular with Tunbridge Wells men, and did excellent work on the Oxted push-and-pull train service for many years.

The 'I3' 4-4-2 tanks were rapidly being withdrawn as new 2-6-4 tanks were allocated to the Oxted line depots. By October 1951 only two remained, Nos. 32075 and 32091, both at Three Bridges; the final survivor, No. 32091, worked the 10.52 am Tunbridge Wells to London Bridge and 7.42 pm London Bridge to Haywards Heath during December 1951.

Between July 1950 and June 1951, Brighton works constructed 41 class '4' 2-6-4 tank locomotives which were virtually identical to the London, Midland & Scottish Fairburn engines of 1945, with 5 ft 9 in. driving wheels. Boiler pressure was 200 lb. per square inch; water capacity 2,000 gallons and coal capacity 3½ tons. All were built for use on the Southern Region; Nos. 42096-106 came first, followed immediately by Nos. 42066-95. The May 1951 allocation of engines required for Oxted line working was: 42080-2, Bricklayers Arms; 42083-5, Stewarts Lane; 42086/7, Newhaven; 42088-93, Brighton; 42095-106, Tunbridge Wells West. (The remainder were at Ramsgate, Ashford and Dover.) Following the departure of Nos. 42083-5 to the North Eastern Region in March 1952 there was considerable reshuffling of those remaining.

These, the first *new* engines for the line since the time of Stroudley, worked almost all Oxted line trains, with the result that variety of motive power largely disappeared. As soon as Brighton works had completed the order it went straight on with constructing BR Standard 2-6-4 tank locomotives, of which Nos. 80010-19 and 80031-33 were specifically intended for the Oxted line. These BR engines were similar in some ways to the LM version, but better looking; they had curved tank and bunker sides to match the profile of BR standard coaches, and the typical sloping front connecting the running plate and the buffer beam. Length over buffers was 44 ft 10 in., height from rail to chimney 13 ft, coupled wheelbase 15 ft 4 in. and total wheelbase 36 ft 10 in. The boiler pressure was 225 lb. per square inch, water capacity 2,000 gallons and coal capacity 3½ tons. Driving wheel diameter was 5 ft 8 in. No. 80010 left the works in July 1951, and on the 20th made its first observed appearance in London when it worked the 11.05 am Brighton to Victoria via East Grinstead. The first 10 were initially allocated to Tunbridge Wells, displacing several LM 2-6-4 tanks, and Nos. 80031-3 went to Brighton in March 1952. All further construction of BR tanks was for other Regions until the final 10, Nos. 80145-54, were built between October 1956 and March 1957; these were all allocated to Brighton. No. 80154 was the last locomotive built at Brighton works, so it was fitting that it should remain on the Southern Region.

Another 'foreign' type of engine started to appear from about October 1951: the LM class '2' 2-6-2 tank locomotive, built at Crewe to an Ivatt design first introduced in 1946 by the LMS. The batch of new engines allocated to the Southern Region, where they were known as 'Teddy Bears', was Nos. 41290 to 41319, of which the 1952 Central District allocation comprised: 41290-7, Stewarts Lane; 41298-41303, Bricklayers Arms; 41304-7, Three Bridges; 41316-9, Eastbourne; and 41313-5, Brighton. As they were not very powerful they never worked the heavy peak-hour trains, but were quite suitable for light trains and were popular with enginemen. Later in 1952 Nos. 41313-15 were transferred to Exmouth Junction and Eastbourne's allocation moved to Tunbridge Wells; Nos. 41304/5 went from Three Bridges to Eastleigh. By June 1955 only Nos. 41318/9 remained at Tunbridge Wells.

Both the LM classes were forbidden to work between Tunbridge Wells West and Tonbridge, but the BR 2-6-4 tanks had no such restriction.

For the two Oxted line freight services during the 1947-52 period Norwood Junction rostered class 'C2x' 0-6-0 engines: Duty 592 took in the 5.10 am Norwood to Groombridge and 5.03 pm Tunbridge Wells to Norwood, and Duty 591 the 7.05 am Norwood to East Grinstead and 2.10 pm return. In summer 1952 a Norwood 'C2x' was booked to take the 3.44 pm (Saturdays excepted) East Croydon-Tunbridge Wells passenger train, but only as far as Upper Warlingham; here, engines were changed and a Three Bridges LM '4MT' tank on Duty 677 took the train from there to Tunbridge Wells.

The Bulleid Pacifics later became regular performers on the line, normally on the semi-fast trains between Brighton and London via Ashurst. The first appearance of a 'West Country' class at Oxted was that of No. 21C101 *Exeter* on its first day in traffic, 21st June, 1945. It worked the 8.00 am Brighton to Victoria and 12.03 pm return (via East Grinstead). Next day, No. 21C103 *Plymouth* worked the 8.00 but suffered from a 'hot box' and remained in London, the 12.03 being taken by an ancient 'B1' 4-4-0, No. 1450.

The next reported sighting of a 'West Country' on the line was not until 28th September, 1948, when No. 34034 *Honiton* worked the 4.50 Victoria to Brighton.

This picture of Oxted dates from 1960 or 1961, for the BR Standard 2-6-4 tank engine shown is No. 80068, which was transferred from the London Midland Region to Stewarts Lane in December 1959. It is working possibly the 2.08 pm Victoria to Tunbridge Wells train, and the stock is Bulleid five-corridor set No. 804. Class 'H' 0-4-4 tank on Oxted-Tunbridge Wells push-and-pull train stands in the down bay. *Lens of Sutton*

Class '4PT/FT' No. 42074, built at Brighton in November 1950, with a Tunbridge Wells to Victoria train at Selsdon, about 1955. Very few Oxted line trains called here in the 1950s. *Lens of Sutton*

Nos. 21C133/5 and 34034/6 were the first of the class to be allocated to Brighton (September 1948), but by the end of the year all four were replaced by Nos. 21C137/8 and 34039/40. They do not seem to have had any regular duties on the Oxted line until early 1950, when the 6.58 am Brighton to London Bridge was booked for one (Brighton Duty 740). Since January 1950 there had been seven Bulleid Pacifics at Brighton, Nos. 34035-41; however, maintenance standards were not high and between 20th July and 12th September no 'West Country'could be spared for this train. From 15th January, 1951, the 10.18 am Brighton to Victoria via Ashurst and 3.52 pm return were worked by a Bulleid Pacific instead of the booked 'U1' class 2-6-0, but this working did not last long. Brighton did not seem to have the ability to look after its Pacifics, and passed them on to other depots that could, receiving as replacements Nos. 34045-8 from Salisbury in June 1951. Once again, there were no booked 'West Country' workings on the Oxted line, the 2-6-4 tanks taking over virtually every train. Bulleid Pacifics did not return, except on odd occasions, until 1958.

The heavily-loaded 6.10 pm from Victoria was a poor timekeeper and the cause of many complaints while worked by a 2-6-4 tank engine. It was decided to work it regularly with a Bulleid Pacific from 15th September, 1958, and from then on there was always one of them on this train. Provided by Brighton Shed, the locomotive came up on the 1.55 pm Brighton to Victoria. The down train left Victoria from Platform 17 and, although banked out by a 'C2x' 0-6-0, which had brought in the empty stock, the Pacific usually slipped on the complicated crossovers leading to the down fast line and continued to slip until the whole train either crawled on to Grosvenor Bridge or stopped just short of it. The departure platform was changed to No. 16 to give the train a slightly straighter run out, but the trouble persisted and the 6.11 pm slow to Coulsdon North could often get as far as Balham before the 6.10 fast thundered by trying to make up time. The Brighton allocation of Bulleid Pacifics in 1960 was 34008/19/38/39/55/57/98. Between June 1961 and June 1962 the 1.55 pm up and 6.10 pm down were entrusted to a Bricklayers Arms rebuilt Pacific - often No. 34101 *Hartland* - working Duty No. 531.

In the mid-1950s maintenance of the 2-6-4 tank locomotives was poor and failures frequent. On 17th November, 1954, for example, No. 42082 seized up at Lingfield while working the 8.03 am London Bridge to Brighton; another locomotive took over the train, which left over 40 minutes late. Two other 2-6-4 tanks failed on the same day while working the 4.40 and 5.09 pm down trains. On 11th July, 1955, No. 42067 failed at Honor Oak Park on the 6.30 pm London Bridge-Forest Row; it got to East Croydon somehow and the engine was coaxed into the siding there. The only replacement was a very leaky 'E6' goods 0-6-2 tank, No. 32413 from Norwood Yard; this machine was duly coaled and watered and staggered off with the 200-ton load. Arrival at Forest Row was 1½ hours late!

Because of the many failures, two of the BR Standard 2-6-0 locomotives, Nos. 76005/6, were loaned from Eastleigh to Brighton in mid-January 1954 and tried out on the line. On 18th January No. 76006 worked the 8.20 am Brighton to Victoria and its sister the 11.02 am Brighton to Victoria and 3.52 pm return. Both did quite well, but apparently were not quite up to scratch and, about April, were transferred to Dorchester. A later batch of these Moguls - Nos. 76053-62 - was allocated to Redhill in mid-1955 and during 1958 one would occasionally turn up on the 3.50 pm Victoria to Brighton instead of the booked Three Bridges tank engine.

Further attempts to supplement the 2-6-4 tanks were made in December 1954, when four class 'U1' 2-6-0s, Nos. 31900-3, were transferred from Stewarts Lane to Brighton. These were booked to work the 6.24 am (SX) or 7.06 am (SO) Brighton to London Bridge and 4.20 pm (SX) or 4.18 pm (SO) return; 8.00 am (SX) Brighton to London Bridge and 5.40 pm (SX) London Bridge to East Grinstead; and 8.20 am Brighton to Victoria, 12.03 pm return, and 5.18 pm Brighton to Victoria. However, these engines were transferred away in May 1955.

In the new timetable of 1955, which actually began on Wednesday 15th June because of the locomen's strike, it was intended that almost all trains should be worked by 2-6-4 tank engines. The summer 1956 timetable was also largely operated by tank engines which were being worked to the limit, and so Stewarts Lane started to send out an 'N' or 'U1' Mogul on the 5.50 pm Victoria to Tunbridge Wells. The situation was eased with the introduction of BR-built tank engines Nos. 80145-54 between October 1956 and March 1957.

The main operating disaster of 1955 was the attempt to run the Tunbridge Wells to Oxted push-and-pull service with 'M7' 0-4-4 tanks. To make way for them several of the successful and well-liked 'H' class were transferred from Tunbridge Wells, their unwelcome replacements being Nos. 30054-9. The enginemen just could not get on with the 'M7' at all; as one driver later wrote: 'Even the inspectors sent to show us how to work them lost time'. To make up for their shortcomings some 'H' class were 'borrowed' from Tonbridge, as well as the last example of the London, Chatham & Dover 'R' class 0-4-4 tank engine, No. 31666, and the last example of the LBSCR 'D3' 0-4-4 tank, No. 32390 (from Brighton). On 20th, 28th and 29th July, 1955, No. 32390 was noted on the 6.36 pm East Croydon to Tunbridge Wells (part of Duty 669); it was withdrawn in October. The 'R' class worked the 6.36 pm on 28th June and 1st and 14th July, and the 6.54 pm Oxted to Tunbridge Wells on 4th and 5th July (Duty 671). In November it was again working Duty 669, but was withdrawn the following month. All the 'M7' locomotives were transferred from Tunbridge Wells in May 1956, being replaced by more 'H' class engines. These ruled the roost until 1963, as far as working push-and-pull trains between Tunbridge Wells and Oxted was concerned.

Another former London & South Western locomotive to appear, but only on rare occasions, was the 'T9' 4-4-0. On 25th May, 1955, No. 30718 of Nine Elms depot worked the 5.18 pm Brighton to Victoria via East Grinstead, having earlier worked an inspection special from Waterloo to Brighton via Eastleigh and Fareham. On Sunday 9th February, 1958, 'T9' No. 30719, also of Nine Elms, worked the 12.55 pm Brighton to Victoria after having been retubed at Brighton works. These are the only known recorded sightings of the class in BR days, apart from the occasion when a Stewarts Lane 'T9', No. 312, worked the 9.09 am Victoria to Tunbridge Wells on Whit Monday, 7th June, 1949.

The Bulleid 'Q1' 0-6-0 was also quite a rarity and, although there were no booked workings, the following were sighted:

No. 33026 (Tonbridge) on the 5.50 pm Victoria-Tunbridge Wells, 29th April, 1949.
No. 33037 (Stewarts Lane) on the same train, 13th August, 1949.
No. C7 (Guildford) on the 3.28 pm Haywards Heath-London Bridge, 9th December, 1949.
No. 33033 (Tonbridge) on the 3.38 pm Victoria-Brighton, 4th August, 1956.
No. 33014 (Hither Green) on the 9.55 am Brighton-Victoria, 19th December, 1957. This train was booked for a Tonbridge 'U1'.

The 'Schools' class 4-4-0 was a rarity on the Oxted line until 1959/60, when some of them were transferred to Brighton. Early sightings included that of No. 30924 (Bricklayers Arms) on 28th March, 1955, when it worked the 7.26 am Edenbridge to London Bridge; No. 30909 on 24th September, 1958, on the 7.19 am Brighton to London Bridge; and 30936 on 29th September and 2nd October, 1958, working the 1.55 pm Brighton to Victoria and 6.10 pm return in place of the usual Bulleid Pacific. Until mid-1961 a 'Schools' usually worked the 7.17 am Brighton to London Bridge and 4.40 pm return (Duty No. 740), when it was replaced by a Bulleid Pacific. As usual, Brighton's low maintenance standards ensured that even a magnificent 'Schools' would be a failure on a modest six-coach load, mainly because the sand-boxes were not kept filled.

In the latter part of 1957 timekeeping of the heavy business trains was very poor. On 4th December, 1957, a 'fog' service was in operation, and the 5.38 pm from London Bridge left 1hr 40 min. late because its crew had been delayed reaching the engine. On another occasion in December the 2-6-4 tank working the 5.38 pm ran out of steam at Upper Warlingham, but managed to reach Lingfield where the passengers were detrained. It was later alleged that the crew were willing to continue nursing the sick engine to East Grinstead, but were under orders to terminate the train at Lingfield.

By August 1958 it was reported that timekeeping of the 5.38 pm London Bridge to East Grinstead had further deteriorated, and the 5.50 pm from Victoria, which from October to December 1957 had never once run to time, was also very bad: on 14th May, 1958, it was stated to have arrived at East Grinstead 1¼ hours late! In January 1959 three BR class '4' 4-6-0 locomotives were transferred from the South Western Division, Nos. 75070/4/5. From February No. 75074 began working the 8.24 am Forest Row to Victoria and 5.49 pm Victoria to Groombridge; No. 75075 was seen on the 8.20 or 9.55 am Brighton to Victoria and 3.50 pm return; and No. 75070 often took the 7.19 am Brighton to London Bridge. There was an improvement in timekeeping almost immediately, possibly because of the presence on the footplate of a motive power inspector during the first few weeks. Even then, the 4-6-0 on the 8.24 am from Forest Row would run out of breath on the long pull up from Lingfield through Oxted, traverse Oxted tunnel at approximately walking pace, and usually flake out just north of the tunnel. Five minutes of firing-up saw it on its way again.

Later, the three 4-6-0 engines were joined by a fourth, No. 75069, and by 1960 this and No. 75074 were allocated to Stewarts Lane, while Nos. 75070/75 were at Three Bridges. Until June 1962 they were booked to work the following two diagrams:

Stewarts Lane Duty No. 503. 6.29 am Victoria to Tunbridge Wells; light engine to turn via Eridge and Ashurst Junction; 1.47 pm Tunbridge Wells to Victoria; 5.49 pm Victoria to Groombridge; again light engine to turn via the Ashurst triangle and return to Victoria on the 9.20 pm from Tunbridge Wells.

Three Bridges Duty No. 677. 7.07 am Three Bridges to Forest Row and 8.24 am thence to Victoria; 3.50 pm Victoria to Brighton via Ashurst and 6.55 pm return; then to Three Bridges presumably on freight or parcels via main line.

If available Three Bridges sent out its other 4-6-0 on the 7.41 am East Grinstead to London Bridge, returning on the 5.37 pm (Duty No. 676). The coaches of this train were shunted at East Grinstead from Low Level to High Level, forming the 7.26 pm to Victoria; the locomotive returned to Three Bridges from Victoria on a van train.

The next major change of motive power was the disposal of all the LM Class '4' 2-6-4 tank engines to the London Midland Region in December 1959 and their replacement by an equivalent number of BR Class '4' required for Oxted line duties. The newcomers were allocated as follows: Nos. 80066-68/81, Stewarts Lane; 80082-85, Bricklayers Arms; 80088/89/94, Three Bridges; 80095, 80137-42, Tunbridge Wells West; 80143/44, Brighton. These joined Nos. 80010-13, 80031-33 and 80145-54, already at Brighton, and 80014-19 at Tunbridge Wells. In mid-1961 Tonbridge depot received several standard tank engines from Ashford (Nos. 80037-43/59/64/65), one from Stewarts Lane (80066) and one from Bricklayers Arms (80085), although there were actually only two Tonbridge duties that included Oxted line workings. No. 80087 was transferred from Ashford to Three Bridges, which thus had four of the class.

Portions of some of the Monday-to-Friday locomotive diagrams in force from September 1961 to June 1962 are quoted below.

Tonbridge Duty No. 222. Class '4' 2-6-4T. 9.55 am Brighton to Victoria and 4.48 pm return.
Tonbridge Duty No. 226. Class '4' 2-6-4T. 9.47 am Tunbridge Wells to Victoria and 7.08 pm return.
Stewarts Lane Duty No. 502. Class '4' 2-6-4T. 10.38 am Victoria to Brighton.
Bricklayers Arms Duty No. 531. Class 'West Country' 4-6-2. 1.55 pm Brighton to Victoria and 6.10 pm return.
Bricklayers Arms Duty No. 533. Class '4' 2-6-4T. 8.01 am London Bridge to Tunbridge Wells; 3.47 pm Tunbridge Wells to East Croydon and 5.27 pm empties thence to London Bridge.
Tunbridge Wells Duty No. 655. Class '4' 2-6-4T. 7.12 am Tunbridge Wells to Victoria and 10.08 am return.
Tunbridge Wells Duty No. 656. Class '4' 2-6-4T. 7.55 am Groombridge to London Bridge; 4.20 pm London Bridge to East Grinstead; light engine to Oxted; 6.54 pm Oxted to Tunbridge Wells (rear portion of 6.10 pm Victoria).
Tunbridge Wells Duty No. 658. Class '4' 2-6-4T. 11.47 am Tunbridge Wells to Victoria and 3.08 pm return; 5.47 pm Tunbridge Wells to Victoria and (probably) 9.08 pm return.
Tunbridge Wells Duty No. 659. Class '4' 2-6-4T. 8.26 am Tunbridge Wells to London Bridge and 5.20 pm return.
Tunbridge Wells Duty No. 664. Class '4' 2-6-4T. 7.03 am Tunbridge Wells to London Bridge; 3.44 pm East Croydon to East Grinstead; 5.26 pm East Grinstead to Victoria; 8.08 pm Victoria to Tunbridge Wells.
Three Bridges Duty No. 674. Class '4' 2-6-4T. 10.47 am Tunbridge Wells to Victoria and 2.08 pm return.
Three Bridges Duty No. 678. Class '4' 2-6-4T. 4.44 pm East Croydon to Tunbridge Wells (rear portion of 4.20 pm ex-London Bridge); 7.47 pm Tunbridge Wells to Victoria.
Brighton Duty No. 740. Class 'West Country' 4-6-2. 7.17 am Brighton to London Bridge and 4.40 pm return.

Brighton Duty No. 742. Class '4' 2-6-4T. 7.35 am Brighton to Victoria; 11.08 am Victoria to Tunbridge Wells; 2.47 pm Tunbridge Wells to Victoria; 6.48 pm Victoria to East Grinstead and light engine to Tunbridge Wells.
Brighton Duty No. 745. Class '4' 2-6-4T. 9.09 am Victoria to Tunbridge Wells; 12.47 pm Tunbridge Wells to Victoria and 5.09 pm return.

Since October 1961 most of the class 'U1' 2-6-0 were operating from Norwood Junction Shed, and these locomotives were now working the Oxted line goods trains in place of the 'C2x' and 'Q' locomotives. The 'Q' could sometimes still be seen, however; on 7th June, 1962, one was on the 7.55 pm Crowborough to Norwood Yard freight, and another most surprisingly on the 7.47 pm Tunbridge Wells to Victoria passenger.

Although the Oxted-Tunbridge Wells push-and-pull service was almost invariably worked by class 'H' 0-4-4 tank locomotives there were occasionally shortages of these stalwarts and, during January 1960, the service was worked by several class 'L1', 'C' or 'D1' tender engines from Tonbridge depot. They had to run round the coaches at Oxted and run tender first in one direction - most unpleasant in the cold weather. Tunbridge Wells sent out its last 'E4' 0-6-2 tank, No. 32581 (which had been allocated there since June 1951) each day from 16th to 20th January, 1960, to work the 3.00 pm to Oxted and 4.04 pm return trains. Although not fitted for push-and-pull working this 'E4' did occasionally cover for the 'H' class, for example on 14th April, 1960, when it worked the 7.24 pm Oxted to Tunbridge Wells. However, even on the 'H' class the air-control gear was not always operable, as R.W. Kidner remembers:

> I recall at Lingfield watching the 6.54 pm Oxted to Tunbridge Wells push-pull and seeing the fireman leaning out to open the regulator on a signal from the guard. I suppose as the driver had the brake it did not really matter.

From 18th June, 1962, Bricklayers Arms Shed was closed and its 'West Country' Pacifics sent to Brighton. Tonbridge also ceased to have any engine workings, although retained for a while as a stabling point. Several 2-6-4 tank engines were transferred away; a Brighton-based 'Schools' class now worked the 7.17 am to London Bridge and 4.40 pm return until 28th December, 1962; after this the 'West Country' class was back on these trains. The 3.54 pm Victoria to Brighton and 4.48 pm Victoria to Groombridge were worked by BR class '4' 4-6-0s during April 1963 and until June. Towards the end of 1962 the last steam class to appear on the Oxted line, the 'W' 2-6-4 tank, began working some of the goods trains, including the pick-up freight train from Norwood Junction that ran to Edenbridge Town on alternate days.

In late June 1963 the only steam-hauled trains observed at Oxted were the 7.00 am Forest Row to London Bridge (a 'Q' class of Three Bridges); the 8.24 am Forest Row to Victoria (a Stewarts Lane class '4' 4-6-0); the 9.55 am Brighton to Victoria; the 4.44 pm East Croydon to Tunbridge Wells; and the 5.06 pm Tunbridge Wells to London Bridge (all Tunbridge Wells class '4' 2-6-4 tanks). 'H' class locomotives now operated the push-and-pull trains in the morning and late afternoon busy periods only.

From 9th September, 1963, all booked steam working through Oxted came to an end and Tunbridge Wells West Shed was closed except as a stabling point.

East Grinstead High Level, and freight train starting to traverse the St Margaret's loop. It is headed by class 'W' 2-6-4 tank No. 31921, a rarity when the picture was taken about 1960.   *P.W. Chapman*

Steam locomotives did appear occasionally, to cover for failed diesel locomotives, but these appearances grew more rare as time went on. Stewarts Lane depot was closed to steam on 9th December, 1963, and Brighton on 15th June, 1964.

Steam traction had had a long life on the Oxted line, and no doubt many people considered that its replacement was well overdue. As long as trains continued to be steam-hauled the schedules were painfully slow: for example, 1¼ hours from London to East Grinstead compared with the 1993 standard electric timing of 52 minutes. Down trains almost always needed to take water at Oxted, for which they were allowed three minutes. But, whatever its shortcomings, from the purely aesthetic point of view nothing could rival a steam-hauled train; whether seen in sunshine or rain the sight and sounds were incomparable.

As an example of how travel by steam train was something to savour, here is another recollection by R.W. Kidner, this time of a foggy winter's evening about 1950. The fog was so dense that men were climbing the signal ladders at London Bridge Low Level to see what aspect was showing. The Oxted line train, hauled by a class 'I3', left from Platform 9 at Low Level

> . . . and I travelled in the raised guard's seat in a 'birdcage' brake end at the front of the train overlooking the engine. I well remember the light from the firebox shining on the fog while going up the bank from New Cross Gate, when the firing seemed continuous. It was something the like of which will not be experienced again.

Chapter Seven

Steam Coaching Stock

LBSCR and SER

At the time of opening, the Stroudley four-wheeled close-coupled sets were becoming numerous. The coaches were only 26 ft long over body and had very cramped third class compartments although the firsts were, in contrast, wide and luxurious. A distinctive feature of these sets was the guard's duckets, or side lookouts, at each brake-end, where the overall width was 9 ft. It is possible that even earlier stock was in use on the line in the 1880s. Under R.J. Billinton's regime some bogie coaches began to appear in 1894, but they were scarce and his 32 ft six-wheeled stock was far more likely to have formed the majority of Oxted line trains. During the Edwardian era most trains were formed with both six-wheeled and bogie coaches, randomly provided, and topped and tailed by a six-wheeled brake van. The plain arc roof was favoured by the 'Brighton', Billinton's version being higher in the centre than Stroudley's.

Main line stock was not unknown, however, and in 1906 it is recorded that one such train, formed of seven six-wheelers plus brake vans, had been fitted with incandescent gas burners and was booked to work the 5.25 pm London Bridge to Tunbridge Wells and 7.40 pm return. On race days the seven-coach 'bogie block' sets were sometimes used, as their seating capacity was high; these sets, built during 1900/1, were unusual in having toplights. Later, much of Billinton's six-wheel stock was converted to bogie, each of the third brakes being made up from a five-compartment third joined to a brake van on a new 54 ft underframe; as the guard's ducket had been in the centre of the van body it was now about halfway along the brake portion of the bogie coach. Several three-coach bogie sets now began to appear, composed of two rebuilt third brakes and a composite, some of which were lavatory-fitted. Nevertheless, the mixed six-wheel/bogie trains continued in use until the early 1920s, and up to 1922 there was still a regular working between London and East Grinstead of a six-wheeled, close-coupled 'long' set. Set numbers were in use latterly, the coaches being lettered on the solebar 'Set Train No. 89', for example; and several trains also bore the set number in large numerals on the brake-end.

Few carriage workings are known. In July 1918 the 6.20 am Brighton to London Bridge via East Grinstead was booked to be formed of Set 78 or 79, plus two bogie composites and a six-wheeled van. In January 1919 Set 55 was in the 10.30 am Brighton to Victoria via East Grinstead, the 5.50 pm (Saturdays) or 6.00 pm (not Saturdays) Victoria to Tunbridge Wells and 9.00 pm return, and the 12.05 midnight Victoria to Brighton via the main line.

The South Eastern's Oxted line service began with very short four-wheeled carriages in sets of nine, each of the first and second class vehicles having three compartments and the thirds four. Later the SER used six-wheeled stock with the odd four-wheeler included, together with a lavish sprinkling of small vans, until about 1910.

Oxted viaduct, view east. An up train, with 0-6-2 tank engine and six-wheeled coaches, is crossing. The photograph was taken not later than 1908.   *A.H. Homewood, Burgess Hill*

London Bridge to East Grinstead train passing Hackenden, about a mile north of East Grinstead. The train, a mixture of 6-wheel and bogie stock, is headed by an 0-4-2. Cook's Pond viaduct is faintly visible in the distance.

By 1909 some of the trains had been given set numbers, but by no means all. A formation comprising two brake vans, a six-wheeled second and a third, plus a bogie first, was booked to work the 9.15 am London Bridge to Edenbridge, 10.41 am Edenbridge to Cannon Street, 12.30 pm Cannon Street to Oxted and 2.26 pm Oxted to London Bridge. A similar formation, but with one of the brake vans replaced by a six-wheeled brake third, was scheduled for the 8.23 pm Charing Cross to Oxted and 9.40 pm Oxted to Cannon Street. A numbered set was, however, booked for the amazing 7.00 am Dover Town to Charing Cross via Tonbridge, Oxted and the Mid-Kent line in 1909: Set 74 or 76 on alternate days, formed entirely of bogie stock and comprising a third brake, lavatory tri-composite, composite (1st and 2nd), lavatory third and third brake. The journey time of this train was not much short of four hours!

Large numbers of three-coach bogie sets, with distinctive 'birdcage' roof lookouts for the guard at each end, were appearing from 1910 onwards, but it is not certain whether these ran on the Oxted line until the 1920s. They were, after all, main line stock. In 1922, for example, only one SECR train was booked to be worked by a three-set, this being the odd 7.46 am Woldingham to London Bridge. The only other SECR trains in 1922 were one up in the morning from Tonbridge to London Bridge and one down in the afternoon or evening, but they were not part of the same carriage working. For the 7.33 am up, two four-coach sets of the 'Caterham/Tadworth' type were used (three six-wheelers and a bogie composite), plus a loose six-wheel second and a loose six-wheel third. On the other hand, the 1.34 pm (Saturdays) and 6.27 pm (not Saturdays) London Bridge to Tonbridge via Oxted used a five-coach set - either No. 256 or 261 - formed of four bogie coaches and a six-wheel second, together with loose stock comprising two six-wheel thirds, a six-wheel second and, except on Saturdays, a bogie composite. All these SECR trains were markedly superior to those of the 'Brighton'; more of the compartments had lavatory access and all the carriages had elliptical roofs instead of the already old-fashioned plain arc roofs of the LBSCR's trains. Moreover, until the LBSCR stock, which was Westinghouse air-braked, could be converted to vacuum braking it was incompatible with the ex-SECR stock.

Southern Railway

Most of the train services continued to be worked by former 'Brighton' three-coach sets until the 1930s, when they began to be withdrawn. Former SECR three-coach sets also worked many of the services and their number increased as the number of ex-LBSCR vehicles diminished. Certain services continued to be operated by specified sets each day, these usually being simple 'out-and-home' workings; in contrast, the three-sets worked complex cyclic diagrams in which the vehicles ended the day often many miles from where they had started.

The February 1926 carriage working notice shows that the 6.47 am Tonbridge-Cannon Street via Tunbridge Wells and Oxted was worked by Set 679, eight close-coupled ex-SER bogies. The return journey was by the ex-SECR main line

Oxted to Brighton via East Grinstead and Lewes train, with a 'D3' class and 1909-built ex-SECR three-coach set at Hurst Green Halt about 1938.   *Lens of Sutton*

A push-and-pull train from Brighton via East Grinstead has just shunted to the down platform at Oxted and the driver of 'D3' 0-4-4 tank engine No. 2367 speaks to a station man while the fireman transfers the route-indicating discs to the other end of the train on 2nd August, 1937.
                                                                                    F.M. Gates

except on Saturdays when it formed the 1.30 pm London Bridge-Edenbridge via Crowhurst Junction. Another long set of ex-SECR stock, No. 698, worked the Saturdays excepted 6.27 pm London Bridge to Tunbridge Wells West via Crowhurst, having worked up in the morning over the Sevenoaks line.

Former LBSCR stock working shown in a September 1928 carriage working notice included the following:

3-set 781 or 782	8.27 am Forest Row-Victoria, 5.50 pm Victoria-Tunbridge Wells West.
5-set 849	6.37 am Tunbridge Wells-Victoria, 4.05 pm return via Three Bridges and East Grinstead.
6-set 891	2.55 pm London Bridge-Oxted, 3.59 pm return.
6-set 917	8.32 am Uckfield-London Bridge, 4.40 pm return.
Part 7-set 935	7.51 am Eastbourne-Eridge-Victoria and 3.45 pm return.
Part 7-set 935	8.05 am Brighton-Eridge-Victoria and 3.45 pm return.

Sets 781/2 were fitted for 'slipping', each set working every other day in the 5.05 pm London Bridge-Forest Row, being slipped from the main train at Horley or Three Bridges. Set 917 was four bogies and two six-wheeled brake vans, and Set 935 ran as seven vehicles between Eridge and Victoria, three bogies and a six-wheeled van being the Brighton portion and two bogies with a six-wheeled van the Eastbourne portion.

More train services were booked to be worked by specified sets by September 1931, as under:

3-set 781 or 782	8.27 am Forest Row-Victoria, rear portion of 6.10 pm Victoria-Tunbridge Wells (not Saturdays); 5.20 pm Victoria-Forest Row via Three Bridges.
5-set 849 (not Sats)	8.32 am Uckfield-London Bridge, 4.40 pm return.
4-set 851	8.32 or 8.40 am Tunbridge Wells-London Bridge and 10.40 am return; 1.08 pm Tunbridge Wells-London Bridge and 8.00 pm (not Sats) return.
4-set 862	8.03 am London Bridge-East Grinstead-Brighton and 11.30 am return.
5-set 882 or 883	8.10 am Lewes-East Grinstead-London Bridge. Next day: 5.08 pm Victoria-East Grinstead-Lewes.
8-set 890	6.58 am Brighton-London Bridge via Eridge. Return via main line.
6-set 891 (not Sats)	Up via main line. Return on 5.20 pm London Bridge-Tunbridge Wells.
5-set 888 (Saturdays)	1.26 pm Victoria-Forest Row, 3.10 pm return.
5-set 934	2.53 pm London Bridge-Oxted, 3.59 pm return.
4-set 935	8.05 am Brighton-Eridge-Victoria and 3.45 pm return.

Most of these sets were composed of ex-LBSCR arc-roofed bogie coaches, some of which were lavatory-fitted. Set 935 was three bogies and a six-wheeled brake van; the Eastbourne portion was now only a single lavatory brake composite (No. 6937 was specified). Sets 882, 883 and 934 were formed of high-roofed stock - often called 'Balloon' stock - and were restricted to ex-LBSCR lines. Set 851 remained in London on Saturday afternoons and Sundays, returning to Tunbridge Wells on a Sunday evening service. On Saturdays an ex-SECR four-coach set, No. 688, worked the 1.38 pm London Bridge to Tonbridge via Edenbridge Town and Tunbridge Wells. Also on Saturdays there was a single unbalanced working of the new Maunsell 8 ft 6 in.-wide corridor stock, when a five-coach set (No. 191, 192 or 220) appeared on

A Bank Holiday duty: class 'I1x' 4-4-2 tank No. 2001 of Tunbridge Wells Shed displays both duty number (603) and train number (366) as it enters Oxted with an afternoon Tunbridge Wells to London Bridge train formed of a Maunsell three-corridor set.

Lens of Sutton

the 5.14 pm Brighton-East Grinstead-Victoria. All other trains were booked to be worked by three-sets, either singly or two together, and mostly of the ex-SECR 'birdcage' type.

Maunsell stock did appear from time to time, especially when certain Hastings line trains were diverted via Crowhurst Junction and Oxted; during the summer Saturday timetable some trains were scheduled to take this route, continuing up the Mid-Kent line. Ex-LBSCR sets disappeared in the late 1930s.

In summer 1938 several Maunsell three-coach corridor sets of the 9 ft-wide type were displaced from the London-Bognor line by electrification and started to appear on the better Oxted line trains, notably the 3.55 pm Victoria-Eridge-Brighton/Eastbourne and presumably the balancing up working, and the 8.29 am Forest Row to Victoria. The two 1925-built 'Ironclad' corridor sets, Nos. 471/2, were reduced in length and began to be allotted certain Oxted line train services, but following wartime reduction in the timetable were spare.

For the May 1941 timetable only three sets were booked to work specified trains. Two of these were composed of ex-SECR coaches: six-set 685 appeared on the 7.00 am Brighton to London Bridge, returning (except on Saturdays) on the 5.20 pm London Bridge-Tunbridge Wells, thence to Brighton at 7.37 pm. On Sundays it returned to Brighton on the 6.40 pm from London Bridge via East Grinstead. Seven-set 902 was on the 7.47 am Tunbridge Wells-London Bridge and 5.50 pm (Saturdays excepted) Victoria-Tunbridge Wells or 12.20 pm (Saturdays only) London Bridge-Tunbridge Wells. Five-corridor set 455 - a mixture of 'Ironclad' and ex-London & South Western vehicles - worked the 8.30 am Tunbridge Wells-London Bridge and 4.40 pm (Saturdays excepted) London Bridge-Uckfield or 1.25 pm (Saturdays) Victoria-Tunbridge Wells. By May 1944 Set 685 had been replaced on the same workings by six-corridor set 471: set 455 by five-corridor set 472; and set 902 by a newly-formed eight-corridor set, No. 194, in which the brake coaches were the second and seventh vehicles. Set 194 was composed entirely of Maunsell 9 ft-wide coaches.

Maunsell corridor three-sets now appeared on several other trains, such as the 6.37 am East Grinstead-London Bridge, 6.45 am Tunbridge Wells-Victoria, 8.21 am Forest Row-Victoria and 7.52 am Eastbourne/8.00 am Brighton-Victoria. In the down direction Maunsell sets could be seen on the 3.55 pm Victoria-Brighton, 5.09 pm Victoria-East Grinstead, 6.10 pm Victoria-Tunbridge Wells and 6.48 pm (Saturdays excepted) Victoria-East Grinstead. Seven Maunsell sets were diagrammed each day. Ex-SECR three-coach lavatory sets were still very much in evidence, however, on both peak and off-peak trains. They seemed to have been around forever.

By 1944 ten three-corridor sets had diagrams on Oxted line train services, being berthed at Brighton, Eastbourne, East Grinstead (two sets), Forest Row, Haywards Heath, Lewes, Tunbridge Wells West (two sets) and Victoria. Also four of the Eastern Section four-corridor sets of 8 ft 6 in. stock were now working on the Central Section, as under:

(1) 6.18 am   Brighton-East Grinstead-London Bridge and empty to Rotherhithe Road. Saturdays excepted: 3.25 pm Charing Cross-Tonbridge-Tunbridge Wells West (via Sevenoaks). Saturdays only: 1.42 pm London Bridge-Tunbridge Wells West via Edenbridge Town (rear portion).

(2)   7.25 am   Tonbridge-Brighton, 10.50 am Brighton-East Grinstead-Victoria, 9.20 pm
            (Saturdays excepted) Victoria-Tunbridge Wells West or 2.30 pm (Saturdays)
            Victoria-Tunbridge Wells West
(3 and 4)   9.28 am Tunbridge Wells West-Victoria, 4.50 pm Victoria-Brighton (front set)
            and Tonbridge via Tunbridge Wells West (rear set).

In 1947 sets Nos. 194, 471 and 472 were still booked for the same trains as in 1944. Seven-corridor set No. 461 (Eastern Section 8 ft 6 in. stock built in 1925) was now berthed at Tunbridge Wells West to work, Saturdays excepted, the reinstated 7.06 am to London Bridge and 6.30 pm return, both via East Grinstead. On Saturdays it formed the 10.52 am to London Bridge and 12.47 pm return.

Many of the Tunbridge Wells-Oxted services were booked to be worked by a two-coach push-and-pull set. In the 1920s a set comprising one 'Balloon' saloon driving trailer coupled to a low-roof compartment composite would come up to Oxted from Brighton. From about 1930 only arc-roof LBSCR push-and-pull sets were seen in the area, the Tunbridge Wells allocation being Nos. 754 and 986. No. 753, based at Brighton, was seen at Oxted also. The 1931 allocation at Tunbridge Wells was Nos. 754/5 and 984, two being diagrammed and the other a relief set. By 1935 only sets 984/7 were stationed at Tunbridge Wells and they were still there in 1939, although by then they had been renumbered 717/20. After this, auto-sets began to move around more and there was no fixed allocation; not only ex-LBSCR sets but ex-SECR ones began to turn up at Oxted.

Working of auto-trains north of Oxted was extremely rare, but during 1941 the 7.24 pm East Croydon-Tunbridge Wells was booked to be a push-and-pull set; its previous working was the 5.12 pm from Tunbridge Wells. By April 1944 this train was being worked by a three-set (not push-and-pull).

British Railways

As far as the operating department was concerned there was no sudden change of policy once the SR had become the Southern Region. Carriages continued for a few years to be painted in the malachite green that had been introduced in 1939. Within a short time some non-corridor sets began to be repainted red and some corridor sets became red and cream; others, however, contrived to remain green at each revarnishing.

The 1948 allocation of sets to work the Oxted line was Nos. 194, 461, 471 and 472, plus a number of Maunsell three- and four- corridor sets and several ex-SECR three-sets. Seven-set 461 was transferred away in May 1949 and ex-SECR seven-set No. 903 arrived to take up the working of the 7.06 am Tunbridge Wells to London Bridge and 12.20 pm (Saturdays) or 5.20 pm (Saturdays excepted) return. No. 903 was now the only ex-SECR 'long set' to be allocated to the Central Section and was one of the few to receive red livery with yellow and black lining. It remained on these workings until April 1956.

Six-corridor set 471 worked the 6.58 am Brighton to London Bridge and 4.40 pm London Bridge to Uckfield thence empty to Tunbridge Wells and return to Brighton at 7.27 pm, all 'Saturdays excepted'. In 1953 it was replaced in these workings by a new six-corridor set, No. 876, at that time the only set that included BR standard coaches to be allocated to the line.

Four-corridor set 472, usually working with a loose coach at one end, was now booked to work (Saturdays excepted) the 8.30 am Tunbridge Wells to London Bridge and 10.45 am return, and the 1.08 pm Tunbridge Wells to London Bridge and 6.30 pm return, all via East Grinstead. On Saturdays it was provided for the 10.06 am Tunbridge Wells to Victoria and 1.25 pm return. Set 472 was transferred from the Oxted line in June 1955.

Eight-corridor set 194 worked the 7.47 am Tunbridge Wells to London Bridge and 5.50 pm Victoria to Tunbridge Wells; on Saturdays for a while it also filled-in on the 10.45 am London Bridge to Tunbridge Wells and 2.10 pm thence to Victoria. From 1951 it did no work on Saturdays. From June 1955 the Monday-to-Friday workings were replaced by a Bulleid eight-set, No. 767, which remained in traffic until 1963. It was berthed at Groombridge, and later the morning train was arranged to start there at 7.55, the 5.50 pm down terminating there also.

At this time few of the business trains were longer than six or seven coaches, eight-set 194 being exceptional. Capacity was adequate and it was not until the mid-1950s that season-ticket holders increased to a level that caused severe overcrowding. In 1949 the 5.40 pm London Bridge to East Grinstead, normally composed of an ex-SECR three-set, a loose corridor third and a Maunsell corridor three-set, still had plenty of room. Some of the 'birdcage' sets had unbalanced workings: for example, two sets came up on the 7.26 am Edenbridge to London Bridge via Crowhurst Junction; one returned to Tunbridge Wells as the rear portion of the 4.20 pm from London Bridge, the other set ran empty to Rotherhithe Road where it remained for the rest of the day. The 8.22 am Lewes to London Bridge (later the 8.00 am from Brighton) was a single three-set which later formed the rear portion of the 5.25 pm London Bridge-Reading, detached at Redhill and continuing to Tunbridge Wells via Tonbridge.

The first Bulleid three-coach sets allocated to the line were Nos. 795 to 802 in 1954. No. 802 was made up to five coaches for the timetable changes of 1955, when it was booked to work the new 7.04 am Forest Row to London Bridge, returning as the 6.30 pm to Forest Row. Set 801 was similarly made up to five vehicles in November 1956, and the two sets then began turn-and-turn-about two-day cyclic working. Sets 795 to 800 were transferred away from the line in 1959.

Workings of five-sets 801 and 802 from 1957 to 1962 were as under:

Day One: 8.26 am Tunbridge Wells-London Bridge and 6.31 pm London Bridge to Forest Row.

Day Two: 7.00 am Forest Row to London Bridge, 5.37 pm London Bridge to East Grinstead, 7.26 pm East Grinstead to Victoria and 9.08 pm Victoria to Tunbridge Wells.

Other Bulleid three-sets transferred to the Oxted line were Nos. 768, 769 and 850 in 1955; four years later they were gone. It was from the mid-1950s that rolling stock showed the greatest variety: SECR non-corridor, Maunsell, Bulleid and BR corridor, LBSCR and SECR push-and-pull sets and, from April 1956, BR non-corridor in the shape of six-set 904, the only such set on the Central Division. Five of the coaches were new, but the sixth was actually an ex-LSWR vehicle, completely non-matching. It was replaced in November 1958 by two Bulleid corridor coaches, so that Set 904 was now seven vehicles. Its regular workings were the 7.03 am Tunbridge Wells to London Bridge and 5.20 pm return.

When Set 904 replaced Set 903 the latter was berthed at East Grinstead and from June 1956 until late March 1957 part of it was used for the front portion of the 7.42 am to London Bridge and the front portion of the 4.20 pm return. Then in June 1957 Set 904 was damaged while being shunted at New Cross Gate; Set 903 was reassembled and was used as a substitute for Set 904 until September or later. It often happened that a 'scratch' set had to be assembled to stand in for the booked set when it was away at works being overhauled or repainted.

Newly-formed Set 804, which comprised four Maunsell coaches and one Bulleid, went into traffic on 1st April, 1957 to replace part-set 903 on the 7.41 am East Grinstead-London Bridge and 4.20 pm return; another similar five-set, No. 803, was made up about the same time as a spare. In November 1958 No. 803 was re-formed to include the brake second from Set 804, which in May 1959 was altered to comprise entirely Bulleid vehicles. Either set could be seen on the 7.41 up and 4.20 down.

There was also a plentiful supply of loose coaches used to strengthen trains at peak and sometimes off-peak times. For many years the formation of the 6.10 pm from Victoria was: two corridor seconds, one corridor first, Maunsell three-set (for Uckfield, later Brighton) and another three-set for Tunbridge Wells. Time was lost with this nine-coach train to Oxted during summer 1958 and the Brighton portion was reduced to five coaches. After the Bulleid Pacifics started working this train it became nine-coach again. Sometimes the rear portion was a four-coach set, making 10 corridors in total - the longest train of the day.

As the amount of corridor trains increased so the number of ex-SECR 'birdcage' sets dwindled until by spring 1958 only seven remained. During March and April the 5.20 am Victoria-Tunbridge Wells was one of the last trains to have a three-set and by August 1958 all were gone, except the few converted for push-and-pull use. Apart from these and Set 904 all trains were now formed of corridor stock.

All sorts of oddities appeared in the Oxted down bay platform. About 1956 one of the two articulated two-coach sets, whose bodies had been converted from SECR steamcars in 1924, was seen waiting to work the 6.54 pm Oxted to Tunbridge Wells - the connection off the 6.10 pm from Victoria. This was during the period that these sets (Nos. 513/4) were working the Clapham Junction-Kensington Olympia service, and R.W. Kidner believes it may have been on its way to Ashford or Lancing. Sometimes seen were the sets (Nos. 731-9) composed of two ex-LSWR 47 ft 6 in. corridor coaches with brass handrails to the corridor windows and standing areas where the lavatories had been. On occasion auto-sets were used to strengthen London trains; on 28th December, 1956, the 10.08 am from Victoria included Set 727 - not a good idea, for its sand-pipe fouled the live rail at Clapham Junction, causing delay.

Around 1959 complaints about the service, its unpunctuality and the inadequacy of the rolling stock (although comfortable, seating capacity was in short supply) reached a shrill level. The Southern, wedded to the idea of set trains with a brake at each end, bluntly asserted that 'the 48-seat brake seconds cannot be replaced by more 64-seat corridor seconds'. Complaints also were made about the now-ancient auto-trains, 'dirty and ill-lighted'; BR admitted they were life-expired but had no plans to renew them as there were hopes to introduce diesel trains. The 4.20 and 5.20 pm from London Bridge had seats to spare, but in order to secure a seat in the 5.38 one needed to board it by 5.20.

Steam heating in winter was not always very reliable. R.W. Kidner writes:

> There was a lot of leaking, mainly at the joinings - I was present once when a flexible pipe burst with a loud report. It was at Victoria and I suppose now would close the station.
> I recall travelling in an ex-SECR 'Continental' coach on the Oxted line with the steam heat supposedly on and a pile of unmelted snow in the corridor.

This would have been, probably, during the 1958/9 winter, when a 'Continental' corridor second was the last coach of the 8.24 am Forest Row to Victoria for some considerable time.

In 1959 two Bulleid four-corridor sets, Nos. 89 and 90, were transferred from the Eastern Section to provide increased comfort for Oxted line passengers. Both were berthed at East Grinstead and their workings took in the following trains, starting on 15th June, 1959:

6.34 am to London Bridge and 8.01 thence to Tunbridge Wells; Rear portion 1.47 pm
    Tunbridge Wells-Victoria, detached at East Croydon;
3.44 pm East Croydon-East Grinstead;
5.26 pm East Grinstead-Victoria and 6.48 pm return (with 100- seat second).

Front portion 7.41 am East Grinstead-London Bridge (with 5-set 803/4);
Rear portion 4.20 pm London Bridge-Tunbridge Wells;
9.20 pm Tunbridge Wells-Victoria and 11.38 pm thence to East Grinstead.

Ex-SECR 100-seat seconds were used to strengthen several trains at this time. Three vehicles were berthed at East Grinstead, two for the 6.34 am up and one for the 5.26 pm up; two at Forest Row for the 7.00 am up; and two at Tunbridge Wells for the 8.26 am up. Certain off-peak trains also included a 100-seater. The 5.37 pm London Bridge-East Grinstead included two, and one of the Tunbridge Wells pair was returned in the 7.08 pm and the other in the 8.08 pm from Victoria. The 6.31 pm London Bridge-Forest Row had two of these austere vehicles leading. R.W. Kidner recalls:

> They were always empty as the rest of the train was more comfortable. They were also rather dirty. To be in the leading compartment was the nearest thing a passenger could do to footplate riding, with the sounds and smell of the 2-6-4 tank engine, including the grinding of the buffers, making a memorable trip.

Of the coaching stock to be seen on the line during the 1960-2 period the Maunsell corridor sets were still very prominent, including Nos. 194, 202, 222-32, 241/5/8, 327, 952-61 (three- sets) and Nos. 181-92 and 449-54 (four-sets). Not all these would be seen during a day's operation, for Oxted line workings formed only a part of their operating cycle. Bulleid corridor sets included three-sets 973-9 (from early 1962), four-sets 81-85, 87-93, five-sets 801-4, six-set 897 and eight-set 767. Three-set 779 turned up in early 1962, having been transferred from the South Western Division. Set 803 was completely re-formed about this time and now comprised six Bulleid vehicles. It appeared on the services booked for Set 897 for several months.

BR standard corridor coaches began to put in an appearance. Six-set 876 was still in traffic, although for much of 1961 it was away at works being repainted green and four-set 869, temporarily made up to six coaches with the addition of two Maunsell vehicles, was substituted. Four-set 868 also was sometimes seen on Oxted line trains, as well as some of the BR three-sets - although none had a booked working. These three-sets were somewhat deficient in seating capacity as only 88 second class passengers could be conveyed seated.

The old push-and-pull sets began to be replaced by conversions of Maunsell brake composites and open seconds, although these could not run on the few trains that still worked from Oxted through to Tonbridge. These 'new' sets included Nos. 600-2, 604-6, 609, 617 and 619. Old sets still working in 1961 were Nos. 652, 656, 659-61 and 663; No. 659 included the last 'birdcage' in traffic. In December 1961 two auto sets were transferred from the South Western to the Central Division: No. 1 arrived at Tunbridge Wells West on 8th January, 1962, and No. 662 on 21st December, 1961. Set 1 comprised a converted LSWR brake composite and an SECR 10-compartment second; Set 662 was two ex-SECR conversions. Both were withdrawn later in 1962 and the Maunsell conversions held sway until replaced by diesel multiple units.

The introduction of diesel trains rendered surplus the Maunsell stock and most of the Bulleid sets. The survivors had their workings altered. Six-set 897 now formed the 4.40 pm London Bridge to Brighton and probably the 7.17 am Brighton to London Bridge; and eight-set 767 was now berthed at Forest Row for the 7.00 am to London Bridge and 6.30 pm return. The solitary non-corridor set 904 now worked the 7.49 am Tunbridge Wells to London Bridge but still returned on the 5.20 pm as before. These workings were maintained until June 1963, when more withdrawals took place.

As type '3' diesel locomotives arrived to take over the remaining steam-worked trains in summer 1963 the authorities had to face the fact that with the coming of winter none of the existing fleet of carriages could continue to be used, for the locomotives had no steam-heating boilers. After September 1963 all were either withdrawn or transferred from the line.

Chapter Eight

The Diesel Era

Because of an increase in the number of passengers using the Oxted line, it was felt that services ought to be improved. Since the line did not look like being electrified, the only way it could be modernised was to use diesel-electric multiple units in order that steam could be eliminated. So, in March 1959, authority was given by the British Transport Commission for the Southern Region to build 19 three-car diesel units at Eastleigh Works. It was said at the time that this was only a temporary measure until the line could be electrified, perhaps in 1964. There was no intention of building sufficient demus to work the whole service, so some of the peak hour trains would have to remain steam-worked. It was planned to run six- or nine-car trains during peak periods, but the off-peak service would need only three-car trains. It was not possible to start building the units until 1961, since Eastleigh was then full up with building Kent Coast electric trains.

However, before these new trains were ready, the line did see occasional demus. One of the first recorded was 'Hampshire' three-car unit No. 1115, which on 27th January, 1960, left Victoria for Oxted at midday to work test trips in the area until February. Also seen from time to time were the narrow-bodied 'Hastings' six-car units, diverted because of engineering works from their regular route via Sevenoaks to work over the Crowhurst spur and via Oxted. This happened on four Sundays in January 1958 and was the first time these then-new units were seen at Oxted.

'Hastings' units were used for possibly the first time by Oxted line passengers when on Sunday, 25th March, 1962, a special Sanderstead-Tunbridge Wells service ran owing to bridge renewal at Selsdon Road. Three 'Hastings' sets were in use, in addition to steam trains, reversing at Sanderstead. Initially drivers were trained on 'Hastings' units in preparation for working the soon-to-be-introduced 'Oxted' demus, the run taking in Woodside, Oxted, East Grinstead, Ashurst Junction, Uckfield, Lewes, Uckfield and Tunbridge Wells Central on 26th-28th March, 1962.

By March the first of the 'Oxted' demus had been built; 18 more followed during 1962 and were numbered 1301-19. The motor coach seated 42 passengers in one five-bay saloon; the other half of the vehicle had a small compartment for guard and luggage and an engine room. Inside was an English Electric pressure-charged diesel engine of 600 bhp, coupled to a main generator, which powered two nose-suspended traction motors. These were on the inner bogie instead of the outer one as on straight electric motor coaches; this was an attempt to distribute the weight somewhat (the motor coach weighed 56 tons). It is a curious fact that, although the traction motors were identical to those on electric multiple unit stock, emus and demus could not work together. In fact demus could work only with other demus and with nothing else. On the 'Oxted' units the engine speed when idling was 450 rpm, but when the electric heating was on, the current being supplied from the main generator, the speed automatically increased to 600 rpm. Consequently one could hear the engine roaring away even though the train was stationary.

The centre trailer was a composite with four first-class compartments, these having more generous proportions than the 'firsts' in the 'Hampshire' units, and a small second class saloon at each end of the coach, with one lavatory. The compartments seated 24 first class passengers, and capacity of the two saloons was 42. This coach weighed 31 tons.

The 31 ton driving trailer coach seated 76 second class passengers in two saloons ; there was no communication between them or between coaches. To have built non-gangwayed trains for main line use at such a late date as 1962 was certainly nothing for the Southern Region to be proud of.

Plastic was much in evidence on the bodywork. The cab front was resin-bonded fibreglass, steel framed, and all doors were of glass reinforced plastic. The interior was panelled in grey plastic sheet, the ceilings being of the same material but white. There was a limited amount of teakwood, this being used for seat ends and around the windows. The windows had aluminium frames, and there were ugly aluminium strips each side of the doors inside which may have been intended to keep out draughts in winter but were completely useless. Body width was 8 ft 6 in.

Running trials of unit 1301 were made between Eastleigh and Alton on 14th March, 1962, and by mid-April it was making its first appearance at Oxted for driver training. On 16th-18th April No. 1301, based at St Leonards diesel depot, worked a schedule for training that included Lewes, Eridge, Oxted, Tunbridge Wells West, East Grinstead, Oxted, Eridge, Lewes and back to St Leonards. Stops were made at all stations, and the Special Traffic Notice instructed 'Stations to ensure passengers do not join'.

On 18th June, 1962, the first demus entered service on some of the busiest peak-hour trains. The total seating capacity of a nine-car train (72 firsts, 480 seconds) was certainly an improvement on the supplanted steam stock, but the riding qualities were none too good. 'Oxted' units gained a reputation for bouncing around in all directions when on the move, and in the motor coach the vibration caused by the engine was considerable whether the train was stationary or on the move. Even the trailers vibrated during the passage of a demu through a tunnel.

It was recorded that diesels worked the 7.41 am East Grinstead to London Bridge and 5.37 pm return, also the 6.38 am Lewes to Victoria and 5.49 pm Victoria to Tunbridge Wells West from 18th June. Only six units were ready by then, so some of the trains booked for demu, such as the 6.10 pm from Victoria, continued with steam for a few more months. On the first day the up service ran well, but the 5.49 pm had brake trouble and left 38 minutes late and was an hour late at East Grinstead. There were several failures of the new trains in the following weeks: the 5.37 pm down on two occasions in July, and the 5.49 pm on 20th August. It was customary for the train in rear to propel the failure to Oxted or East Grinstead, where a fitter could be called to have a look at it.

The last of the 19 demus entered traffic in August 1962 and the planned diagrams at last could be introduced. From Victoria demu-worked trains left at 9.09 and 10.09 am for Tunbridge Wells, 10.38 am for Brighton via Uckfield,

11.09, 12.09 and 1.09 for Tunbridge Wells, then at 5.09 pm (front six coaches for Tunbridge Wells, rear three for Brighton), 5.49 pm for Tunbridge Wells, 6.10 pm (front six coaches for Brighton, rear three for Tunbridge Wells), 8.09, 9.09 and 10.09 pm for Tunbridge Wells. Up trains to Victoria were the 6.41 am from Tunbridge Wells, 6.38 am from Lewes, 7.35 am from Brighton, 9.24, 12.47 and 1.47 from Tunbridge Wells, 1.55 pm from Brighton, 2.47, 3.47, 5.47 pm from Tunbridge Wells, 7.26 pm from East Grinstead and the 7.47 pm from Tunbridge Wells. London Bridge was served by demus at 7.41 am from East Grinstead and 7.08 am from Tunbridge Wells, and 5.37 pm to East Grinstead and 6.15 pm to Tunbridge Wells. It seems that all 19 units were diagrammed, but this included three that were used on an empty working between Eastbourne and St Leonards for maintenance and interchange purposes.

Theoretically the diagrams were arranged so that each unit visited St Leonards every 10 to 14 days for maintenance and renewal of brake blocks. A fuelling point was set up in part of the goods yard at Tunbridge Wells West and every unit in traffic had to pay at least one visit there each day. The planned stock provision was three units starting at Brighton, six at Eastbourne, three at East Grinstead (these having worked empty from Tunbridge Wells the previous night), one at Tonbridge and six at Tunbridge Wells.

On Saturdays almost all trains were now demu and only the 5.20 and 6.29 am down continued to be steam-worked.

From 17th June, 1963, the journey time from Victoria to East Grinstead was cut by nine minutes to 65 minutes and demus now began working most of the Oxted-Tunbridge Wells local services in place of push-and-pull trains. The 9.09 am down now left Victoria as a nine-car train; the rear unit was detached at Oxted to form the 9.57 am to Tunbridge Wells and the middle unit came off at East Grinstead in order to work Three Bridges locals. The 3.40 pm from East Grinstead was a six-car train formed of the 3.08 pm from Three Bridges and the 2.09 pm from Victoria; at Oxted the train attached to the 3.05 pm from Tunbridge Wells and the resulting nine-car train later made the 5.09 from Victoria.

The diagrams were further altered on 9th September when the 7.55 am Brighton-Victoria and 6.15 pm London Bridge-Tunbridge Wells became locomotive-hauled trains in place of demus. All the Oxted-Tunbridge Wells connecting trains were now demu-worked and Tunbridge Wells steam depot was closed from that date. Stock provision was now two units starting at Brighton, six at Eastbourne, one at East Grinstead and 10 at Tunbridge Wells West. The 6.43 am Tunbridge Wells-Victoria was now a nine-car train and formed the 8.09 am down; the front unit was detached at East Grinstead to work the Three Bridges shuttle and the rest of the train continued to Tunbridge Wells. The 5.38 pm from London Bridge now included a portion for Brighton, detached at Oxted; at East Grinstead the train further divided, one unit being for Three Bridges and the other returning to London at 7.30 pm. The Three Bridges shuttle was berthed at East Grinstead overnight to form the front portion of the 7.46 am to London Bridge next day. After the empties of the 7.46 am had worked from London Bridge to New Cross Gate, two sets then ran empty to Victoria to form the 11.09 and 12.09 down trains. The third remained to form the 4.25 pm London Bridge to Tunbridge Wells, a newly-introduced train. The nine-car 7.18 am Tunbridge Wells to London Bridge later formed the 5.38 pm from London Bridge.

With the timetable changes of 6th January, 1964, almost all trains using East Grinstead now started and finished their journeys in the Low Level station; only in the peaks was there a through service via Forest Row. Apparently it was then that overnight stabling of demus at East Grinstead ceased, possibly because of objections from the local council. The 7.46 am from East Grinstead now started as empty stock from Tunbridge Wells at 6.56, and the 5.38 pm from London Bridge after arrival at East Grinstead ran empty to Oxted where it was divided to form the 7.41 pm Oxted to Lewes and 7.58 pm Oxted to Brighton.

With such intensive use of the demus it is not surprising that failures occurred, leaving trains running short of stock. One of the earliest noted was on 12th November, 1965, when the 5.38 pm from London Bridge was six cars instead of nine (divided at Oxted). It was 35 minutes late arriving at East Grinstead. As some of the older 'Hampshire' (3H) demus were now spare, it was decided to transfer half a dozen of them to St Leonards to help out. These, unlike the 'Oxted' (3D) units, were 9 ft wide in the body and seated five passengers each side in very cramped conditions. The first class and lavatory were stuck at one end of the unit instead of being in the middle, and there were only two first class compartments per unit. The trailers rode better than those of the 'Oxted' units, but apart from that there was little to commend them. They were prohibited from running between Tonbridge and Tunbridge Wells West. Nos. 1113 to 1118 were the units transferred.

More 'Hampshire' units were introduced for the start of the timetable changes of 10th July, 1967, and several locomotive-hauled trains were replaced by demus, as was the daily working of trailer set 601 (detailed later). BR alleged that demus were 'not so susceptible to breakdowns' as locomotives, but a passenger wrote in the local press that 'The comfort, noise and general riding characteristics of the multiple-unit trains are appalling by comparison with the locomotive-hauled trains, which seem to have attracted so much criticism.'

The theoretical provision of demus from 10th July, 1967, was:

Brighton	Three	3D,	three	3H
Eastbourne	Six	3D		
Tonbridge	Two	3D		
Tunbridge Wells West	Eight	3D,	one	3H

It still seemed that all 19 3D units were diagrammed, but in the event of failures there were at least a few 3H units to fall back on.

With the closure of the Forest Row line it became necessary to send empty units into traffic from Tunbridge Wells to East Grinstead via Oxted. The 6.45 am from East Grinstead had to start empty at Tunbridge Wells at 5.40, and the 7.47 am at 6.40, reversing at Oxted. The last three down trains terminating at East Grinstead all had to return empty to Tunbridge Wells the same way. The 7.47 am East Grinstead to London Bridge, a nine-car train, returned in the afternoon as three separate trains: the 4.20 pm to East Grinstead (with a 3H unit that had worked up as the 1.55 pm Brighton to London Bridge), the 4.25 pm to Hurst

Green, and the 4.40 pm to Lewes. This was quite a reduction in seating capacity compared with the previous provision. The stock of the 9.09 am from East Grinstead to London Bridge worked round empty to Victoria, where it was attached to the 3.09 pm down to make that train nine cars. This later formed the 5.54 pm down. The nine-car 6.10 pm from Victoria was now formed from an empty train that had left Oxted at 5.20 pm; this in turn had been made up from the 3.30 pm Lewes-Oxted and the 4.05 pm empties from East Grinstead.

Considerable alterations to demu working were made following the closure of the Uckfield-Lewes section. As this route to St Leonards depot was now unavailable it meant that empty trains now needed to run from Victoria via Haywards Heath, Lewes and Eastbourne for maintenance and return the same way. The amount of empty mileage increased phenomenally. Trains could not even run direct from Tunbridge Wells to Oxted any longer, since the short Groombridge Junction-Ashurst Junction connection was closed; instead, empty trains ran via Eridge and reversed.

One of the most interesting changes was that, for the first time, a 2H unit was booked to be formed in one train each way, as from 6th January, 1969. It worked at the rear of the 7.34 am Uckfield-Victoria (due 8.50) with two three-car units. This train then ran empty to St Leonards. An empty train left St Leonards at 2.05 pm, formed of two different three-car units and a different two-car, and more than two hours later was in Victoria to form the 5.36 pm down - the only train of the day that could be announced 'the first five coaches are for Crowborough', as the 2H was the leading unit. The rear three-car unit was detached at Oxted for East Grinstead. The 2H units based at St Leonards were Nos. 1119 and 1120; they were the same as the 3H units apart from the lack of a centre trailer, but had a solitary second class compartment at the end of the driving trailer. In the three-car units this compartment had been stripped to accommodate luggage. Around 1976 this luggage compartment was fitted up with extra first-class seats, increasing the total seating capacity in the St Leonards-based units from 13 to 19 firsts per unit.

The demus allocated to St Leonards for the Oxted line during the 1968-72 period were 3D Nos. 1301-19 and 3H Nos. 1104, 1112-18. Berthing arrangements were now three 3D at Brighton, three 3D at Tonbridge, eleven 3D and five 3H at Tunbridge Wells West, and one 3D and one 3H at Victoria.

Many of the workings were very complex because of the efforts made to provide maximum service with minimum provision of stock. The nine-car 7.47 am East Grinstead-London Bridge now returned empty to Oxted, the front two units continuing to Hurst Green to form the 9.45 to Victoria and the rear unit shunting to the down bay to form the rear of the six-car 10.54 am Oxted to Eridge. Later this same unit worked up empty from Tunbridge Wells to East Croydon to form the 3.55 pm to East Grinstead, formerly a locomotive-hauled train. The 8.21 am East Grinstead to Oxted on arrival shunted to the up siding, then formed the front part of the 9.13 to Victoria, the 8.27 am from Uckfield attaching to the rear in the platform. Later in 1969 the 10.10 am Uckfield to Oxted was extended to Victoria, where it was attached to the front of the 12.09 down. The 4.20, 4.25 and 4.40 pm from London Bridge, all three-car trains, used the stock of the nine-car 7.55 am Uckfield-London Bridge; when this was only six cars an extra unit was attached to the afternoon St Leonards up empties and run as a special empty train from East Croydon to London Bridge to form the 4.40 pm to Uckfield.

From 1st May, 1972, the 7.32 am Uckfield-Victoria and 5.36 pm Victoria-Crowborough/East Grinstead were strengthened to nine-cars and the 2H units were seen no more. The six-car 9.09 am East Grinstead-London Bridge, instead of later forming part of the 3.09 pm from Victoria, now made the 3.55 pm East Croydon-East Grinstead, the rear unit being detached at Oxted to form part of the 5.22 pm empties to Victoria, which in turn formed the 6.10 pm down. The afternoon empty train from Tunbridge Wells that used to form the 3.55 pm from East Croydon now ran to Oxted to form an unadvertised school train from Oxted to East Grinstead at 4.08 pm.

Three more 3H units, Nos. 1109-11, were transferred to St Leonards in 1973 and No. 1104 was sent back to Eastleigh. It was now possible to diagram an extra demu, the total being 18 3D and nine 3H workings in the Monday-to-Friday timetable. But still there never seemed to be enough units in actual practice and many were the trains that ran short of stock or, on occasions, not at all. During bad periods, when perhaps two units would be away at Eastleigh for overhaul, another two failed somewhere, and one or two in for maintenance at St Leonards, things were really desperate, and units had to be 'borrowed'.

The main change of 1973 was that the 3.09 pm from Victoria to East Grinstead, which had become very overloaded since it had run as only three cars, was now a six-car train, but only as far as Oxted, where the rear unit was detached to form the unadvertised school train. The empty train from Tunbridge Wells now made the front of the 4.12 pm Oxted to Victoria, to which were attached the 3.12 pm from Uckfield and the 3.51 pm from East Grinstead. The 4.40 pm London Bridge to Uckfield, a popular train with the BR staff from Essex House, Croydon (Central Division headquarters) was strengthened to six cars, one unit off the 7.55 am from Uckfield as before, the other having worked empty from Victoria off the 12.51 pm from East Grinstead. An extra unit was also provided on the 6.30 am Uckfield-Victoria to make this train nine cars.

From 6th May, 1974, a 3D unit was booked to work the new 9.00 am Uckfield-Victoria, an additional unit being formed in from Oxted, this having come off the 8.52 am empties from London Bridge. On some days during summer 1974 the 9.00 was six cars throughout. A year later the 7.55 am Uckfield-London Bridge began to run as a six-car train to Oxted, where the 8.22 am from East Grinstead was now attached. Two of these units later formed the 4.20 pm down, now six cars to Oxted and three thence to East Grinstead; the third unit formed the rear part of the 4.40 pm from London Bridge. The stock of the 9.09 am from East Grinstead was used to form the 4.25 pm London Bridge to Uckfield and the front portion of the 4.40 pm to Uckfield. From Victoria, the new 3.40 pm to East Grinstead used the stock of the 9.00 from Uckfield; the 3.54 pm Victoria to Uckfield, which formerly was the balance of the 9.45 from Hurst Green, was now only three cars off the 11.49 am from East Grinstead. To work these services needed a provision of 18 3D units and 10 3H units, the berthing stations being Tonbridge (one 3D), Tunbridge Wells West (12 3D and eight 3H) and Victoria (two 3D). Additionally three empty 3D units started from Brighton and two empty 3H units from St Leonards.

The 1974 allocation of 3H units was Nos. 1108-18; by 1976 it was 1106-9/12-8/23. Despite this, it was a rarity if every peak service ran with its full complement. 3D unit 1318 was under repair at Slade Green depot for many months, and on 9th August, 1976, 'Hastings' six-car unit No. 1005 was used for the 7.55 am Uckfield-London Bridge and 4.40 pm return. The 1977 provision was the same as for 1975 except that only eight 3H units were booked - all starting from Tunbridge Wells. Stock shortage continued into 1978.

It is curious that little effort was made to form trains with their booked stock, 3D and 3H units being regarded by shunters as interchangeable as long as there was no Tonbridge-Eridge working as part of a 3D diagram. The pious hopes of the carriage working planners were largely ignored:

> To ensure that cyclic diagrams (specially designed to facilitate regular servicing and maintenance) are adhered to, it is essential when berthing stock in sidings . . . and similarly when starting from sidings . . . that it is strictly in accordance with the details shown.

When wrong stock appeared on a train it often meant that a particular unit's turn to visit St Leonards had been put off for a few days and sooner or later the result would be - *failure*. Units were always arranged to fail at Oxted, where they could be easily withdrawn, and the up siding was regularly occupied by a dud unit awaiting movement for attention at Selhurst.

The new timetable introduced on 8th May, 1978, appeared to give a more frequent service with fewer units; but in practice it did not work, and there was still a stock shortage, many peak trains running shorter than booked. The 5.05 pm London Bridge to East Grinstead and Uckfield often ran without the East Grinstead portion. On 4th September, 1978, it was a locomotive-hauled train of eight vehicles throughout from London to Uckfield. The 5.38 pm Victoria to Uckfield and East Grinstead sometimes ran without the Uckfield portion, and on 5th June, 1978, the Uckfield portion was a 'Reading-Redhill' 3R unit without first class facilities.

The planned provision of stock for the Oxted line was 14 3D units and 10 3H units, of which Tonbridge was supposed to provide one 3D, Tunbridge Wells 11 3D and seven 3H, and Victoria two 3D and two 3H. In addition St Leonards provided a 3H for the afternoon to cover for a 3D which worked on the South Eastern Division during that time. This 3D unit worked in the 6.13 am Victoria-East Grinstead and 7.53 thence to London Bridge, then ran empty to Tonbridge via Redhill. In the afternoon it was attached at Tonbridge to the 4.40 pm Hastings-Charing Cross, returning in the 6.45 pm down, being detached at Tunbridge Wells Central and running empty to the West station. The 3H ran up specially from St Leonards in order to work in the 5.05 pm London Bridge-Uckfield, then ran empty to Tunbridge Wells West, empty from there to Redhill via South Croydon, and back to St Leonards as part of the 11.38 pm Redhill-Hastings mail train.

By August a 'Hastings' six-car unit had been diagrammed to work a regular group of trains, since the shortage of stock seemed to show no sign of ending. Running empty from Tonbridge, it then worked the 6.27 am Uckfield-London Bridge, 8.01 empties to Hurst Green and 8.45 Hurst Green-London Bridge. In the afternoon it was on the 4.17 pm London Bridge-East Grinstead, 5.24 pm East

Demu No. 1319 with an up train from East Grinstead at Hurst Green Junction, 2nd October, 1984.   *P. Barnes*

Grinstead-Victoria and 6.42 pm return, then working back to Tonbridge empty via Oxted, Eridge and Tunbridge Wells. The six-car unit workings lasted for a few months, but by April 1979 a single 3H unit formed the 4.17 pm from London Bridge.

The stock of the 6.43 am Uckfield-Victoria, a six-car train, ran empty from Victoria to Oxted, whence the front unit formed the 9.05 to East Grinstead and next the 9.49 up; and the rear unit (detached at Oxted) shunted to the up siding, later to attach to the 9.00 am Uckfield-Victoria. Two units off the 7.53 am East Grinstead-London Bridge ran empty back to Oxted, where they were berthed in the up siding from about 11.20 until 4.55. They were then attached to the front of the 4.12 pm Uckfield-Victoria, making a nine-car train, which later formed the 6.08 pm Victoria-East Grinstead/Uckfield.

At Victoria, the unit off the 9.00 am from Uckfield later formed the 3.47 pm to Uckfield, but the unit that had been attached to the up train at Oxted worked empty to New Cross Gate and was later booked to be the rear portion of the 4.35 pm London Bridge to Uckfield/East Grinstead.

The only major change in May 1979 was that the 6.13 am Victoria-East Grinstead now started at East Croydon at 6.31, the stock forming it having come up from St Leonards; and the 6.20 pm East Grinstead-Victoria terminated at East Croydon, returning empty to St Leonards. This allowed two units to be examined overnight at the depot. The booked provision of units was now 12 of each type, an increase of two 3H and consequent reduction of two 3D units.

In the 1980 timetable a new semi-fast train from East Grinstead at 9.24 am was created by diverting the 8.12 am Victoria-Uckfield to East Grinstead, where on arrival it was divided in the platform to form the 9.24 and 9.49 slow. Previously the 9.49 had been formed from the 9.05 from Oxted, a connection off the 8.13 am from Victoria. There was a planned reduction of one 3D unit, leaving a total of

11 3D units and 12 3H units diagrammed. The 6.58 am Uckfield-London Bridge was reduced from nine to six cars, and the 4.17 pm London Bridge-East Grinstead, 5.25 pm East Grinstead-Victoria and 6.40 pm return were reduced from six cars to three. Sometimes an extra unit did run. The 1980 allocation of 3H units at St Leonards had now grown to 16, being Nos. 1105-10/2-20/3. 2H units 1119/20 had been converted to 3H. It is not at all clear why the ancient and decrepit 3H units should have been more and more diagrammed in favour of the relatively young 3D units, but in practice the two were still used indiscriminately - although care was taken to ensure that only a 3D appeared on any diagram that included a run between Eridge and Tonbridge. 3H units could never work these train services, being too wide for the tunnels.

Occasionally Oxted was overwhelmed with defective units, one such day being 9th May, 1980, when the 9.09 am East Grinstead-London Bridge was held at the up home signal for six minutes while they were sorted out. When the train entered the station four units could be seen standing around: No. 1310 in the down siding, No. 1119 in the down bay, No. 1118 in the down platform and No. 1110 in the up siding. At 9.30 am only the up siding should have been occupied!

Diversion of Oxted trains to and from London Bridge from October 1981 did not affect the carriage working very much. The 5.25 am Victoria to Oxted (3D, 3H) continued to run; one unit was provided off the 10.49 pm from East Grinstead the previous night, the other off the 9.10 pm Uckfield-London Bridge, which ran empty to Victoria for berthing. The 6.54 am from Uckfield was restored to nine cars and the 4.15 pm London Bridge to East Grinstead restored to six cars. Stock provision was back to 24 units, of which 13 were 3D and 11 3H (in theory). Use of a Central Division unit on the 6.45 pm Charing Cross-Tunbridge Wells Central service ceased.

The 1980s were a dismal time for Oxted line passengers. Not only were the demus wearing out and breaking down, but often there were insufficient drivers or guards to man the units that *could* work and Oxted, being a point where crews were changed, became notorious for turfing passengers out of trains whose relieving crews had failed to show up. On 21st August, 1982, the 2.15 pm London Bridge-East Grinstead had no driver to take it from Oxted, so passengers were delayed an hour. Apparently when it did leave it was further delayed at Dormans upon running out of water!

From 14th May, 1984, the Victoria service was restored and the entire Oxted line service became demu-worked with the exception of one locomotive-hauled train each way between London Bridge and East Grinstead. Units 1101, 1102 and 1124 were transferred from Eastleigh to strengthen the fleet. The 9.25 am East Grinstead-Victoria was now formed from the 8.17 am ex-Victoria, while the following 9.49 am up was formed from a unit off the 8. 10 am ex-London Bridge; in other words, these two trains departed in reverse order of arrival. The 8.10 am London Bridge-East Grinstead was six cars. At East Grinstead the two units were divided, one forming the 9.49 am up and the other the 10.18 up. The working of these trains was altered in May 1986: the 8.08 am from London Bridge formed the 9.24 am East Grinstead-Victoria, the 8.17 from Victoria returned at 9.51, and the 10.19 up was formed from the rear unit of the 9.08 ex-London Bridge, the other two units shunting to the sidings.

3D unit No. 1316 works a London Bridge to Uckfield train, the East Grinstead portion of which has been cancelled. However, at Oxted a connecting service to East Grinstead is provided, leaving from the down bay on the right. 12th January, 1982.   *Author*

Although the Oxted line was not electrified until 1987, the section from Selsdon Road to Sanderstead had been electrified in 1935 as part of the Woodside & South Croydon Railway electrification scheme. In this view 2-EPB electric unit No. 5763 has just arrived at Sanderstead on the 4.10 pm from Elmers End on 10th May, 1983. Note the SR replacement footbridge.

Author

From mid-July 1986 6L unit 202001 (1013 renumbered) regularly worked as the rear portion of the 4.08 pm London Bridge-East Grinstead, a three-car unit leading. From 3rd October it disappeared and the formation became two 3H units. However, from April 1987 the 6L was back again, and continued to work regularly until 2nd October, 1987, when it worked the 4.08 for the last time. It was in terrible external condition, virtually a rust-heap on wheels, and in August 1986 one passenger was heard to remark: 'They were declared sub-standard for Hastings, so we get them.' Actually they were withdrawn from the Hastings line because electric trains had replaced them in May.

Winter 1986/7 was particularly deplorable for passengers, with late trains, short trains, or no trains. BR candidly announced in March: 'We are not going to spend a vast amount on overhauling at the moment. We are just trying to keep the trains going; they are worn out and odd faults are bound to occur from time to time.' Even renumbering the entire fleet did not make any noticeable improvement to the running. Electrification was on its way, and the last booked demus ran to East Grinstead on 3rd October, 1987, on the 10.26 pm from Victoria: Nos. 205015 and 205002 (formerly 1115 and 1102).

It was not quite the end, though, for demus were still required for working the Oxted-Uckfield line, and there were even a few through trains over the electrified tracks between Oxted and London in the peak hours. Most of the 3D units were withdrawn for scrap and surprisingly it was the ancient 3H units which were favoured for retention. Maintenance was now carried out at Selhurst, much more conveniently placed than St Leonards, which had closed soon after the electrification of the Hastings line.

Surviving units noted between 1988 and 1990 were: 3H Nos. 205001/2/8/9/ 12/15/16/18/24-27 and 3D Nos. 207001/2/4/11/13. Only about eight or nine of these were required to maintain the service: six on the through morning and evening trains and three for the Oxted-Uckfield shuttle.

A few words about livery and other changes. When new the demus were in the then standard Southern Region green, with grey roofs and black underframes and body ends (except the driving ends). In 1966 a small yellow patch was applied to the outer ends, bottom centre, in the hope that it would make an approaching train more visible to men working on the track. 'Hampshire' units had a yellow 'V' painted on the drive-end of the motor coach to indicate that there was no luggage compartment at the other end of the unit; later this indication was changed to an inverted solid black triangle on a yellow ground. Matt blue, applied with an airless spray brush, was used for body sides and ends from about July 1966, with small numerals in white. Later repaints in blue displayed larger numerals and the blue was glossy, although unvarnished. Green took a long time to disappear: Unit 1318 was still green in February 1969, but by January 1970 No. 1315 was the last remaining to be repainted blue. Full yellow ends were standard from 1968.

From 1977 to 1979 several 3D units were outshopped from Swindon, who also took the opportunity to introduce some modifications. The outmoded string-mesh luggage racks were replaced by metal slats, some of the internal timbers were renewed, and outside the continuous footboard was replaced by short individual footboards, one below each door. 3D unit 1317 was the first to receive these modifications (February 1977) and Nos. 1301/4/5/10/13 were similarly dealt with by Swindon during 1977. No. 1312 was outshopped by Swindon in November 1978, then 1311/14 in November 1979. Other units continued to be overhauled by Eastleigh, who retained the continuous footboards.

The next livery change was to blue and grey with white lining, hitherto used only for main line stock. 3D unit 1315 was the first to wear this livery, from July 1980, but blue repaints continued into 1981. 3H units 1113/14/06 were the first three of this type to change to blue and grey, towards the end of 1980. The entire fleet was so-transformed between 1981 and 1984, and No. 1309 was the last remaining blue unit by May of that year.

During 1984-6 some units were again sent to Swindon for overhaul, and this time some much needed new seat covering, of an attractive blue colour, replaced the depressing grey-striped seat covering which the units had had since they were new. The new coverings brightened up the interiors considerably. Units with improved interiors were Nos. 1301/10/13 in 1984; 1302/4/5, 1102/8 in 1985; and 1101/9 in 1986.

Surviving units retained for the Oxted-Uckfield service began to appear in 'Network SouthEast' colours (red, white, blue, grey stripes and yellow ends) in 1988, 3D No. 207002 in March being the first of these mobile paint pots.

Most demus kept their original formations throughout their lives. The first permanent re-formation was in September 1974, when 3H unit No. 1108, while retaining its original centre trailer, took the coaches of 2H unit No. 1121, the original end coaches of No. 1108 going to 2H unit 1121. Other re-formations seen were only temporary, until February 1986, when unit 1309 lost its motor coach which was replaced by a 'Hastings' type motor coach from unit 1037; it was completely non-matching in body style and this unit presented a very odd appearance. 3H unit 1107 also received a 'Hastings' motor coach as replacement about July 1985, but in April 1986 3H unit 1113 did one better for it received a 'Hastings' motor coach *and* trailer, so that only the driving trailer of this unit was the original vehicle.

A 4L unit was made up from surviving 'Hastings' vehicles, painted in original Southern Region green in June 1987 and numbered 203001. Regarded virtually as a museum-piece, it did in fact work in ordinary service from time to time on the Uckfield line, although having no first class accommodation. As it had full yellow ends, it was not really an authentic representation of a 'Hastings' unit as in 1957, although green was an improvement on NSE livery.

Renumberings of units began around August 1986, when Nos. 1101 etc. became 205001 etc., Nos. 1301 etc. became 207001 etc., and the surviving 6L unit 1013 became 202001.

From time to time in the 1970s units allocated to the Reading-Tonbridge line (the 'Tadpole' sets, so-called because the driving trailer was 9 ft wide while the other two coaches were only 8 ft) would appear on Oxted line trains when stock was short. These comprised an ex-'Hastings' motor coach and trailer, gangwayed together, plus a non-gangwayed driving trailer that had originally been part of an electric unit. For example, on 27th December, 1969, the 8.09 am Victoria-East Grinstead was formed of two of these, Nos. 1206 and 1205, so that there was no first-class seating anywhere in the train.

Chapter Nine

Diesel-Electric Locomotive Working

The first diesel-electric locomotive regularly to work over the Oxted line was No. 10800, built in 1950 by the North British Locomotive Co., Glasgow. Actually it was intended for branch-line working on the London Midland Region, and saw its first trials between Euston and Watford in November 1950. The 827 hp locomotive was transferred to the Southern Region in August 1952 and from the 18th of that month took up regular duties from Norwood depot.

It was not a large or powerful machine by any means; length over buffer beams was 38 ft 6 in., the two bogies had a wheelbase of 8 ft 6 in. each, and there were four nose-suspended axle-hung traction motors powered by a Davey, Paxman diesel engine. A steam-heating boiler was included, there was a single cab about three-quarters of the way along the body, and the external livery was plain black.

From 18th August, 1952, its booked duties were: 5.05 am London Bridge to Brighton via Dorking, Horsham and Steyning, 10.18 am Brighton to Victoria and 3.52 pm return (both via Oxted and Eridge), 6.49 pm Brighton to Tunbridge Wells West and 9.01 pm thence to Victoria, 11.04 pm Victoria to Oxted (Wednesdays and Saturdays excepted) or East Grinstead (Wednesdays and Saturdays only). These workings were to Norwood Duty No. 610.

However, not only was it underpowered (so that time was lost on the banks with even a modest load of six coaches) but it was unreliable, and broke down frequently. Locomen knew it as the Wonder Engine: 'I wonder if it will go today?' Certainly it spent more time in works being repaired than ever it did working trains. No. 10800 was active for short spells during January and April 1953, but most of the latter part of that year was spent in Brighton Works; then on 9th February, 1954, it took up Duty 610 again. Alas, while working the 3.52 pm on 30th March, the locomotive totally failed at Streatham Common and had to be towed to Norwood, its diesel engine badly damaged. No. 10800 was towed to Brighton works via Oxted and Sheffield Park on 6th April, repairs taking until December to complete. On 11th December, 1954, it left the Southern Region for all time, being transferred to Plaistow, on the London, Tilbury & Southend line. No. 10800 was condemned in 1960.

Remembered with far more affection were the type '3' (later class '33') locomotives, the first of which were delivered in 1960, and which had a continuous association with the Oxted line from 1963 to 1986. They were built by Birmingham Railway Carriage & Wagon Co. with Sulzer diesel engines and Crompton-Parkinson electrical equipment and were the first BR locomotives to be equipped for train electric heating. Steam heating boilers were heavy and their elimination kept the total weight of the locomotive down to 73½ tons and allowed the use of a 1,550 hp 8-cylinder engine instead of the 6-cylinder one used in the similar type '2' locomotive. Each locomotive, which had two 4-wheeled bogies, had four traction motors axle-hung and nose-suspended to the bogie frame; bogie wheelbase was 10 ft. Length over buffer beams was 46 ft 9 in; the body was straight-sided but the ends were rounded and there was a two-digit headcode panel positioned between the driver's windows. In total there were 98 of these type '3' locomotives, Nos. D6500-97, of which the last 12 had narrow bodies for the Hastings line although they were often seen on Oxted trains too. It was stated that there was sufficient reserve of power to work the electric train heating without affecting traction, but when hauling a heavy eight-coach train up the banks during the depths of winter the type '3' did tend to lose time.

Type '3' locomotives began to work certain of the formerly steam-hauled passenger trains during the currency of the 1962/3 timetable, but not, if observation is any judge, on a regular basis.

Further type '3' locomotives were introduced for the summer 1963 timetable, so that by the end of July almost all the trains not booked to be formed of multiple units were diesel-hauled and steam became a rarity. Even the Victoria-Lingfield race specials on 24th August, 1963, were diesel worked (by D6580 and D6540).

But a little problem manifested itself with the coming of winter: the operating people still had a fleet of carriages equipped for steam-heating but no diesel locomotives able to heat them, and unless something was done quickly the passengers were going to freeze. What happened was that several dual-heated coaches were hastily transferred from the Western Region, still in maroon livery, and formed with the few dual-heated Southern Region coaches into 'business sets', which went into service in September 1963. Steam-heated carriages were banished from the line.

From 9th September, 1963, the following trains were booked to be locomotive-hauled, Mondays to Fridays:

Down	Up
am	*am*
5.20 Victoria-Brighton	6.40 East Grinstead-London Bridge
6.25 Victoria-Tunbridge Wells	7.08 Forest Row-London Bridge
7.55 London Bridge-East Grinstead	7.55 Tunbridge Wells-London Bridge
pm	7.20 Brighton-London Bridge
3.09 Victoria-Tunbridge Wells	8.28 Forest Row-Victoria
3.52 East Croydon-East Grinstead	7.55 Brighton-Victoria
3.54 Victoria-Brighton	8.26 Tunbridge Wells-London Bridge
4.20 London Bridge-East Grinstead	8.34 Brighton-Victoria
4.40 London Bridge-Brighton	9.38 East Grinstead-London Bridge
4.48 Victoria-Groombridge	9.25 Brighton-Victoria
5.20 London Bridge-Tunbridge Wells	10.02 Brighton-Victoria
6.15 London Bridge-Tunbridge Wells	*pm*
6.31 London Bridge-Tunbridge Wells	5.30 East Grinstead-Victoria
6.48 Victoria-Forest Row	5.47 Tunbridge Wells-Victoria
7.09 Victoria-East Grinstead	5.49 East Grinstead-Victoria
8.09 Victoria-Tunbridge Wells	6.55 Brighton-Victoria

Empty stock trains in connection with the above, plus parcels and freight trains, also were diesel hauled, although on occasions steam traction was substituted.

The timetable alterations of 6th January, 1964, saw some locomotive-hauled trains being replaced by diesel multiple units, as well as a reduction in the number of Tunbridge Wells services. The 3.09 and 8.09 pm Victoria to East Grinstead became demu workings, as did the retimed 9.45 am East Grinstead to Victoria; both the 9.25 am Brighton-Victoria and 5.47 pm Tunbridge Wells-Victoria disappeared. The 8.26 am from Tunbridge Wells now started at East Grinstead at 9.11. The 8.31 pm East Grinstead-Victoria became locomotive-hauled instead of demu. In the down direction the 6.25 am Victoria-Tunbridge Wells was diverted to Brighton, the 6.15 pm London Bridge-Tunbridge Wells ran to Lewes and the 6.31 pm from London Bridge now terminated at East Grinstead.

A diesel-hauled parcels train for East Grinstead left East Croydon at 5.24 am, calling only at Oxted and Lingfield. It was balanced by an up parcels train at 8.10 pm from East Grinstead, which at Oxted combined with the 8.05 pm parcels from Tunbridge Wells to London Bridge. The engine of the down train worked an up business train, and the engine of the up parcels train was used after working a down business train. Apart from this there was considerable light-engine mileage to work the services.

Even on Saturdays there were a few diesel-hauled services: the 5.24 am East Croydon-East Grinstead parcels, the 5.20 and 6.25 am Victoria-Brighton, 10.54 am Victoria-Brighton, 12.48 pm London Bridge-Forest Row, 9.09 pm Victoria-Tunbridge Wells; and the 7.49 am East Grinstead-London Bridge, 7.19 am Brighton-London Bridge, 8.34 and 9.52 am Brighton-Victoria, 6.58 pm Brighton-Victoria and the 9.45 pm van train from Tunbridge Wells to London Bridge via East Grinstead.

In 1965 some formerly demu-worked train services became locomotive-hauled with a corridor set: 7.24 am Tunbridge Wells-London Bridge, 3.09 pm Victoria-East Grinstead and 4.32 return, and 5.49 pm Victoria-Tunbridge Wells.

From about February 1966 until July 1967 a push-and-pull trailer set, No. 601, made from converted electric stock was in use with D6580, which had been equipped with the necessary controls to work with it. After trials between New Cross Gate and Tunbridge Wells during December 1965 it went into service on the following trains, the engine always being at the London end.

	dep.
East Grinstead	6.46
London Bridge	7.55
East Grinstead	9.12
London Bridge	*Empty*
New Cross Gate	*Empty*
London Bridge	4.20
East Grinstead	5.32
Victoria	6.49
East Grinstead	-

It was an unusual sensation riding in Trailer Control set 601 when the locomotive was propelling. R.W. Kidner recalls:

6-TC set No. 601 made from 4-COR motor coaches and 6-PUL trailers, now made into a non-motor train, at East Grinstead carriage sidings, 11th June, 1966.   *Author*

Class '33' diesel locomotive No. 6555 and eight-set No. 71 at Hurst Green with the 6.29 pm London Bridge to East Grinstead train on 14th July, 1972.   *Author*

When one was in the leading coach at Victoria (the diesel locomotive was at the rear) one could hear the engine begin to roar, and then quite a bit later a very sudden acceleration.

The combination was not wholly reliable; even in summer 1966 the 6.49 pm from Victoria was noted as a bad timekeeper, and on 13th January, 1967, the 5.32 pm up failed at Lingfield. To rescue the train a standby locomotive from Oxted took it to Oxted, where it was terminated. The 6.49 pm down was cancelled as a result.

A standby engine had been provided at Oxted during the morning and evening peaks since December 1965, following a spate of locomotive and demu failures the previous month. All that can be said is that the locomotives were somewhat more reliable than the demus, but the heating provided for the corridor sets was sometimes hit-and-miss.

From 10th July, 1967, there was a small reduction in the number of locomotive-hauled trains, with the 4.42 pm East Grinstead-Victoria, the 7.57 am Brighton-Victoria, the 3.09 and 5.54 pm Victoria-East Grinstead and the 4.40 pm from London Bridge, as well as all the trailer set workings, being turned over to demu operation. The following services remained locomotive-hauled:

Down	Up
am	*am*
5.20 Victoria-Brighton	7.19 East Grinstead-London Bridge
6.25 Victoria-Brighton	8.03 East Grinstead-London Bridge
pm	7.57 Crowborough-London Bridge
3.55 East Croydon-East Grinstead	7.24 Brighton-London Bridge
3.55 Victoria-Brighton	8.41 East Grinstead-Victoria
4.50 Victoria-East Grinstead	8.27 Brighton-Victoria
5.20 London Bridge-Crowborough	10.00 Brighton-Victoria
5.34 London Bridge-East Grinstead	*pm*
6.15 London Bridge-Brighton	5.54 East Grinstead-Victoria
6.30 London Bridge-East Grinstead	6.53 Brighton-Victoria
7.09 Victoria-East Grinstead	8.31 East Grinstead-Victoria

On Saturdays, only the two morning Victoria-Brighton and return trains remained locomotive-worked, plus an unbalanced 7.04 pm Brighton-Victoria. During the Monday-to-Friday business periods, a standby locomotive continued to be provided at Oxted until well into 1969, the morning one running light from Lingfield, and the evening one running light from Norwood Yard.

Upon closure of the line between Lewes and Uckfield the number of locomotive-hauled passenger trains diminished to four each way, peak-hours only and none at all on Saturdays. These four were maintained until May 1978, being the 7.19 and 8.03 am East Grinstead to London Bridge, 8.30 Hurst Green to London Bridge (empties from East Grinstead), 8.41 am East Grinstead to Victoria, and 5.20 pm London Bridge to Uckfield, 5.34 pm London Bridge to East Grinstead, 6.15 pm London Bridge to Hurst Green (empty to East Grinstead) and 6.30 pm London Bridge to East Grinstead. In order to return the

Double-headed 5.57 am empty coaching stock train from New Cross Gate to East Grinstead, near Lingfield at 6.35 am. The train engine would work the coaches back as the 7.25 am East Grinstead to London Bridge, and the pilot locomotive would work the 9.09 up. 22nd June, 1979.
Author

The 3.53 pm East Croydon to East Grinstead train, hauled by class '33' diesel locomotive No. 33065, crosses Riddlesdown viaduct on 8th May, 1979.   *Author*

stock from Uckfield to form the 8.41 am up next day, the 6.59 pm Uckfield-Oxted was worked as a locomotive-hauled train, continuing empty stock to East Grinstead. In 1975 this was changed to an empty train continuing to New Cross Gate, saving a running-round operation at Oxted; the stock next day was worked empty from New Cross Gate to East Grinstead to form the 8.41 am up. To work the services from East Grinstead three engines had to run light from Norwood Yard in the morning and three ran back again after the evening services; two of the engines ran coupled. In 1969 there was an early morning parcels train from Victoria to East Grinstead, the locomotive of which worked an up passenger train; and in the evening the locomotive that had worked the 6.30 pm down returned with the parcels train at 8.35 pm to Victoria. This parcels train had been discontinued by 1972, however.

The only other changes were the starting of the 8.30 from Hurst Green as a passenger train from East Grinstead at 8.11 in 1972, and the extension of the 6.15 pm from London Bridge as a passenger train to East Grinstead in 1974.

There was no longer a standby engine provided at Oxted, but in any case reliability of the 'Cromptons', as they came to be known, was very good; still, failures did occur. On 28th May, 1969, No. D6584 on the 8.03 from East Grinstead failed at Hurst Green. The 8.30 Hurst Green-London Bridge drew into the station, coupled to the failed train and pushed it to Oxted (16 coaches, two locomotives). The failure, complete with its train, was put in the sidings and the second train left for London half an hour late. On 15th January, 1973, No. 6586 on the 8.11 East Grinstead-London Bridge failed at Hurst Green and was pushed to Oxted by demus in rear. At Oxted No. 6586 came off and No. 6571 took over, but the train was terminated at East Croydon 45 minutes late.

On 3rd May, 1976, the locomotive of the 5.19 pm London Bridge-Uckfield developed a fault so the train was terminated at Oxted, the driver not wishing to risk a total failure at some point down the line. The train was backed into the down siding and five coaches left there; the front three coaches were then shunted across to the up siding. Thus the decanted passengers were given about 40 minutes' worth of free entertainment as they watched all these complicated manoeuvres, which had totally blocked the down line for the whole of that time, causing a considerable stacking-up of peak-hour trains.

In 1974 the type '3' locomotives - which had been known as class '33' since 1968 - began to be renumbered into a sequence which bore no relationship to the old '6500' numbers. The standard class '33' became 33001 etc., the push-and-pull fitted variety became 33101 etc., and the narrow-bodied locomotives were renumbered 33201 etc.

There was a small increase in the number of locomotive-hauled trains in the new timetable that began on 8th May, 1978. These now included the 5.57 and 6.42 am empties from New Cross Gate to East Grinstead, 7.29 am and 3.53 pm East Croydon to East Grinstead, 5.20 pm London Bridge to Uckfield, 5.35, 5.50 and 6.21 pm London Bridge to East Grinstead; and 7.25, 8.01, 8.25, 9.09 am, 4.59 pm East Grinstead to London Bridge, 7.15 and 7.37 pm empties East Grinstead to New Cross Gate, and 7.12 pm Uckfield to Oxted, thence empty to New Cross Gate. This 7.12 pm was extended as a semi-fast passenger train to East Croydon from May 1979. However, from 1st June, 1981, there were fewer locomotive-hauled trains, the 3.53 pm and 6.18 pm down and the 4.59 pm up being turned over to demu. The 9.09 am up was withdrawn.

One bizarre development was the naming, 20 years after they were built, of certain class '33' locomotives. During 1980 and 1981 these newly-named machines were seen on the Oxted line, 33008 *Eastleigh*, 33025 *Sultan*, 33027 *Earl Mountbatten of Burma*, 33052 *Ashford* and 33056 *The Burma Star*. They were usually kept in clean condition, although No. 33027 was particularly smart when it turned up on the 3.53 pm East Croydon to East Grinstead on 14th April, 1981.

From October 1983 there were even fewer trains for the '33s' to work, when the 8.01 up and 5.50 pm down became demus, and on Friday, 11th May, 1984, No. 33 107, with special headboard lettered 'Uckfield Crompton Farewell', worked the final 5.20 pm London Bridge to Uckfield - a train known to a certain Edenbridge Town stationwoman as 'The Big Beastie'.

Now there would be only one locomotive-hauled train each way: the 8.26 am East Grinstead to London Bridge and 5.50 pm return, the 5.34 pm becoming a demu. For those who revelled in the luxury of smooth-running corridor coaches it was a dismal prospect. However, early in 1986 an additional locomotive-hauled train was rustled up, partly because of the never-ending shortage of demus and partly to improve timekeeping and reliability, and the 7.11 am Uckfield to London Bridge and 5.08 pm London Bridge to East Grinstead were turned over to locomotive haulage. These were short-lived for, without even waiting for the electric services to begin, the operating authorities did away with Cromptons on passenger trains in May 1986. On Friday, 9th May, No. 33010 worked the 5.08 pm for the last time, and the 5.50 pm London Bridge to East Grinstead was in the hands of No. 33201.

All that remained for the class '33' was to work engineer's and ballast trains on days when tracklaying was being carried out and, during the 'leaf-fall season', work a daily railcleaning train. These had run every autumn since 1974.

Other types of diesel-electric locomotive were rare visitors. A class '31', No. 31113, worked a troop special from Royston (Eastern Region) to East Grinstead on 30th November, 1976, returning with the empty stock to Stratford. Examples of the big class '47' (Brush type '4', as it was originally known) were seen more than once. On 16th October, 1972, No. 1952 arrived at East Grinstead with empty stock from Old Oak Common (Western Region) to form a special train to Plymouth via the West London line. Class '47' locomotives worked a troop special from Swansea to East Grinstead on 1st August, 1976 and, two weeks later, a special from Cardiff to East Grinstead and back to Swansea. On 7th April, 1979, one of the big and powerful class '50' locomotives, No. 50016, worked an enthusiasts' special around some of the Southern Region lines, including that to East Grinstead. 'The Southern Invader' was quite a spectacle as it crossed Cook's Pond with its train of Western Region corridor stock.

A class '47' was even recorded as having worked one of the scheduled passenger trains in place of the booked class '33' when on 18th September, 1979, No. 47238 was in charge of the 8.01 am East Grinstead to London Bridge.

The class '73' electro-diesel locomotive was another rare visitor to the Oxted line. These machines could work as electric locomotives when taking current from a third rail, but also had a small generator to power the traction motors in the absence of a third rail. However, they were severely underpowered in this mode, and could not normally work passenger trains. Nevertheless, on 24th February, 1972, two class '73s', Nos. E6011 and E6017, were seen on the 8.41 am East Grinstead-Victoria ; and on 30th March the same year the 5.20 pm London Bridge was double-headed by No. E6040 and a 'partly-failed' class '33', No. 6568.

A regular electro-diesel working, entirely within the electrified area, was to take the empty stock off the 8.41 am East Grinstead-Victoria round to New Cross Gate; and for many years the empties forming the 6.30 pm London Bridge-East Grinstead were brought in from New Cross Gate by an electro-diesel. The high-pitched whine of its brake compressor was a distinctive sound which, once heard, was never forgotten.

On 19th September, 1987, electro-diesel locomotive No. 73004 paid a special visit to East Grinstead for the purpose of being named *The Bluebell Railway* by the celebrity Johnny Morris, who was a vice- president of the Bluebell Railway. The ceremony was attended by British Rail and Bluebell officials, including Gordon Pettitt (SR general manager) and Bernard Holden (Bluebell Railway's superintendent of the line).

Hunslet-Barclay class '20' locomotives top and tail the Chipman's weedkiller train at East Grinstead on 29th May, 1989. Nearest the camera No. 20901 is seen pushing the train, the leading locomotive is No. 20904.   *P. Barnes*

Chapter Ten

Diesel Locomotive-Hauled Coaching Stock

It was never the intention of the Southern to build sufficient diesel multiple units to work the whole Oxted line service. Locomotive-hauled coaches would be used for many of the business trains as well as certain through trains between Victoria and Brighton via Eridge. A handful of Southern-allocated BR standard coaches had been fitted with electric heaters in 1959, but rather than equip more the authorities decided to transfer from the Western Region several standard coaches, some built as recently as 1962, that already were dual heated. Between June and October 1963, 47 such arrived on the Southern; some were sent to Lancing Works to be repainted from maroon to green livery but most entered service in time for the introduction of the winter timetable on 9th September, 1963, still in maroon. Twenty-nine of them were allocated to sets, but over the next few months coaches were withdrawn in twos and threes for repainting and there can hardly have been a set that ran in its booked formation during that winter. Six-set 427 was formed entirely of ex-Western Region BR stock and went into traffic in green livery. The other sets were a mixture of Southern and Western Region coaches. Six-set 551 is believed to have been ready by 12th September. Seven-set 766 was repainted during January and February 1964. Eight-set 548 was repainted during April and May 1964, and eight-set 985 had its maroon coaches repainted during January 1964. There were also five re-formed three-coach sets (open second, corridor brake second, corridor composite), Nos. 545-7/9/50, which were used in pairs on the Victoria-Brighton and some East Grinstead trains.

Also formed, just in time to enter service on 9th September, 1963, was seven-set 900. This comprised the two coaches of 2-BIL electric unit No. 2006, minus the motors and shoebeams, with five 4-SUB electric trailer coaches in between. One of these was fitted up as a composite, the middle seven compartments being first class. Jumper cables were fitted for electric heating supplied from the locomotive. Although the train looked like an electric that had escaped from the third rail, it was in fact hauled by a diesel locomotive just as though it were an ordinary set; it presented a very odd appearance.

From 9th September, 1963, the booked workings of these six 'new' sets were as under:

6-set 427	7.20 am Brighton-London Bridge, 6.15 pm London Bridge-Tunbridge Wells and 9.36 pm Tunbridge Wells-Brighton.
6-set 551	6.40 am East Grinstead-London Bridge and 7.55 am return. 9.38 am East Grinstead-London Bridge, 3.52 pm East Croydon-East Grinstead, 5.49 pm East Grinstead-Victoria and 7.09 pm return.
7-set 766	Empty Groombridge-Tunbridge Wells, 6.36 am Tunbridge Wells-Brighton, 7.55 am Brighton-Victoria and 4.48 pm Victoria-Groombridge.
7-set 900	(Berthed at Eridge) 7.55 am Tunbridge Wells-London Bridge and 5.20 pm return.
8-set 548	8.28 am Forest Row-Victoria, 4.20 pm London Bridge-East Grinstead, 5.30 pm East Grinstead-Victoria and 6.48 pm Victoria-Forest Row.
8-set 985	Empty East Grinstead-Forest Row, 7.08 am Forest Row-London Bridge and 6.31 pm London Bridge-East Grinstead.

Set 551 had to be shunted three times each day at East Grinstead, for every arrival was in the Low Level but every departure was from the High Level. Presumably this was less trouble than having the locomotive run round the train ; by reversing the whole train up the goods spur and then drawing it into the High Level station it was facing London and ready for departure.

Some of the workings were altered from 6th January, 1964, but all six sets remained in use until 1965/6, when the use of numbered sets was temporarily abandoned, except for No. 900. The requirement was now for one six-coach train (7.27am Brighton-London Bridge and 4.40 pm return); one seven-coach train (6.48 am Eridge-Brighton, 7.59am Brighton-Victoria and 6.15 pm London Bridge-Eridge); seven-set 900 (7.58 am Crowborough-London Bridge and 5.20 pm return); one eight-coach train (7.21 am East Grinstead-London Bridge and 6.31 pm return); one eight-coach train (8.32 am Forest-Row Victoria and 4.48 pm Victoria-East Grinstead-Tunbridge Wells); and a set of coaches that was a mixture of corridor and non-corridor vehicles and still retaining steam heating. To provide the heat a steam-heating boiler van was attached. This set (presumably the old No. 904 with additions) was put on in place of formerly demu-worked train services: the 7.25 am Tunbridge Wells-East Grinstead-London Bridge, 3.09 pm Victoria-East Grinstead and 4.32 pm return, and the 5.49 pm Victoria-East Grinstead-Tunbridge Wells. This experiment was unfortunately not successful, and the set of coaches and associated heating vans, which excited the derision of East Grinstead's urban district council chairman John Andrews, was withdrawn in December 1965.

In February 1966 Set 900 was renumbered 701 in a series begun for trailer sets and trailer set 601 was introduced. This was made up from 4-COR electric motor coaches (demotored) and four corridor trailers from withdrawn Brighton line express units and was fitted with through cables enabling it to be hauled or propelled by a type '3' diesel locomotive. It was berthed at East Grinstead during weekends. It was really a testbed for push-and-pull operation shortly to be introduced on the Bournemouth-Weymouth line, but regular passengers were unimpressed by it. One correspondent to the *East Grinstead Observer* described it as the 'wooden-bodied horror worked on the push-pull principle, which, though a good idea, has not been a success'.

6-TC set 601 continued working until July 1967, when it was replaced by demus; after being repainted in rail blue it was transferred to the Clapham Junction-Kensington Olympia line where it worked until damaged in a collision in June 1970 and withdrawn, being scrapped in 1972. Trailer set 701, which was never fitted for push-and-pull operation, was painted blue in July 1967 and the old headcode panels were removed. Shortly after returning into service it suffered slight damage by fire in September 1967 and never worked again, being withdrawn officially in May 1969. Its place on the Crowborough-London Bridge services was taken by an ordinary corridor train.

Meanwhile the steam-heated train had been replaced by a nine-coach dual-heated corridor train with as high a seating capacity as possible, to work the heavily-loaded 7.25 up and 5.49 down. There was only a single brake second in the middle, with an open second at each end, plus four corridor seconds, a first and a composite. This made an exceptionally heavy train for a type '3' diesel locomotive, especially in winter with heating on, and as the corridor seconds all had Commonwealth bogies they were heavier than normal. Later in 1966 the corridor first was one of the new Mark II vehicles allocated to the Southern Region and distinguished by a domed roof at each end.

7-trailer set No. 900 at Oxted, 7th February, 1966. Nearest the camera car No. S12107S was formerly in 2-BIL unit No. 2006. If the Southern had electrified the Oxted line the trains might have looked like this.   *Author*

Free entertainment for commuters turned out of their evening train; five coaches of the 5.19 pm London Bridge to Uckfield are backed into the Gasworks Siding at Oxted. The other three coaches had to be placed in the Up Siding. 3rd May, 1976.   *Author*

Later in 1966 locomotive-hauled coaches started to be repainted in blue and grey livery, a matt finish applied by airless spray brush. At the same time any coach intended for use on the Oxted line was converted to air-braking and had the steam heaters removed. When sufficient coaches had been converted they started to be assembled into temporary sets and by March 1967 all the 'business trains' were air-braked, only the three-coach sets remaining vacuum-braked until July as they usually ran with parcels vans. Gradually, throughout 1967, the new sets were assembled until in October all had been formed with their correct coaches. The new sets maintained the following workings from 10th July, 1967, until 2nd January, 1969:

3-sets 15-19	Victoria-Eridge-Brighton services.
7-set 51	7.57 am Crowborough to London Bridge and 5.20 pm return.
7-set 52	7.24 am Brighton to London Bridge and 6.15 pm return.
8-set 67	8.41 am East Grinstead to Victoria and 4.50 pm return.
8-set 68	7.19 am East Grinstead to London Bridge and 6.30 pm return.
8-set 69	8.03 am East Grinstead to London Bridge and 5.34 pm return.

Set 69 was the 'high-capacity' equivalent of the nine-coach formation introduced in 1966, and was originally intended to be nine-set 81; however, second thoughts prevailed and, minus one composite, Set 81 was renumbered 69.

In January 1969 three-sets 15-19 were withdrawn and the five remaining sets were re-formed. Each one was now eight coaches, formed with a brake second in the centre, two composites, three corridor seconds and an open second at each end. These sets were now numbered 67 to 71, certain coaches from No. 52 going to Set 70 and some of those from Set 51 going to No. 71. Four sets were required in traffic, Mondays to Fridays, and the fifth was spare. Sets 68 and 69 continued in the same workings as before; Set 67 worked the 8.41 am East Grinstead-Victoria, 5.20 pm London Bridge-Uckfield and 6.59 pm Uckfield-Oxted, and Set 71 at first worked the 8.30 am Hurst Green-London Bridge and 6.15 pm return. Later, the sets were juggled around from working to working.

Sets 67 to 71 were maintained with minor alterations until 1975, when coaches began to get muddled. After this no attempt was made to keep the sets intact and set numbers disappeared. The five Oxted line locomotive-hauled train formations were again altered, the two composites per set being replaced by a Mark II corridor first and the three corridor seconds per set by four open seconds. Many of these had come from Ocean Liner boat trains and had carpeted aisles, curtains to the windows and fixed tables. The tables were surprisingly unpopular with commuters - after all, what better than a table to rest one's newspaper on? - and were soon removed.

The locomotive-hauled trains were far more comfortable than the demus, but some passengers still complained about them. Sometimes the lighting was rather feeble, as speeds were so low that often the batteries could not be recharged by the dynamo. And heating was sometimes non-existent, especially in the rear coach, where for some odd reason the electrics failed to function. In up trains, drivers had a habit of turning off the heating at East Croydon, still with 10 miles to go! But to bowl along of a summer's evening in an open second between Hurst Green and Lingfield, accompanied by the throaty rasp of a Sulzer engine, was one of the great pleasures of rail travel, now sadly missed.

Chapter Eleven

Electrification

The first definite scheme to electrify the Oxted line was the LBSCR's in 1919, when it was proposed to extend its AC overhead system over several lines, including some SECR ones. It seems that the SECR services to Caterham, Tattenham Corner, Oxted and Reigate were to be electrified and worked by the LBSCR on behalf of the SECR; but in 1922, with Grouping imminent, it was decided not to go ahead. The SECR had a scheme of its own, using third and fourth rails with 1,500 volts DC fed into each rail, and in 1921 it was proposed to electrify several suburban services on this system, including South Croydon-Oxted-Crowhurst Junction and Redhill-Tonbridge. Whether it was seriously contemplated to employ two systems of electrification over the Oxted line is unclear, but the plans were abandoned when Grouping was seen to be inevitable. The LSWR became the dominant constituent of the Southern Railway, and it was the LSWR system of electrification (600 volts DC third rail) that became standard. Even before Grouping the South Western Board was putting pressure on the SECR not to saddle it with a third incompatible system of electrification, although it did allow the Brighton to finish off its Coulsdon North extension as so much work had already been done.

Electrification on the overhead system through South Croydon to Coulsdon North was inaugurated on 1st April, 1925, and on the third rail system to Caterham and Tattenham Corner on 25th March, 1928. Thus until the overhead system was abolished on 22nd September, 1929, South Croydon saw three different kinds of traction working at the same time.

The third rail continued to advance: almost the whole of the suburban area was converted by 1930, and all the ex-LBSCR main lines and some branches by 1938. The Oxted line remained steam-worked, and continued to be shown in black on 'Southern Electric' carriage maps, where almost all was red. Then in June 1939 the Southern Railway Board authorised electrification of the line to Oxted, East Grinstead and Horsted Keynes but the declaration of war in September of that year caused the abandonment of this plan. If done, there would presumably have been an alternative through service between London and Brighton via East Grinstead, Horsted Keynes to Haywards Heath having been electrified since 1935. Possibly the empty countryside south of East Grinstead would have become a vast subtopia, for the presence of electric trains always encouraged house-building.

After the war, the ever forward-looking Southern was full of plans. On 31st October, 1946, the General Manager, Sir Eustace Missenden, announced that the Board had approved plans for further electrification in order to eliminate steam traction completely from the former SECR and LBSCR lines. These lines included, among others, 'the secondary main line to Haywards Heath and Brighton from Croydon via Oxted, East Grinstead and Horsted Keynes'. Diesel traction was to be used for feeder services and for local goods trains.

Presumably these lines included Oxted-Edenbridge Town-Tunbridge Wells, the link line from Three Bridges to Tunbridge Wells, and the Uckfield and Heathfield routes, all of which would have lost their through services to and from London. The Southern hoped that the work would be completed by 1955, but once again a major scheme for electrification was abandoned because of a shake-up in railway ownership; this time it was the Nationalisation of 1948.

The new Railway Executive was not much interested in electrification, because of the high cost; and even less interested in diesel traction, preferring steam because of its relative cheapness. However, once the Executive had been abolished, things changed. In 1955 the Modernisation Plan was announced, and over the next few years millions of pounds were spent on electrification and dieselisation all over the country. The new standard system of electrification was 25,000 volts AC overhead, and this was used in many parts of Britain but not by the Southern, who would have nothing to do with it. The Southern preferred to stick with its third-rail, low voltage system.

In 1958 it was officially announced that, once the lines in Kent had been electrified, work would begin on the Oxted, East Grinstead, Ashurst and Uckfield lines, through services running between London and Brighton. As the line south of East Grinstead had now been closed services would perforce terminate there. Completion date for this work was put at 1964. The new station at Hurst Green was to be used for joining and dividing electric trains so that through services could use both the routes to East Grinstead and to Tunbridge Wells via Edenbridge Town.

Because of increasing numbers of passengers, and complaints about the 'inadequacy' of the steam trains, BR decided that six years was too long to wait for the fruits of electrification. Diesel-electric trains were ordered instead, only as a temporary measure until such time as electrification was completed. In fact, the 'temporary' demus served East Grinstead for 25 years, from 1962 to 1987, as the money just could not, or would not, be found to electrify; since the demus were there anyway it was expedient to keep them in use until they were worn out. Moreover, there were doubts as to whether there was sufficient traffic on the Oxted line to justify the cost of electrification, and in addition demus were cheaper to run than electric trains, although their maintenance costs were much higher.

Many passengers thought the line was being 'run down' in preparation for closure, although on several occasions BR swore that it had no intention of closing the line. Despite this, the engineers reported at the end of 1980 that if the demus were not replaced by 1987 at the latest the line would have to close, there being no alternative as the trains would be unsafe to operate.

In 1983 BR announced its plans to electrify lines to Cambridge, Norwich, Hastings and East Grinstead at a cost of £40 million. At last, in May 1985, authorisation to electrify the East Grinstead line was given; work was to start 'almost immediately' and the cost would be £7 million. Apparently the alternative, to refurbish the demus, would have cost about £4 million. The short section between South Croydon Junction and Selsdon had already been energised by March 1984, and from May a local service, peak-hours only, between London and Sanderstead had been introduced.

Yet again, the opportunity to electrify at the BR standard 25,000 volts AC overhead system was wasted and the technically outmoded 750 volts DC third rail system was chosen. Much of the expense of this was caused by the desire to protect the line with new barbed-wire and chain-mesh fencing, and the need to build several sub-stations and track-paralleling huts. On the other hand, with the third rail there was at least no need to raise clearances of bridges of tunnels. If the line had formed part of a high-speed Channel Tunnel route, as was originally intended, maybe overhead wires would have been used.

On 16th May, 1986, the ceremony of the laying of the 'golden pot' and the first length of conductor rail was performed at Lingfield station by the Southern Region General Manager, Gordon Pettitt. This ceremony, which marked the start of electrification work, was attended by two local Members of Parliament and several council chairmen - and even representatives of the Bluebell Railway. Mr Pettitt said that the electrification had not needed Government sanction - it was being paid for out of BR's own revenue. Platforms at Lingfield, Dormans and East Grinstead were to be lengthened to hold eight-car trains; substations would be built at Upper Warlingham, Oxted, Hurst Green and Dormans and track-paralleling huts at Riddlesdown, Lingfield and East Grinstead. Mr Pettitt also promised that the off-peak service would be run with new, sliding-door stock (one-class only) although peak trains would have to use old swing-door stock. Later, it was decided that modern trains could not be allowed to pass through Oxted tunnel.

By August 1986 the conductor rail was mostly in place from Sanderstead to Oxted and by March 1987 it had reached Lingfield. Usually the work was carried out on Sundays, the line being closed to traffic.

The line was energised on 20th July, 1987, in a ceremony at East Grinstead that went badly wrong. Six firework thunderflashes had been rigged up to go off one at a time in sequence, but because rainwater had seeped through they all exploded together, causing temporary deafness to the onlookers. The flashes were supposed to show the danger of trespassing on the track but, as one of the unfortunate bystanders commented: 'It sounded as if someone had let off half Woolwich Arsenal.'

Test running of electric trains soon began, and continued throughout August. 4-CIG Brighton main line units were used, with much flashing at the pick-up shoes as they scraped over the rusty conductor rail.

On Saturday, 19th September, 1987, the first electric train (a 4-CIG unit) to carry passengers on the Oxted line rolled into East Grinstead station. Among these passengers, who were invited guests of BR, was the broadcaster Johnny Morris, who in his capacity as vice-president of the Bluebell Railway Preservation Society was there to perform a naming ceremony on a class '73' electro-diesel locomotive. He unveiled the nameplate *The Bluebell Railway* and a handsome badge that included the railway's motto *'Floreat Vapor'*. The ceremony was attended by British Rail and Bluebell Railway representatives, the town mayor and the president of the Chamber of Commerce, and music was provided by the Copthorne Silver Band playing on the down platform, from which the general public could view the proceedings. Only guests were admitted to the up platform.

A really big event was staged for the following weekend, 26th and 27th September: the Gala Days. There were special £1 tickets for each day giving freedom of the line. The first public electric train to leave East Grinstead was the 6.52 am up (4-VEP units 3166 and 3162). Noteworthy was a special train chartered by the Rotary Clubs of East Grinstead and Titsey which left East Grinstead at 8.15 am for Bournemouth (due 11.00) calling only at Lingfield, Hurst Green and Oxted. The fare was £7.50 (1st class £12.50) and nearly 400 passengers were carried, along with plenty of liquid refreshment. Stock used was two 4-CIG units, Nos. 1268 and 1728. The advertising poster for this special proclaimed 'An electrifying experience. Be part of history - join the first charter of an electric train from East Grinstead to Bournemouth - and back!!' The train was due to leave Bournemouth at 5.30 pm and be back in East Grinstead at 8.10.

On both Saturday and Sunday a special train service operated, with four 8-car trains per hour between East Croydon and East Grinstead, every fourth train running approximately in demu timings as the regular Victoria-East Grinstead service. Apart from a temporary loss of power very early on Saturday at Dormans, the special service ran very well, and large numbers of people were carried.

There were many attractions at several stations. At Upper Warlingham the entertainments were pitched at young children, and the Romney, Hythe & Dymchurch Railway locomotive *The Bug* was in steam hauling a few RHDR coaches on a temporary track set up in the up-side car park. At Woldingham stalls were selling 'collectables' on the up platform. At Oxted diesel locomotive No. 33008 *Eastleigh*, electro-diesel locomotive No. 73004 *The Bluebell Railway* and diesel shunter *Ivor* were on display, and in the former goods shed was a model railway exhibition. Green-liveried 4L diesel unit No. 202001 was working between Oxted and Uckfield on the Saturday, and the £1 tickets were valid on this line, although no Sunday service was operated.

At Lingfield the now-disused signal cabin was open to the public, buffet refreshments were organised in the booking hall (possibly for the first time in the station's history) and at nearby Lingfield Park Racecourse a huge steam rally was the main attraction, with reduced admission charge to railway ticket holders.

East Grinstead's attractions included the Bluebell Railway's 'P' class No. 323 *Bluebell* on a low-loader and an almost continuous free service of vintage buses between the station and Sheffield Park, Bluebell Railway; at nearby East Court the town museum had a railway display, a model railway was on show to the public and there was a miniature passenger-carrying railway in the grounds. The Network SouthEast Marching Band paraded in Railway Approach.

The weekend was a huge success, over 16,000 passengers travelling. BR had gone to a great deal of trouble to give the public an unforgettable two days of enjoyment; seldom before had BR shown itself to have a human face. It was perfectly possible for a passenger to find himself in the same compartment as the General Manager, Gordon Pettitt, or the area manager, Don Gallop (whose picture adorned all the Oxted line stations)!

And then, most oddly, instead of continuing with electric trains, the line reverted to demus for another week - almost as though the Gala Days had never

The scene at East Grinstead on 4th August, 1987, when electric and diesel trains could be observed together. 4-CIG unit No. 1279 on a crew-training run, and 3D unit No. 207013 on the 2.19 pm to Victoria.   *Author*

These advertisements for the 'Gala Weekend' were displayed on all the demus operating the Oxted line for several days before the event.   *Author*

happened. On 30th September, 1987, the electrification was officially 'inaugurated' at East Grinstead by the Secretary of State for Transport, Paul Channon, who cracked a bottle of champagne over the buffers of the electric multiple unit that had brought him, the BR Chairman Sir Bob Reid, the Network SouthEast manager Chris Green, the Southern General Manager and the local MP, Tim Renton, to the station. Other guests included East Grinstead's town mayor, the president of the Chamber of Commerce, and local Members of Parliament. In fact there was such a concentration of bigwigs that the station had, before their arrival, been patrolled by sniffer dogs.

Mr Pettitt referred to his announcement of the electrification go-ahead in May 1986:

> I was advised by a lot of people that I was holding myself as a hostage of fortune for I as good as promised that electrification would be delivered on time - now 16 months later the new service is a reality.

The special train that had brought in the guests was then used to take out a party of 200 local schoolchildren to London for sightseeing.

Even after this 'inauguration' the demu service continued operating; so many different dates for the start of electric train running make the historian's task rather difficult, but the date that public electric services began running to a new timetable is probably the only important one. This was Monday 5th October, 1987, the last regular demus having run on Saturday, 3rd October.

The initial timetable was an admirable one. A half-hourly off-peak service operated, alternate trains running to and from London Bridge or Victoria; in the late evenings and on Sundays the service was hourly to and from Victoria. The main service was operated by 4-VEP and 4-CIG units, with 2-EPB suburban units used as strengthening in the peaks to give a high seating capacity. Every train was supposed to include a proportion of first class and be lavatory-equipped. Running time of stopping trains was about 50 minutes, and a few fast trains were included in the peaks: the 7.25 and 8.01 am East Grinstead to London Bridge were fast from Oxted to East Croydon, and the 5.25 pm from London Bridge to East Grinstead called only at East Croydon, Oxted, Lingfield and Dormans and was accelerated by eight minutes. There were new trains at 7.34 am from East Grinstead to London Bridge and at 6.09 pm return.

In contrast, Uckfield line passengers were worse off, as their line remained diesel worked, most trains reversing at Oxted; previously most trains had run through between London and Uckfield. But at least there was same-platform interchange at Oxted, the trains shunting from the up platform to the down bay just like their push-and-pull predecessors. At peak times there were a few demu through trains, so it was still possible to ride in a diesel over the electrified tracks; diesel trains left Victoria for Uckfield at 5.02 and 6.02 pm, and from London Bridge at 5.30 pm. There were many occasions when these trains did not run, owing to staff or stock shortage, and life for the Edenbridge Town or Crowborough commuter grew steadily worse, with half-hour or longer waits for 'the next train to Uckfield'. Later the 5.02 pm was withdrawn altogether.

VEP No. 3916 crosses Oxted viaduct on 25th January, 2003 with the 15.38 East Grinstead-Victoria service.

P. Barnes

The new electric service started off well, passengers approving of the much smoother ride and quicker running, particularly noticeable on the up grades. Flashing at collector shoes added interest to the journeys, but this phenomenon soon disappeared as the conductor rail became polished.

Barely had the trains got into their stride when disaster struck. On 16th October, 1987, a storm of great ferocity, with hurricane-force winds, struck the south-east. Many trees were blown on to the line, which had to be closed for three days while they were cleared away. Unfortunately, many of the green leaves remained, and when the trains began running again on the 19th they slipped very badly, causing great damage to wheels and motors and much late running for several days afterwards.

There was slow progress on the 8.36 pm Victoria to East Grinstead on 20th October. The train had struggled to Woldingham and a passenger asked his companion wearily: 'Where are we?'

'Somewhere north of Oxted, where we have to change on to one of the ropey old diesels,' was the response.

'Ropey old diesels?'

'Yes, I think they're going to retain them as a tourist attraction.'

VEP No. 3916 passes Oxted signal box with the 14.23 Victoria-East Grinstead service on 25th January, 2003. *P. Barnes*

Chapter Twelve

Special Trains

For many years special trains - that is to say, any trains run as additional services not in the timetable - were run in connection with the Lingfield horse-races. For two such trains from London Bridge to Lingfield in about 1905 the motive power was 'B1' class 0-4-2 No. 173 and 'B4' 4-4-0 No. 51, both of New Cross depot. The running of these specials caused some problems before 1920. There were sometimes as many as six trains, which had to run on empty to East Grinstead for berthing in the Low Level yard, the locomotives continuing light to Horsted Keynes to take water. On arrival back at East Grinstead they turned by using the spur to the High Level station, thence to St Margaret's Junction and so back into the Low Level station. In 1920 a water crane was installed at the west end of the down platform at East Grinstead High Level and the siding space at Lingfield was increased. Before World War I two or three locomotives coupled would go up to Oxted for water, and apparently this practice continued during the 1920s also. Three trains could be berthed at Lingfield.

The 9.05 am Victoria-Tunbridge Wells via Edenbridge Town would sometimes be diverted via Lingfield (for the use of racecourse staff, it is thought) and the 10.07 push-and-pull from Oxted ran via Edenbridge Town instead.

Lingfield specials often included one or two Pullman cars in the makeup. During 1954 BR or LM 2-6-4 tank locomotives worked the trains, to save turning at East Grinstead, but they lost time. They ran light to Oxted for water. On 12th November SR 2-6-0 locomotives were used on all the specials except one from Cannon Street; No. 42080 on the 4.03 pm Lingfield-Victoria managed to lose 25 minutes. Specials also ran from Brighton to Lingfield. On 20th August, 1955, LM class '4' tanks Nos. 42082/8 and BR Class 4 tanks Nos. 80012/122 worked specials from Victoria to Lingfield, No. 80121 worked one from Brighton, and the 12.33 pm special from Cannon Street, in the hands of class 'N' No. 31812, was the only one anywhere near to time. Mogul - haulage of Lingfield specials became normal: for example, one in June 1960 used class 'U1' No. 31894 of Stewarts Lane.

By 1963 the number of race specials for each meeting had declined to two, as a March 1963 special traffic notice shows. For the steeplechases of 20th and 21st March specials from Victoria to Lingfield at 12.02 and 12.30 pm were booked, calling only at East Croydon and taking about 50 minutes on the journey. Each train comprised eight corridors and a Pullman car. One train was berthed in the dock road, the other in the down siding. The locomotives then ran coupled to East Grinstead for water, then back to Lingfield to work the return specials to Victoria at 4.50 and 5.05 pm. Two first class coaches were to be provided for the exclusive use of Lingfield Race Club members in the 12.02 down and the 5.05 return.

By 1965 race traffic had declined even more, and in May retiring signalman Charlie Smith, who had worked at Lingfield since 1926, remarked 'The traffic

A class 'E5' 0-6-2 tank locomotive heads a seven-coach bogie block set past Hurst Green Junction. The headcode suggests that the train is a return Lingfield to London Bridge race special. *Lens of Sutton*

has gone down to nothing on what it used to be on race days. We had two or three horsebox specials and up to 10 passenger specials in those days.'

In demu days a special sometimes ran, but only by using existing stock that otherwise ran empty. On 20th February, 1970, an additional empty three-car demu left Oxted for Lingfield to form an additional 5.05 pm to Victoria, extra units being attached at Oxted. Rather more satisfactory arrangements were made on 7th August, 1970, when an extra nine-car demu ran from Lingfield to Victoria at 5.13 pm, taking the place of the scheduled empty 5.15 pm Hurst Green-Victoria. To form the train special empty trains ran from both Oxted and East Grinstead. In the down direction specials seldom ran, and the ordinary stopping trains, strengthened to six or nine cars, were considered adequate. 'Hastings' units 1034/5 did, however, work a Victoria-Lingfield special on 19th August, 1972.

On 28th June, 1985, a Pullman race special ran from Basingstoke to Lingfield, hauled by class '33' diesel locomotive No. 33017, and another locomotive-hauled race special ran on 2nd July, 1986. These were unusual events, as demus had been used normally.

Before World War II hop-pickers' specials and specials for hop-pickers' friends were a big traffic on the Eastern Section of the Southern; many went via the Oxted line and the Crowhurst spur to Paddock Wood and other places. Use was made of 14-coach six-wheeled carriage sets, then quite common. After the war, ex-SEC bogie stock was used. On Sunday 7th September, 1947, five return specials were routed via the Crowhurst spur and Oxted to London Bridge, and were very full.

On the evening of 20th September, 1953, the following return trains came round the Crowhurst spur and up the Oxted line: 5.12 pm from Staplehurst, 5.10 from Hawkhurst, 6.05 from Goudhurst, 6.10 from Wateringbury, 6.38 from Goudhurst, 7.10 from Marden, 6.05 from Northiam via the Kent & East Sussex line and Headcorn, 7.56 from Maidstone West, and 7.45 from Hawkhurst. Of these, the 7.10 pm from Marden was the only one that called at Oxted.

On 21st September, 1958, only three return hop-pickers' friends specials were routed via Oxted: the 5.02 pm Headcorn to London Bridge, with 'E1' 4-4-0 No. 31507; the 5.44 pm from Ashford, with class 'V' No. 30934; and the 6.08 pm from Hawkhurst to London Bridge, in charge of class 'C' goods locomotive No. 31267. With the mechanisation of hop-picking, special trains ceased running in about 1961.

Ramblers' specials were very popular during the 1950s. On 22nd March, 1953, Bulleid Pacific No. 34071 worked a ramblers' excursion from Victoria to Sheffield Park; it was the first time since 1945 that one of these locomotives had run via East Grinstead. On 8th September, 1957, Bulleid Pacific No. 34068 worked a ramblers' special to Ardingly via East Grinstead. Unfortunately a coupling broke at East Croydon and removing the front coach caused a delay of 50 minutes; arrival at Ardingly was an hour later than intended. An 11-coach excursion from Victoria to Groombridge, worked by class 'V' No. 30908, ran on 6th October, 1957.

On 11th May, 1958, another interesting ramblers' excursion, named 'The Bluebell Special', ran from Greenford, Western Region, to Haywards Heath via Oxted and East Grinstead. It was noteworthy for being hauled by Great Western 4-4-0 *City of Truro* as far as East Croydon, but this engine was permitted to go no further and class 'K' 2-6-0 No. 32342 worked the train from East Croydon to Haywards Heath.

Ramblers' excursions, organised by Mr G. Platt (the rail transport organiser of the Ramblers' Association), were accompanied by group leaders who would set off with parties from the destination station and return to the train some hours later. The excursions' popularity waned in the 1960s, as many people came to dislike the idea of being 'organised'. A 12-car 'Hastings' demu was used for a Victoria-Stonegate ramblers' excursion on Sunday, 8th April, 1962, outward via Oxted, Crowhurst Junction and Tonbridge, return via Tonbridge and Redhill.

There were also school specials, mainly for Ardingly College, during the 1950s, when it was customary for the 'end-of-term' special to be steam-hauled via East Grinstead and the 'start-of-term' special to be electric via Haywards Heath. To work the end-of-term special on 21st December, 1954, class 'V' No. 30917 *Ardingly* was appropriately used; the carriages had come down empty from New Cross Gate the previous day.

A series of 'no-passport' excursions for schoolchildren was organised by R.H. Clark of British Railways. One such ran on 25th May, 1960, from East Croydon to Folkestone Harbour via Oxted, Crowhurst Junction and Ashford hauled by 'West Country' No. 34098 *Templecombe*, conveying parties from Lingfield and Oxted schools among others. Mr Clark had managed, against much internal opposition, to organise a three-coach special from Lingfield to Oxted in connection with the main train; an additional train in the direction of the peak-hour flow was quite an event!

During the summer advertised excursions, which were shown in the timetable, ran on only a few days of the year, and cheap tickets were sold in connection with them. Before 1914 many excursions ran to Brighton via Oxted, Horsted Keynes and Haywards Heath. In 1953 a Sunday train ran from New Cross Gate to Oxted at 10.00 am, calling at Forest Hill (the only steam train to do so at that time); the return from Oxted was at 6.28 pm and it ran through to London Bridge. In 1961 a 10.01 am Forest Hill to Margate ran on only four Sundays (9th and 23rd July, 13th and 27th August) via Oxted and Crowhurst Junction, the return train at 6.40 pm taking the same route. This was the only timetabled train to use the Crowhurst spur that year, and it did not run in 1962.

Before 1914 there were special trains to Hever for *The Times* annual staff parties given by Major Astor, the owner of Hever Castle. Hever was also the destination for expensive excursions by the preserved Pullman car train known as the 'Venice Simplon Orient Express' during the 1980s; 2nd October, 1984, was one day that it ran there and it was stabled overnight at Tunbridge Wells West.

Troop trains ran during World War II and for several years afterwards. During 1944/5 there was a fast Sunday train from Victoria to Heathfield at 9.50 pm, not advertised to the public as it was intended for troops on short leave. On 22nd April, 1945, the eight-corridor train was worked by class 'Q' No. 541. On 8th April, 1953, a troop train at 10.18 am from Lingfield to Weybourne (Eastern Region) was scheduled. To work this the stock, an eight-coach corridor set plus a third, had left Eardley sidings (Streatham) at 5.12 am.

Entire farms could be moved by trains in those days too, the machinery and livestock being conveyed in wagons. On 25th February, 1955, a farm removal special from Lenzie left Bricklayers Arms at 9.30 am for Tunbridge Wells via Oxted and Edenbridge Town.

Railway enthusiasts' specials gained in popularity during the 1950s, reaching a peak in the 1960s. Here the idea was for societies to charter a train, arrange for it to be hauled by unusual motive power, and visit a succession of lines during a day's outing. Specially high fares were charged, for these specials took a great deal of organisation. Here is a list of special trains known to have covered some part of the Croydon, Oxted & East Grinstead:

The 'Wealden Limited' (Railway Correspondence & Travel Society) on 14th August, 1955. Included Lewes-East Grinstead-Oxted-East Croydon. Class 'H2' No. 32426 *St Albans Head*, eight corridors of Set 938 plus Pullman buffet car.

'The Southern Counties Ltd' (Locomotive Club of Great Britain) on 24th February, 1957. Included Lewisham-Oxted-Horsted Keynes. Class 'H2' No. 32424 *Beachy Head*.

'Bluebell Special No. 2' (Bluebell Railway Preservation Society) on 22nd April, 1961. Included Three Bridges-East Grinstead-Oxted-Eridge-Polegate. Class 'E4' Nos. 32503 and 32564 (one at each end), six-corridor Set 869.

'Sussex Coast Limited' (Locomotive Club of Great Britain) on 24th June, 1962. Returned from Eastbourne to London Bridge via Heathfield, East Grinstead and Oxted. Class 'M7' No. 30055 and class 'T9' No. 120; seven-set 237. The 'M7' assisted from Eastbourne to Eridge.

The 'Sussex Downsman' (RCTS/LCGB joint) on 22nd March, 1964. Returned from Brighton to Victoria via Uckfield and Oxted. Set 237.

The 'Maunsell Commemoration Tour' (LCGB) on 3rd January, 1965. Included Tonbridge-Crowhurst Spur-Oxted-Mid-Kent Line to London Bridge. Class 'N' No. 31411, Set 770. Thought to be the last train to use the Crowhurst spur.

The 'Surrey Downsman' special train, headed by 'West Country' class No. 34102 *Lapford*, enters Oxted at 12.02 pm on Sunday 5th March, 1967. BR class '4' No. 75077 waits on the up line to work the train back at 12.20.   *Author*

'Southdown Venturer' (Southern Counties Touring Society) on 20th February, 1966. Included Victoria-Oxted-Uckfield-Brighton. 'West Country' class No. 34013 *Okehampton*. The 'Surrey Downsman' (LCGB) on 5th March, 1967. Included Lewisham-Oxted-Norwood Junction. Class 'WC' No. 34102 *Lapford* hauled the train to Oxted, arriving there at noon, and BR class '4' No. 75077 worked the train from Oxted northwards at 12.20. No. 34102 followed shortly afterwards, running light, and was therefore the last steam locomotive to be seen at Oxted.

The 'Sussex Venturer' (Bulleid Pacific Preservation Society / LCGB) on 4th January, 1969. Included Norwood Junction-Oxted-Tunbridge Wells West-Uckfield-Lewes. Class '33' diesel locomotive No. 6565. Nine coaches including buffet restaurant car.

The 'Southern Invader' on 7th April, 1979. East Croydon-East Grinstead-East Croydon. Class '50' diesel locomotive No. 50016 *Barham* and 10 Western Region Mk I coaches including restaurant car.

Relief trains were sometimes laid on at busy times. On several occasions the 3.55 pm Victoria to Brighton/Eastbourne ran as two complete trains, one to Brighton at the normal time and another to Eastbourne about seven minutes later. This occurred on 22nd and 23rd December, 1944; Maundy Thursday and Easter Saturday, 1945; 3rd and 4th August, 1945; 21st and 22nd December, 1945; 18th April, 1946; 3rd April, 1947; the pre-Christmas period, 1952. After this, duplication became a rarity although on 15th January, 1957, because of heavy school traffic, trains for Brighton and Eastbourne, each of six corridors, left Victoria at 3.50 and 3.55 pm respectively. On 29th March, 1945 (Maundy Thursday), even the 6.10 pm from Victoria was divided, a special for Tunbridge Wells leaving at 6.13.

Until the early 1960s special services, often with extra trains, operated on Bank Holidays ; but for many years now the Southern Region has considered that a standard Sunday service is all that is required. Until the 1950s locomotives operating Bank Holiday trains carried a train number board on the smokebox; all trains, from whatever line, were supposed to arrive at Victoria or London Bridge in numerical sequence and departures also were in numerical order. The numbers were displayed to assist signalmen to regulate the trains at these busy times.

In recent years the only time when anything like a special train service was operated was at Christmas Eve, when office workers would leave London during the afternoon. The evening trains worked by locomotive-hauled trains would be cancelled, and instead these trains would run at approximately hourly intervals during the afternoon from London Bridge to supplement the normal hourly Victoria service. The 'Christmas Eve' service ran in most years from 1971 to 1982 but not in 1973 (although additional trains were advertised they did not run).

A special train, chartered by the Rotary Clubs of East Grinstead and Titsey, ran from East Grinstead to Bournemouth and back on 26th September, 1987, and again on 17th September the following year. Although very popular these trains were not repeated as, apparently, crews could not be spared to work them.

Hastings unit No. 1031 on a railtour passing through Lingfield on 17th September, 1983.
P. Barnes

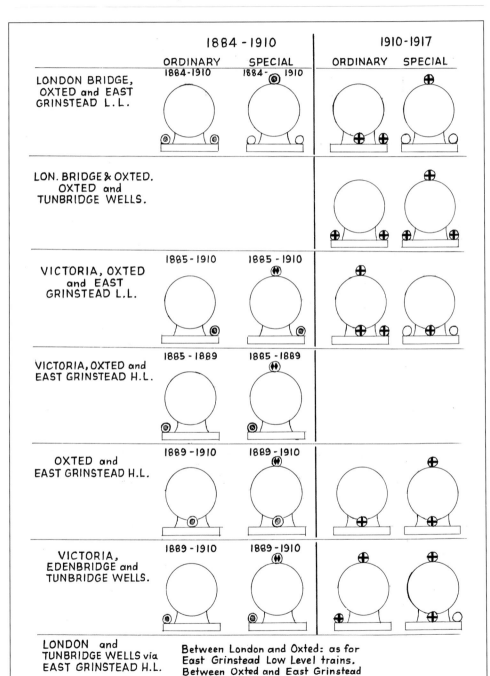

Chapter Thirteen

Headcodes

All the southern railway systems went in for means of identifying the destination and route of their trains, using 15-inch diameter metal discs secured by brackets on the front of the locomotive. Those used by the Brighton on the Oxted line until 1910 were green with a white rim, whilst the South Eastern's Oxted trains carried a disc with black spot and white rim. For special trains the Brighton added a disc with two black diamonds painted on, and the SER's specials had a large oval plate hung at the top of the smokebox. In 1910 the Brighton's headcodes were entirely altered, and only two types of disc were now used: plain white, and white with black cross. This system was short-lived for in 1917 the 'black cross' was eliminated, the codes being changed yet again, and the variety of positions for discs was increased by adding two more brackets. The SECR, for its part, did not simplify its headcodes until 1917, when all the weird assortment of stripes and blobs was eliminated and only white discs and 'black cross' discs were used. The Southern Railway in 1923 did away with the 'black cross', but the LBSCR codes were maintained until March 1934.

There were several three-disc codes in use on the system, and for reasons of economy the Southern wished to eliminate as many as possible, replacing them with two-disc codes. In effect this meant that practically every code had to be changed, and the March 1934 codes lasted until the end of steam.

East Grinstead Low Level, *c.*1921, with train bearing the Oxted-East Grinstead code; possibly it was the 5.05 pm from Victoria. Class 'D3' 0-4-4 tank No. 390, with Billinton 6-wheel stock. *C.E.K. Nutt*

1917 - 1934

VICTORIA & OXTED.
OXTED & BRIGHTON
via ERIDGE.

FROM JUN. 1917

LON. BRIDGE & OXTED.
OXTED &
TUNBRIDGE WELLS.

FROM JUN. 1917

OXTED & EAST
GRINSTEAD H.L.

JUN. 1917 till AUG. 1922

OXTED & EAST
GRINSTEAD L.L.

JUN. 1917 till AUG. 1922

OXTED & TUNBRIDGE
WELLS via EAST
GRINSTEAD H.L.

FROM AUG. 1922

OXTED & BRIGHTON
via EAST GRINSTEAD
L.L. and LEWES.

FROM AUG. 1922

FROM MAR. 1934

VICTORIA, OXTED
& TUNBRIDGE WELLS
via HEVER.

LON. BRIDGE, OXTED
& TUNBRIDGE WELLS
via HEVER.

OXTED & BRIGHTON
via ERIDGE.

OXTED & BRIGHTON
via HAYWARDS
HEATH.

OXTED & TUNBRIDGE
WELLS via EAST
GRINSTEAD H.L.

OXTED & BRIGHTON
via EAST GRINSTEAD
L.L. and LEWES.

FROM AUG. 1949:

VICTORIA & BRIGHTON
via ERIDGE.

FROM AUG. 1949:

VICTORIA & BRIGHTON
via EAST GRINSTEAD
and LEWES.

LON. BRIDGE & BRIGHTON
via ERIDGE.

LON. BRIDGE & BRIGHTON
via EAST GRINSTEAD
and LEWES.

FROM 1884:

LONDON BRIDGE,
CROYDON, OXTED,
CROWHURST JN.
and TONBRIDGE.

FROM FEB. 1917:

LON. BRIDGE, CROYDON
& OXTED LINE.

FROM FEB. 1917:

LON. BRIDGE, MID-KENT
& OXTED LINE.

FROM MAR. 1934:

LON. BRIDGE & DOVER
via E.CROYDON, OXTED,
CROWHURST JN.
and TONBRIDGE.

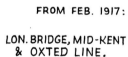

FROM MAR. 1934:

LON. BRIDGE & HASTINGS
via MID-KENT, OXTED,
CROWHURST JN.
and TONBRIDGE.

Curiously there were never separate codes for 'Victoria (or London Bridge) and Tunbridge Wells via East Grinstead', and in practice the 'Tunbridge Wells via Hever' codes were always displayed. The apparent intention was that the codes should be changed at Oxted, but this rarely if ever happened. Not until 1949 were there separate codes for the London-Brighton via Eridge or East Grinstead services, and these were three-disc, giving an air of distinction to these trains.

Numerical headcodes came in with the diesel trains. There was not much logic to them, apart from the fact that they continued the SR system with main line electric trains of having even numbers for Victoria services and odd numbers for London Bridge ones. The initial 1962 codes were as follows:

1	Oxted and Tonbridge.
22	Victoria and Tunbridge Wells West via East Grinstead.
33	London Bridge and Tunbridge Wells West via East Grinstead.
44	Victoria and Tunbridge Wells West via Hever.
47	London Bridge and Brighton via Eridge.
60	Victoria and Brighton via Eridge.
77	London Bridge and Tunbridge Wells West via Hever.

To these in 1965 were added:

55	London Bridge and East Grinstead Low Level.
60	Also used for Oxted and Brighton or Lewes.
66	Victoria and East Grinstead Low Level.

Codes 22, 33, 44 and 77 fell into disuse following service changes and closures.

Following closure of the Uckfield-Lewes section, the codes from January 1969 were now:

1	Oxted and Uckfield.
47	London Bridge and Uckfield.
55	London Bridge and East Grinstead.
60	Victoria and Uckfield.
66	Victoria and East Grinstead.

In May 1978, for no very clear reason, almost all the Central Division headcodes were altered to coincide with a replanned timetable. The Oxted line codes were now more logical than before, and 'Oxted-Uckfield' lost its separate code '1'.

66	Victoria and East Grinstead.
77	London Bridge and East Grinstead.
88	Victoria and Uckfield.
99	London Bridge and Uckfield.

Upon electrification of the East Grinstead line these codes were not altered, and the through diesel trains between London and Uckfield also continued to carry the same codes. However, the shuttle service between Oxted and Uckfield, from October 1987, carried the new code '5'.

Chapter Fourteen

Incidents

In 100 years on the Oxted line there have been no serious accidents to trains involving loss of life, but there have been countless 'incidents': derailments, collisions and delays caused by obstructions on the line or by atrocious weather conditions.

On 19th July, 1935, class 'I3' No. 2075 while working the 5.18 pm from Brighton to Victoria via East Grinstead derailed at Streatham Junction. The locomotive had been running bunker first at high speed, and afterwards drivers were instructed not to exceed 40 mph with engines running in reverse. Another 'I3', No. 2090, had derailed at Balham on 17th December, 1932, while working the 3.07 pm Forest Row to Victoria.

On 17th July, 1946, an Oxted line train was involved in a collision at Victoria. Class 'I3' No. 2090, while shunting two wagons, hit the second coach of the 2.30 pm to Tunbridge Wells just as that train was leaving Victoria. The first coach of three-set No. 542 was derailed and the second knocked right over, blocking much of the Central Section part of Victoria. The 5.50 and 6.10 pm trains were cancelled, and the 6.48 pm to East Grinstead left from the Eastern Section.

On 13th and 14th March, 1947, owing to earth slips on the Brighton main line, the 6.00 pm Victoria to Brighton ran as an eight-corridor steam train via Oxted and Horsted Keynes, taking over three hours on the journey. The 7.40 am Brighton to Victoria next day was also steam-hauled via Oxted and arrived nearly an hour late.

Class 'I3' No. 32021 was working the Sunday 8.36 am London Bridge to Brighton via East Grinstead on 11th September, 1951, just past Dormans when the locomotive's main steampipe burst. Driver Alfred Johnson was scalded, but applied the brake before jumping off the engine with fireman Reginald Bowden. The train pulled up on Cook's Pond Viaduct, from which the 50 passengers were able to admire the view for 1½ hours before another locomotive arrived to take the train on.

A cable fire at Victoria on 16th December, 1957, caused the diversion to London Bridge of morning business trains. Newspapers normally carried by the 5.20 am from Victoria were taken by road to London Bridge and loaded on to the 8.01 am. Fire was also a problem with Cook's Pond viaduct during each summer, when hot ashes from locomotives caused the timbers to ignite on two or three occasions a year; the local fire brigade always managed to extinguish these fires before any serious damage was done. The viaduct had provision for piping up water from the pond.

The severe winters of 1961/2 and 1962/3, with their heavy falls of snow, badly affected running on the Oxted line. On 31st December, 1961, snow-laden trees were overhanging the track and points were frozen. Next day some trains were delayed at Oxted for nearly two hours. The *East Grinstead Observer* recorded that on 30th December, 1962, a down train was stuck in a snowdrift at Riddlesdown.

R.W. Kidner recalls that on one occasion, about 1963 or 1964, after the goods trains began to be worked by diesel locomotives, a type '3' backed on to some empty coal wagons in the westernmost siding at Oxted and accelerated so rapidly that the first wagon jumped in the air and came down off the track.

Another severe winter occurred in 1968. After a heavy fall of snow on 9th January an evening train was derailed at Selsdon and blocked the line. Replacement buses ran between East Croydon and Sanderstead, but passengers aboard the 5.09 pm from Victoria to East Grinstead had the time of their lives, for their train was diverted via Haywards Heath, Lewes, Uckfield and Hurst Green, not arriving at East Grinstead until 9.50 pm! Next morning, because of frozen points, there were no trains after the departure of the 7.19 until 8.36 (the 7.47 running late), and the 8.21 to Oxted was extended to London, leaving East Grinstead at 9.01 am.

Heavy and continuous rain on 14th and 15th September, 1968, caused flooding in many parts of south-east England, but the Oxted line was one of the least affected. A landslip between East Grinstead and Lingfield closed the up line on the 15th, but the down line remained in use. For some two weeks, trains through Oxted tunnel were reduced to a crawl as water poured through the roof and down the air shafts.

On the afternoon of 1st July, 1968, a diesel unit while reversing on the north crossover at Oxted station became derailed and blocked both running roads. The train service between East Croydon and Oxted was cancelled, although there were shuttle trains between Oxted and East Grinstead. Passengers from London Bridge rode to Caterham, whence special buses were running to Oxted via Godstone; passengers for Lingfield and East Grinstead travelled to Three Bridges, thence by special coaches. Passengers on the 6.10 pm from Victoria, however, were detrained at East Croydon and found waiting for them outside the station a rather unsatisfactory substitute - an ancient Guy 'Utility' double-deck bus in very poor condition. R.W. Kidner, who was a passenger that evening, believes it was ex-Southdown, for such vehicles were not normally seen in the Croydon area at such a late date. He records:

This left and duly called at all stations, although in fact everyone aboard was for Oxted or south (not surprising for passengers off a train non-stop to Oxted). After calling at Woldingham station, the bus tackled the long steep hill up to the Downs, apparently in bottom gear. Halfway up there was a gasp from the seventy-odd passengers when the bus lost what little speed it had as the driver appeared to search for an even lower gear. He found it; he had been in second! On arrival at Oxted the commuters (usually courteous in a crisis) thanked the driver for having got them there, but were glad to note that from Oxted southwards trains were running.

On at least three occasions trees were blown on to the line by fierce winds. On 16th January, 1974, the 5.36 pm Victoria to Crowborough ran into a large tree that had fallen on the line between Upper Warlingham and Woldingham. Some windows were broken but there were no serious injuries to passengers and the train was not derailed; however, the line was blocked for the rest of the evening. Much more serious was the occasion when, in high winds, a train was hit by a falling tree that thrust itself into the side of the front coach, seriously injuring two passengers, one of whom was trapped, the other being thrown from the train through the hole made by the tree. This very unpleasant business occurred near Dormans on 27th March, 1987, and the diesel unit involved was No. 205002 which, although quite badly damaged, was repaired and back in traffic by mid-May 1987.

From time to time obstructions were deliberately placed on the line by mischievous persons, but nothing could compare with the 'obstruction' caused when a stolen motor car was crashed on to the railway by an exceptionally careless motorist. This happened just south of Upper Warlingham station, where the line is in cutting, on 21st February, 1975. The car was hit by the 6.09 pm from Victoria and trapped under the buffers of the front unit (No. 1319), which pushed it ¼ mile before the driver could brake the train. The line was blocked for two hours, passengers for East Grinstead being diverted to Three Bridges, thence by bus.

Apparently most things have been on the Oxted line, quite apart from trains, over the years: trees, autumn leaves, cars and even the traditional herd of cows. On 12th May, 1968, eight cattle broke through a fence between Lingfield and Dormans, and three of the beasts were killed when an up train hit them.

On 22nd August, 1975, a demu working the 4.05 pm Uckfield-Oxted derailed at Hurst Green Junction, blocking the lines. The 4.20 pm from London Bridge was one of the trains held up. There was something wrong with the signalling equipment: the points had been set for the East Grinstead line and the newly-installed Edenbridge up home signal should have been at danger but was in fact 'off'. East Grinstead passengers at East Croydon were advised to travel to Three Bridges, thence by bus, but passengers for Lingfield, Dormans and the Uckfield line were left to fend for themselves.

On at least three occasions trains ran off the trap points at the up end of East Grinstead's up platform. Two were engineers' trains (on 22nd August, 1981, and 20th June, 1987) but on 3rd November, 1988, a passenger train actually managed to do this, the front coach of 4-CIG electric unit No. 1266 ending up at an angle of 45 degrees. It is believed the guard gave the 'right-away' without checking the signal aspect. Two passengers were injured.

The year 1985 was not a particularly good one for the Oxted line. Trouble started early: on 7th January there was a fall of snow and the 8.03 am from East Grinstead was cancelled. Then on 4th February there was an earthslip at Merle Common, between Hurst Green and Lingfield, rendering the up line unusable; several trains were cancelled and others delayed as single-line working was put into operation. On that same evening, according to Mrs Johnson-Rooks of Felcourt, her train limped down as far as Woldingham, where it remained for over 25 minutes. 'For most of that time the guard lounged at the front of the train and made no effort to tell passengers what was the problem (in fact it was yet another signal failure).' When a passenger remonstrated with the guard he was told, 'This isn't PR, it's BR.'

On 31st May, 1985, there was a collision at Battersea Park station, when a Gatwick Express ran into the rear of the 8.51 am from East Grinstead, which was moving at about five mph. Injuries to passengers were minor. The 9.20 from Gatwick Airport, which was travelling at 20 mph, had passed a signal at danger.

This class '33' locomotive ran off the trap points at East Grinstead early on Saturday morning, 20th June, 1987. The line was already closed to passenger traffic as the engineers had possession. Here, *Broadlands* is being rerailed.   *Author*

Incidents of a different sort occurred on two occasions at Oxted, where passengers at last began to rebel at the treatment meted out to them by BR. On 1st October, 1985, the Uckfield portion of the 5.25 pm from London Bridge was terminated at Oxted for want of a guard. Six irate commuters for Crowborough and Uckfield 'sat-in', as the following train was due to terminate at Eridge and was of no use to them. Oxted station called the police, who invited the passengers to leave the train, but the passengers won as the train crew decided they would take the train on. More ugly scenes at Oxted were observed on 14th November, 1986, when the 5.32 pm from Victoria, which had left at 6.00, arrived 50 minutes late and was terminated there. Furious passengers threatened the driver, and police were again called by BR 'to protect their employees from commuters' wrath', and to prevent a fight from starting. There had been five days of delays that week, and passengers' endurance had been goaded beyond all limits. In the end it took them 2½ hours to get from London to East Grinstead that night.

There was a very heavy snowfall on 11th January, 1987, and on the 14th a further fall and drifting caused the complete closure of the East Grinstead line for one day. Trains were snowbound on the Edenbridge line, which was closed for three days. The snow completely covered the track in many places, giving the uncomfortable impression of an abandoned trackbed. The East Grinstead line was reopened on 15th January with an ad-hoc train service.

In the small hours of Sunday 5th July, 1987, a ballast train ran into the rear of a stationary engineers' train just north of Dormans station. The three men on the moving train managed to jump clear before the collision, which derailed the locomotive and three wagons, but four engineers on the stationary train were injured. Locomotive No. 33003 was later written off. Work on the line was delayed until 7.10 pm and reopening to passenger traffic was at 6.30 am on Monday, the first train being replaced by a bus between East Grinstead and Hurst Green.

After electrification, delays and failures became very rare occurrences, although cancellations because of staff shortage did not abate. On 4th November, 1987, fire broke out in the rear carriage of the 5.53 pm London Bridge to East Grinstead, and the train halted just beyond Sanderstead for some time; a diesel locomotive was sent to bring it back to Sanderstead. Apparently no train arrived at East Grinstead until shortly after 9.00 pm that evening.

On 11th April, 1988, the 5.06 pm London Bridge-East Grinstead failed at Lingfield. The following train, the 5.25 pm from London Bridge, was terminated at Hurst Green (at which it was not even booked to call) and returned empty to London. The passengers who were decanted at that rather bleak station began to wonder if they would get home that night, as the 5.32 from Victoria failed to show up, but at last the 5.53 pm London Bridge to East Grinstead arrived, and then ran to Lingfield at a crawl (because of the failure being 'in section') and at Lingfield coupled on to the waiting train. The dead train was then pushed the rest of the way to East Grinstead, arrival there being two hours 15 minutes after it had left London.

Oxted-Uckfield diesel trains were unable to travel to and from Selhurst depot for refuelling on 17th October, 1992, because only two lines were in use through South Croydon. To overcome this little problem the units were refuelled by road tanker at Oxted.

Chapter Fifteen

Strikes and Other Disputes

When railway staff 'withdraw their labour' their motives can be the desire for increased pay, improved working conditions, or protest against dismissal of a colleague. In the the early days of strikes the men usually managed to get their way, but in more recent times, as their jobs became more vulnerable, striking was completely counter-productive and, quite naturally, caused a great deal of resentment among passengers. When there were only partial strikes (the so-called 'work-to-rule') and a train service of sorts was operated, season-ticket holders were unable to claim any refund; they just had to suffer monstrous inconvenience.

There was a major railway strike in September 1919 for higher wages, and in May 1926 the trades unions really flexed their muscles by calling a general strike. Any trains that did run were manned by volunteers; on 6th May no passenger trains ran to or from East Grinstead, but there was a service from Three Bridges to London.

Enginemen ceased work for two weeks in spring 1955, although other railwaymen worked normally. On Whit Sunday, 29th May, no trains ran, and there was nothing to London via Oxted on the bank holiday. On the 31st three Oxted line trains each way ran, the engine crews being members of the National Union of Railwaymen, who were not in dispute. These trains were timed at 8.30 am and 2.30 pm from Tunbridge Wells West to London Bridge via East Grinstead, and 11.30 am and 5.30 pm return; and at 9.00 am from Tunbridge Wells West to Victoria via Edenbridge Town and 11.05 am return. This service, using nine-coach trains, seems to have been maintained for the rest of the week. On 4th June the 2.30 up and 5.30 down trips were cancelled, being replaced by a 3.30 pm Tunbridge Wells to Victoria, 6.10 pm Victoria to Uckfield and 8.15 pm Uckfield to Tunbridge Wells. The 8.30 am up was well-used, approximately 130 people boarding it at East Grinstead. The strike ceased on 14th June, 1955; although much damage had been done, viewed as an attempt to paralyse the country it was a failure. Road transport had come to the rescue, and carriage of freight by rail began its sharp decline.

However, this was the last of the major, prolonged strikes. In future it was found more expedient to stay absent on isolated days in the week, so that very little pay was lost. Somehow this also affected train working on the following day, as rolling stock always seemed to be in the wrong place. A one-day strike occurred on 3rd October, 1962; no trains ran on the Oxted line, but the stations were staffed.

When drivers 'worked-to-rule', as they did during the early part of December 1967, it seemed to imply that to work normally meant breaking the rules. The Press called these bouts of non-cooperation 'go-slows', and the result certainly was late-running trains and cancellations. Another 'go-slow' was in force from 24th June to 7th July, 1968. On the first day several peak-hour trains did not run and others were about half an hour late; off-peak trains were only a few minutes late. No trains at all ran on Sunday 30th June.

There was a signalmen's strike for a few days in July 1969. Most trains ran but on the 10th the last two from Victoria (10.09 and 11.09 pm) were cancelled.

The 1970s and early 1980s were the years of seemingly never-ending disputes, and passengers were given a rough time. They were not interested in the reasons why the unions and the BR Board were in perpetual conflict; all the passengers wanted was a reliable train service. Many people took to commuter road coaches in desperation. Here are some of the major problems that Oxted line passengers had to cope with during that time.

17.4.72   Drivers' dispute. Only three morning trains left East Grinstead, and the line from there to Lingfield was closed after 3.00 pm as the signal cabins were unmanned.

18.4.72   9.45 am Hurst Green-Victoria did not run. A Victoria train turned up at 10.27, was delayed at Oxted awaiting a guard; arrived Victoria 11.53. No resemblance to advertised service.

21.4.72   Poor service again; East Croydon announced at 3.30 pm that there would be no Oxted line trains until the 5.20 pm from London Bridge.

14.5.72   BR shutdown; no trains anywhere.

23.11.72   No trains on Southern Region because of strike.

28.2.73   Drivers' strike; no trains ran. Also on 8th March, 11th March and 1st May.

16.12.73   No trains on nine consecutive Sundays until 17th February, 1974.

8.1.74   Norwood drivers on strike, so no locomotive-hauled trains ran. Normal demu service.

15.1.74   One-day strike of drivers.

28.1.74   Guards and signalmen not working. Very few trains ran; three up in the morning and only one down.

20.2.75   Signalmen's strike; no Oxted line trains.

22.4.80   All the Tunbridge Wells drivers were on strike so very few demu services ran, but all locomotive-hauled trains ran normally.

1.5.81   Strike by men at Tunbridge Wells depot. Only four business trains ran up in the morning and three down in the afternoon. Also on 6th, 7th and 8th May. At London Bridge on 8th May the 5.50 pm was announced dramatically as 'the one and only train leaving London for East Grinstead this evening'.

13.1.82   Drivers' strike; no trains at all. Also on 16 other random days until 18th February.

28.6.82   NUR strike. Only two trains ran. Also on 29th June, when the 9.46 am from East Grinstead was the first up train.

4.7.82   Drivers' strike; lasted two weeks until 18th July. A few trains ran. During first week a Tunbridge Wells driver worked a special diagram: 6.31 am East Grinstead-London Bridge and 7.40 am return; 9.30 am East Grinstead-East Croydon and 10.30 am return. During second week a locomotive and eight coaches worked a special diagram: 7.52 am East Grinstead-London Bridge and 9.14 am return; and 10.25 am East Grinstead-East Croydon. On first day of 'normal' working, 19th July, there were at least five demu failures, two cancellations and much stock displacement.

20.10.83   Strike of guards, including those at Tunbridge Wells. Special locomotive-hauled train at 10.20 am from East Grinstead to London Bridge. 5.20 pm London Bridge-Uckfield ran, but East Grinstead passengers off this had over one hour to wait at Oxted.

21.10.83   Second day of guards' strike. 9.15 pm London Bridge-East Grinstead did not run, but a demu ran at 10.18 to East Croydon. The only Oxted line train thence was at 11.30 pm to Eridge. Oxted laid on a special coach for East Grinstead passengers.

19.8.85   Guards' strike over driver-only trains (which never ran on the Oxted line). Only five trains left East Grinstead in the morning and two arrived in the afternoon. In the evening there was no train back from East Croydon until 9.40 pm.

Since then, the line has remained reasonably strike-free as the Unions came gradually to realise the futility of going against the will of the British Railways Board in such things as flexible rostering of drivers, which the Board was determined to implement. But no matter whether one supported the Board or the Unions, it was always the passenger who suffered and the suffering was probably worse on the Oxted line than elsewhere because, in addition to strikes, the line was afflicted by stock shortages, crew shortages and train failures. The end result was just the same: 'grotesque inconvenience', as the Member of Parliament for Crawley (Nicholas Soames) once described it.

Chapter Sixteen

Fares and Tickets

In Joint Line days, separate stocks of tickets, headed 'LB&SC&SE&C RYS', were held by the joint stations. Ordinary tickets were available for return in either company's trains. During the Great War, thanks to the severe reduction in train services, interavailability of tickets was increased further and passengers could use their return halves to Edenbridge and Tunbridge Wells by either the SECR or LBSCR routes, and SECR tickets could be used on the Brighton company's Oxted line trains.

LBSC season tickets in 1912 were available for one or two weeks, and one, two, three, six or twelve months - a far greater choice than today. On the joint line seasons could be used in either company's trains, and in addition there were joint seasons (first class only) issued at the joint stations for use to London Bridge, Victoria, Charing Cross, Waterloo Junction and Cannon Street by LBSCR or SECR routes. These cost around 10 shillings more than the normal type.

Ordinary single tickets were available only on the day of issue. Ordinary returns were available for eight days at Selsdon Road, Sanderstead, Upper Warlingham and Woldingham, and for six months at stations south thereof. First class was considerably more expensive than third class, probably because Government duty was levied (not abolished until 1929). Second class had been abolished in 1911 by the LBSCR but the SECR continued to maintain it until September 1923.

The LBSCR published rates for conveying horses and carriages by passenger train: one, two or three horses and a two-wheel or four-wheel carriage by open carriage truck all commanded different fares with a five shilling surcharge if conveyed by covered carriage truck. The service was not cheap, but only the well-to-do would be expected to travel around in trains taking their horses and carriages with them. From London to East Grinstead the charges in 1912 were 10 shillings for one horse, 17s. 6d. for two horses, 11s. 8d. for a two-wheeled carriage and 17s. 6d. for a four-wheeler. These could not be handled at Selsdon Road, Sanderstead or Dormans.

Another facility was the collection and delivery of passengers' luggage in advance, which could be handled at all Oxted line stations except Dormans. The service cost a flat rate of one shilling door to door or sixpence if the luggage was brought to the station by the passenger.

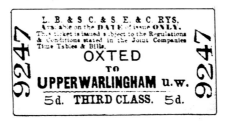

There was also a parcels service. The consignee would be charged according to distance and weight of the parcel, and 'frail or bulky' parcels were charged 50 per cent more when carried at the railway's risk or 25 per cent more at the owner's risk. These rates had to calculated on the spot by overworked station clerks. In 1912 a 2 lb. parcel from Oxted to London cost fourpence, a 3 lb. parcel fivepence, a 5 lb. parcel sixpence, and so on.

Here is a 1912 list of return fares and one-monthly season ticket rates between Oxted line stations and London.

	Returns				Seasons				
	First		Third		First			Third		
	s.	d.	s.	d.	£	s.	d.	£	s.	d.
Selsdon Road	2	11	1	6	2	3	6	1	5	0
Sanderstead	3	1	1	7	2	3	6	1	5	9
Upper Warlingham	4	0	2	1	2	12	6	1	15	0
Woldingham	4	6	2	5	2	15	0	1	18	0
Oxted	5	6	2	10	3	5	9	2	7	6
Lingfield	7	1	3	10	3	17	3	2	11	3
Dormans	7	10	4	2	4	0	0	2	13	9
East Grinstead	8	10	4	11	4	2	6	2	16	3

Special cheap tickets were very restricted in scope. Some were available only during the summer, others only by certain trains and on certain days of the week. In May 1922, for example, cheap day returns to London every Wednesday were being advertised from Oxted, Lingfield, Dormans and East Grinstead:

	First		Third	
	s.	d.	s.	d.
Oxted	7	5	3	11
Lingfield	10	2	5	1
Dormans	10	9	5	4
East Grinstead	11	8	5	10

Fares had been considerably increased during the Great War, so that these 'cheap' tickets were now more expensive than the pre-war ordinary fares. The Southern Railway seemed to have no intention of giving East Grinstead daily cheap tickets and by summer 1928 neither Lingfield, Dormans nor East Grinstead had them, yet Oxted did. As for season tickets, East Grinstead issued a quarterly

ticket that was valid for travel via Lingfield or Three Bridges for £8 1s. There was no ticket solely for the direct route, and a resident calculated that if there were it would have cost only £7 1s. It was particularly unfair as Guildford, another place with alternative routes to London, did not charge extra for the longer route.

'Go as you please' cheap day tickets were advertised during the summer of 1934. They were issued daily from London to Sanderstead: 2s. 10d. first, 1s. 8d. third; Riddlesdown: 3s. 3d., 2s.; Upper Warlingham: 3s. 6d., 2s. 3d.; Woldingham: 4s., 2s. 6d.; and Oxted: 4s. 6d., 2s. 9d. There were issued only on Saturdays and Sundays to Lingfield: 5s. 9d. first, 3s. 6d. third; and Dormans: 6s., 3s. 9d.; and daily to East Grinstead: 6s. 6d., 4s. These fares, a considerable reduction in cost since 1922, were only about twopence more than ordinary singles. By 1938 the first class fares had been reduced by about threepence or fourpence, though the third class class fare remained the same.

Weekend returns were available to and from London on Fridays, Saturdays and Sundays for return the same weekend; they were more expensive than day returns but cheaper than ordinary returns. There were also summer tickets to and from London and stations Oxted to East Grinstead at 8s. 6d. first class, 5s. third class. Later the summer tickets became 'monthly returns' all year round.

Many of these concessionary fares disappeared and by July 1949 all that remained were ordinary singles and returns, monthly returns and, to certain stations, day returns. These were now not permitted to be used between 4.30 and 6.30 pm Mondays to Fridays or 12.0 noon and 1.30 pm on Saturdays. The table below shows the comparative costs of day and monthly returns in summer 1949:

	Day Returns				Monthly Returns			
	First		Third		First		Third	
	s.	d.	s.	d.	s.	d.	s.	d.
Selsdon					5	3	3	6
Sanderstead					5	5	3	7
Riddlesdown	4	8	3	0	6	3	4	2
Upper Warlingham	5	4	3	4	7	5	4	11
Woldingham	5	11	3	9	8	0	5	4
Oxted	7	1	4	5	9	2	6	1
Hurst Green Halt	7	4	4	8	9	9	6	6
Lingfield	9	1	5	10	11	0	7	4
Dormans	9	7	6	1	11	8	7	9
East Grinstead					12	3	8	2

East Grinstead had a very restricted range of cheap tickets. Day returns were issued on Wednesdays, Thursdays and Saturdays by the 12.08 or 1.48 pm trains at a cost of 4s. 3d. Even cheaper evening returns could be had on Tuesdays, Wednesdays, Thursdays and Saturdays for travel on the 4.05 or 6.10 pm to London at 3s. 6d.

From 1st October, 1950, day returns were sold for use on any train between any two stations within the London Transport area. Cheap evening fares were retained until the mid-1950s, available by any train after 4.00 pm (5s. from East Grinstead, 4s. 6d. from Lingfield and Dormans in 1954). A mid-week shopping ticket was in vogue between 1955 and 1962 on Wednesdays and Thursdays only;

available after 9.30 am for return before 4.30 or after 6.30 pm. East Grinstead to London cost 5s. with this ticket; increased to 5s. 6d. in 1960 and 6s. 3d. in 1961.

Season ticket sales increased considerably over this period. Oxted was the busiest station, issuing nearly 11,000 seasons during 1957; East Grinstead was not far behind, the sale of season tickets between 1955 and 1957 having risen by 138 per cent to 7,540. In 1954 there were only 175 season-ticket holders from East Grinstead to London; by 1958 there were 574; and in another four years the number had increased to 855. At Dormans in 1962 there were only 111 and at Lingfield 144, but it was Woldingham that remained the least-used station on the CO&EG. The number of season-ticket holders at East Grinstead declined in the 1960s, was up slightly in the 1970s, but by December 1980 it had reached 960, following a spate of house-building in the area. Dormans had now 170 and Lingfield 280 season-ticket holders to London.

Day returns were now available by any train, and in 1960 the cheap off-peak ticket was brought in. It was a few shillings less than the day return and at first could be used on the 6.34 am from East Grinstead, which arrived at London Bridge before 8.00 am. It could not then be obtained until after 9.30 am, and the holder had to leave London before 4.30 or after 6.30 pm. It was not at first sold on Saturdays or Sundays. Cheap off-peak tickets were coloured pink, and a year or two later became the standard cheap ticket, all other kinds being swept away. Full-fare ordinary singles or returns had to be purchased for travel in the peak hours, a restriction intended to discourage casual travel at that time. From 8th September, 1968, ordinary returns were valid on the day of issue only.

Fare increases were relatively rare events in those days, although the amount of increase was usually quite considerable. For example, the East Grinstead-London off-peak return fare in 1960 was 7s. 8d., increased to 8s. 6d. in 1962 and to 9s. 9d. in 1968. From 1971 fares were increased with phenomenal rapidity; indeed in four short years they had doubled. It was very discouraging to passengers, who must have felt that the fares they were paying were sufficient to *buy* the train in which they rode. And it seemed that each fare rise coincided with a reduction in service, so that passengers were paying more to get less.

Two small concessions to travellers were made in 1970. From 26th April tickets were available to any Southern Region London terminus at no extra charge, and off-peak ticket holders were allowed to leave London between 4.30 and 6.30 pm, although the tickets still could not be purchased before 9.30 am.

The tickets themselves, from the earliest days until 1987, were standard Edmondson card, white for first class and green for third (later second). 'Excursion' tickets were buff. About 1965/6 the design was changed so that the ticket no longer needed tearing in half for the return journey. The old date-stamps were replaced by cash registers which recorded the fare and date in purple ink on the ticket. For the most popular journeys a separate machine at each booking office issued paper tickets similar in style to Bell Punch 'Ultimate' tickets used on some municipal bus systems. All these were replaced virtually overnight by 'APTIS' tickets of a totally standard design which could be issued from any station to any other station.

Between June 1973 and January 1977 there were no fewer than seven fare increases, three of these being in 1975 and two in 1976. Fares in 1977 were almost double what they had been in 1973 and well above the rate of inflation. Off-peak day returns, for both first and second class in September 1975, are shown below; cheap first-class tickets were abolished soon afterwards.

	Day Returns	
	First	Second
	£	£
Sanderstead	0.92	0.62
Riddlesdown	1.05	0.70
Upper Warlingham	1.17	0.78
Woldingham	1.22	0.81
Oxted	1.44	0.96
Hurst Green	1.50	1.00
Lingfield	1.72	1.15
Dormans	1.95	1.30
East Grinstead	2.03	1.35

From 1972 to 1979 the number of single tickets issued rose, as did the number of season-ticket holders to East Croydon. The rise in the cost of a season ticket was enormous: the monthly season from East Grinstead to London was £10 2s. in 1967/8, £68 in 1981, and £97.20 in 1986. Between November 1981 and May 1984 - while there was no Victoria service - season-ticket holders were permitted to use trains between Three Bridges or Horley and Victoria at no extra cost (except the cost of getting to and from Three Bridges or Horley!). This special concession was quickly withdrawn when the East Grinstead - Victoria service was restored.

In the 1980s 'Railcards' became available for several categories of traveller, where for the cost of the card one was entitled to reduced-fare journeys. From 12th May, 1985, annual season-ticket holders could obtain a railcard for £5, which would give them a year's entitlement to half-price day return tickets, Fridays excepted. Several other concessionary-fare tickets, announced with much trumpeting, were quietly withdrawn a few years later.

On 11th June, 1986, the most useful ticket ever devised was introduced with a great deal of publicity. Called the Capitalcard, it provided for one return trip over the line outside the Greater London area plus unlimited travel over any BR or London Transport railway and any bus service within the Greater London area for only 80 pence more than the normal day return. The day return from East Grinstead then being £4.10, the Capitalcard was only £4.90; if purchased within Greater London (at Riddlesdown or Sanderstead stations) it cost £2.50. Originally, special pink season-sized tickets were printed, but in 1987 they were replaced by APTIS standard tickets. The Capitalcard was renamed the Day Travelcard in 1989, by which time the cost was £6. But it was, and remains, superb value for a day's unlimited travel around London.

The south end of Selsdon station, showing Brighton-style signal cabin, disused Oxted line platforms, and electrified Woodside & South Croydon platforms.   *Lens of Sutton*

An up train is held at Upper Warlingham signal cabin on 29th December, 1976, and the signalman leans out to tell the driver the reason. The snowy conditions suggest a signal failure.
                                                                                              Author

Chapter Seventeen

Signalling

From South Croydon Junction to Selsdon Road Junction signalling was installed by the LBSC, and from there to a point south of Upper Warlingham it was installed by the SER. Woldingham had a small sub-standard LBSCR frame, and Oxted and beyond was standard Brighton signalling. Signal cabins at Selsdon Road, Sanderstead, Upper Warlingham, Woldingham, Hurst Green Junction and Crowhurst Junction North were LBSCR structures of standard brick construction, but Riddlesdown Tunnel and Oxted cabins were of timber planking, a style favoured by the South Eastern.

Selsdon Road signal cabin was located on the up side just south of the platform and controlled the junction with the Woodside & South Croydon until the closure of that line in May 1983. The double junction was replaced by a trailing connection with the down line and a facing crossover immediately south. The cabin was closed, and demolition occurred in February 1985.

Sanderstead signal cabin (12 levers in 1889) was unusual in being located in the middle of the down platform. From 30th September, 1935, to 13th May, 1983, it was kept busy reversing electric trains off the Mid-Kent line. There were fouling bars on the down line here; as long as the train wheels kept these depressed the signalman could not accept another train. The electric train would draw out of the station and reverse into the up platform using a crossover just south of the road overbridge. On 5th September, 1958, the cabin was struck by lightning during a storm, but survived until August 1987, when it was demolished.

Riddlesdown Tunnel Intermediate, opened for race specials, was 150 yards south of the tunnel, on the up side. It was abolished about 1963 and the signals it controlled were replaced by colour-lights controlled from Sanderstead and Upper Warlingham, but not quite in the same places. The box stood out of use and was demolished by about 1969.

Upper Warlingham cabin was situated immediately south of the up platform, and latterly controlled a mixture of semaphore and colour light signals. Replacement of the semaphore up starting signal by colour lights came at the time the platform was extended at the up end. This cabin also controlled Nichols Siding from 1886 until its abolition; there were 14 levers in all. The structure was demolished in 1987.

Woldingham box, opened in March 1885, was a small 12-lever cabin on the up side, south of the station. Long after most signals had been replaced by SR-type upper-quadrants, Woldingham retained a lower-quadrant down advance starting signal on a lattice post, until 1973. There was no down home signal at Woldingham in later years , only a down distant. In times of staff shortage in the 1970s, Woldingham was not infrequently switched out, resulting in a very long section between Upper Warlingham and Oxted. If it covered the rush-hour period it affected the timekeeping of the batch of trains due to arrive at Oxted at virtually 10-minute intervals (the 5.53 and 6.10 pm from Victoria and the 6.15 and 6.30 pm from London Bridge). The cabin was demolished in September 1987.

Woldingham station had one of the smallest signal cabins found on the Oxted line. Behind, part of the vast expanse of Marden Park is seen. 18th February, 1984.   *Author*

Last days of the old wooden signal cabin at Oxted, about to be replaced by the new brick-built structure on the left.   *Author*

Oxted Lime Siding was originally controlled by a ground frame on the down side, with connection only with the down line. In 1900 this was replaced by a new wooden signal box on the up side, with 15 levers, controlling new signals and new trailing crossover. Owing to the 1 in 132 gradient no up goods train was allowed to do any work in the lime siding, which continued to be served only by down trains. The box was closed after 1948.

Oxted signal cabin, at the south end of the down platform, seems to have been bodily moved a few yards south when the down platform was extended in 1889. The cabin then contained 17 levers. When the gasworks siding was laid three years later the number was increased to 20. Additional pointwork put in in 1896 resulted in a further enlargement, and there were now 28 levers; the Board of Trade inspector reported that a new cabin had been erected alongside the old cabin. At the time the up platform was lengthened (1963) and some sidings and connections removed, there were several alterations to the signalling. The up home and starting signals were replaced by colour lights, still controlled from the old wooden cabin, only the down home and starting signals remaining semaphore. The up home signal, previously just short of the down end of the platform, was moved to a position south of the sidings. It incorporated a 'calling-on' aspect so that approaching demus could attach to trains already in the platform. A repeater at the down end of Oxted up side was installed by the SR but was replaced by a BR type around 1969.

The entire signalling between South Croydon Junction and Oxted was replaced by power signalling in 1985, controlled from Three Bridges 'signalling centre'. It was intended that power signalling from Oxted to East Grinstead and Uckfield should be controlled from a new box at Oxted, and this was duly built. A neat little structure of brick, it was brought into use on 11th June, 1987, and the old box closed, being demolished in August.

Hurst Green Junction cabin, opened in December 1887, increased in importance upon the opening in June 1961 of Hurst Green station and the later reversing of empty demus between East Grinstead and Tunbridge Wells. There were 18 levers. The station itself was signalled with colour lights from the outset; the Hurst Green down starter had a junction indicator for the Ashurst line, replacing semaphores that had themselves replaced the tall and magnificent junction semaphore signals south of the road bridge. Yet Hurst Green Junction retained, until 2nd May, 1971, the last LBSCR signal on BR. This was the up main home (from East Grinstead), and it was replaced by a colour light. After this only the up home (from Edenbridge Town) and both down advance starters remained semaphore until power signalling controlled from Oxted was extended to Hurst Green, the cabin being closed in June 1987 and demolished in September 1987.

Hurst Green Intermediate was another 'occasional-use' cabin, opened on days when race specials ran. It was on the down side between Hurst Green Junction and Crowhurst Junction North. Opened some time during the late 1880s, the box was probably abolished in early SR days.

Crowhurst Junction North was opened only for the Tonbridge-Oxted-London trains for a short time each day, and on race days. Later it was opened for a few hours during each morning rush peak period for the East Grinstead-London service. Following total closure in 1965 it stood empty, its lever frame rusting, until 1973.

3H unit No. 1101 passes Hurst Green Junction signal box on 2nd October, 1984.   *P. Barnes*

At Hurst Green Junction on 27th February, 1954, the 12.20 pm (Saturdays) from London Bridge takes the Edenbridge Town line, the direct route to Tunbridge Wells. 'LM4' class 2-6-4 tank No. 42103 is in charge of seven-set 903, formed of ex-SECR coaches. The public footpath at this point was replaced by a hideous footbridge about 1968.   *D. Cullum*

Crowhurst Junction North on 31st January, 1953; East Grinstead line to left and spur line to Crowhurst Junction South in foreground.   *D. Cullum*

Lingfield Intermediate, opened around 1890, and situated on the up side 1¾ miles north of Lingfield, was used to control the Brick Siding, served by one goods train daily. It was opened for race traffic also. Apart from this, it saw little use and was abolished in August 1958, being replaced by a ground frame.

Lingfield station signal cabin was at the London end of the up platform. As siding accommodation was increased in stages during the 1890s the number of signal levers was increased from 14 to 29, and in addition there were two ground frames - the north one containing eight levers and the south one containing twelve. The cabin had to be enlarged to accommodate the extended frame. Latterly Lingfield was opened only for the morning and evening peak periods; it was entirely closed in July 1987 and demolished in October. Power signalling between Hurst Green and East Grinstead (exclusive) was brought into use on 11th/12th July, 1987.

Dormans station was signalled originally; the cabin was at the London end of the up platform. The SR abolished it, probably in the 1930s, and made Lingfield-St Margaret's Junction into one section.

St Margaret's Junction cabin was brought into use in October 1885 after having been closed for a few months; it was situated in the fork between the low level line and the loop line. From June 1955 until June 1963 it would have been used in the peak periods only, as trains did not use the Low Level at any other time. It closed in January 1967. Its junction signal lost its right-hand bracket and the left-hand one was now controlled from East Grinstead. The down distant became 'fixed', the only fixed distant on the line.

East Grinstead Low Level formerly possessed North and South cabins, but only the South cabin - at the down end of the up platform - survived into recent times. The North cabin was opened only occasionally to operate the north crossover, but control of this was transferred to the South cabin in the 1920s. East Grinstead South (with 15 levers) was a timber box, its roof clad in canvas. The station was later signalled so that up trains could start from either platform, although arrivals were limited to the down platform until July 1987. East Grinstead's cabin worked for the last time on 17th July, 1987 (it was 105 years old) and its signalman, Clive Emsey, marked the occasion by dressing in traditional signalman's uniform. The new layout, with power signalling, was introduced on 20th July, 1987.

Pictures of St Margaret's Junction are hard to find. Here is one taken on a Sunday in April 1959 when, owing to engineer's possession of the loop for track blanketing, all trains worked into and out of East Grinstead Low Level, with consequent bunker-first running in the up direction.

P.W. Chapman

On 8th January, 1982, locomotive No. 33063 approaches coaching stock berthed overnight in East Grinstead's up siding ; it will then work the train to London Bridge. The charming little signal cabin, with its canvas-covered roof, lasted until 1987.   *Author*

Chapter Eighteen

Some Passengers and Some Railwaymen

Among the regular daily passengers on the Oxted line there were many who were on high salaries and rode first class. For them, the business trains included a good proportion of compartments with what BR termed 'superior accommodation', and these 'top people' tended to form little enclaves, so that their morning journey was something of a social occasion. During the early 1960s one such enclave could be found on the 8.24 am Forest Row to Victoria; of the four persons occupying the same compartment every day one was Lt Col. Frank Harding, General Manager of the Pullman Car Company, and another was Dr Richard Beeching, BR Chairman from March 1961 till May 1965.

Dr Beeching, of Lewes Road, East Grinstead, was on a salary of £24,000 (of which, after tax, he saw just over a quarter). He would drive to East Grinstead station and board the 8.35 am up and return home by the 6.10 pm fast train from Victoria. The *East Grinstead Observer* recorded that on 19th April, 1961, he left his free pass at home and a travelling inspector made him pay 15*s*. 3*d*. for a first class return.

In March 1963 Beeching, a resident of East Grinstead since 1958, published his 'Reshaping of British Railways' report, which included details of 'non-paying' lines and their suggested fate; and it was enthusiastically acted upon by the Government - both Right and Left. Of the lines to East Grinstead only the CO&EG was spared, this being the one upon which the doctor travelled each day!

Other big names who used the line about this time included Jeremy Thorpe, future leader of the Liberal Party, and Sir John Benn, the publisher, who favoured the 9.13 am fast train from Oxted to Victoria.

Some of the second class compartments had their little enclaves too. During 1968 a compartment in the rear coach of the 7.24 am Brighton to London Bridge was always occupied by a maker of rostrum cameras from Ashurst, a cigar-importer and a letterer of strip-cartoons from Hurst Green, a man from Woldingham who was in the music business, and a solicitor from Sanderstead. All these people had become acquainted with each other simply by travelling in the same compartment every day, yet on arrival at London Bridge all went their separate ways. The cigar-importer was notable in wearing a bowler hat, some years after such accoutrements had ceased to be *de rigeur* for businessmen.

Although until the mid-1960s Oxted line businessmen dressed alike (dark suit, bowler and rolled umbrella) they tended to have a rather more independent attitude than their fellows on some other lines. R.W. Kidner, himself a regular passenger from 1955 to 1974, recalled that one morning, when the 8.41 am East Grinstead to Victoria was at Oxted waiting to leave, a late passenger arrived at the station car park, brakes screeching. In the up bay road (which was between the car park and the up main platform) a few wagons and a goods brake van were quietly sitting. The bowler-hatted passenger leapt across the verandah of the van, gained the platform, and as the startled guard appeared at his door gave him a cheery wave, shouting, 'Thank you, my man; have it there again tomorrow!'

As for the station staff, theirs was often not a happy lot, for they took the brunt of passengers' ire when the trains were not running properly. Some merely snarled back at the passengers; others, such as Bob Blackford, senior railman at East Grinstead, showed unfailing courtesy and tact. It was tough being in charge of a station at the end of the line, late at night, when some drunken passenger (like as not having passed his destination) would stagger out of the train and proceed to throw up all over Bob's nice clean station. Commuters showed their appreciation of 'the human face of British Rail' by presenting Bob with a tankard and cheque for £235 to mark his retirement in August 1996.

Until 1965, stations were presided over by station masters: awe-inspiring figures often remote from the public. They were replaced by station managers, a post which has since been abolished. In fact the frequent reorganisation and renaming of railway grades has become too confusing to keep track of. In September 1964 a new post of area manager was created, and the Oxted line was the first to receive one. Joe Russell, formerly station master at Herne Hill, was directly responsible to George Weeden, the line manager, and controlled 17 stations in the area taking in Sanderstead-East Grinstead-Ashurst from a new office at Hurst Green. Assisted by the uniformed station managers, the bowler-hatted Mr Russell was supposed to be 'in touch' with the passengers. In the 1980s station managers were no longer in uniform, and were in charge of several stations, but tended not to stay on one line for any length of time. For example, Gordon Dudman was the Oxted and East Grinstead station manager for only 18 months, from March 1983 to September 1984, but in that short time became a familiar figure as he toured the outposts of his empire by train; for his part he knew most of the 750 regular travellers at East Grinstead by sight. The fact that he wore a bowler hat seemed to enhance his standing.

Until the mid-1960s there were 'best-kept station' competitions, and some station masters took these very seriously. Fred Steddy, who was promoted to Lingfield from the Oxted booking office in May 1958, leaving Lingfield for Burgess Hill and Wivelsfield in March 1963, was one such individual, and during his time at Lingfield his station came top in 1961 and second place in 1963 for the Central Division. Sadly, in later years, such things as tending station flowerbeds became officially regarded as unproductive use of a railwayman's time.

Charlie Smith, signalman at Lingfield from 1926 to 1965, was featured in the *East Grinstead Observer* for 21st May, 1965, at the time of his retirement. He started as a junior porter at Mayfield in 1916 and became a signalman in 1923. Clearly one of the old school of dedicated railwaymen, he remarked that when he came to Lingfield he never thought he would spend the rest of his life there, 'but I'd do it again if I had my way.' He disapproved of Nationalisation: 'You have got to have a certain amount of competition. They have made it better for the travelling public in some ways, but we never used to have half the complaints that we have now.'

A retired railwayman, H.G. Morris, in 1972 sent in some reminiscences of the time that he was a relief man who often worked at Lingfield although based at

East Grinstead in the 1930s; he also drove a 2 ton Thornycroft lorry with solid tyres, as well as a 2 ton Karrier, a Ford and a Scammell.

In 1931 my head station was East Grinstead and my wage as Porter II was 38 shillings per week; insurance stamp was sevenpence weekly. I was 'spare' so I was sent to other places to relieve for a week (daily travelling) and just one shilling and sixpence extra if I was away during my usual meal break - not that I had any meal: perhaps a mug of cold tea from a tin bottle and a raw onion and slice of dry bread. Other times during my week of relief duties I had to go to cattle pens anywhere. We never had protective clothing then or anything for one's hands.

There was a porter-signalman (Charlie Smith) stationed at Lingfield who, when he was on platform duties seeing to trains, used to call out 'Lingfield, luvverly Lingfield, luvverly Lingfield!' The last time I covered there was in 1955 although I was then a relief signalman stationed at Horsham. My job at Lingfield was to open up the ground frame (14 levers) which stood in rear of the down platform: I refused to work it because there had not been any work done on the frame for many weeks. It needed oil and it needed the fitters on it as every time I pulled one or two levers the slot wouldn't stay up and the frame locked itself. There was race traffic about too and things had to wait until fitters came along to see to it. The authorities didn't like it but the crews of the locos did because I had no point protection.

The Oxted line was always very special to me; it was the first Southern line I ever rode on, and in my boyhood it was always associated with exciting day trips to London or to the coast. During 1961/2 many hours were spent at Oxted station for the cost of a platform ticket, when the train formations were observed and an attempt was made to compile a record of engine workings by actually asking each driver for the duty number of his locomotive! For by then only Tonbridge and occasionally Stewarts Lane depots ever displayed the duty numbers on the headcode discs. Most drivers were co-operative; some were not.

North end of Lingfield's down platform in the early 1950s, with signalman Charlie Smith (of 'luvverly Lingfield' fame) and signal inspector Tom Mann.   *Lens of Sutton*

After Solari destination displays came into general use a supply of wooden boards was retained for emergencies. Here senior railman Bob Blackford is about to pop one such board into its bracket at East Grinstead on 29th September, 1988. *Author*

In 1967 I became a regular traveller on the line and was able to observe all the day-to-day changes; fortunately I was able to secure the comforts of a locomotive-hauled train in both directions. On one occasion in 1968 the 7.24 am Brighton to London Bridge was for some reason travelling very slowly on the approaches to Norwood Junction when it came to a *dead* stop - like hitting a wall. All the 'face-to-engine' occupants of the compartment in which I was riding found themselves on the floor, looking very surprised. At the time I assumed that the driver was giving a demonstration of just how powerful air brakes were, for after a while the train continued to London Bridge as though nothing had happened. No explanation was given to passengers for such odd behaviour.

On another occasion in 1968 the 7.24 totally failed at Honor Oak Park. As there are no platforms by the fast lines it meant that all the passengers were invited to climb down on to the track (I jumped down!) and walk across to the platform on the up slow line in order to complete their journey. One assumes that the current had been turned off first before the passengers were decanted, but it was all quite exciting.

From 1970 to 1990 I travelled on the Oxted line two or three times a week, avoiding whenever possible those days when a proper service was not being run; believe it or not, there *were* occasions when trains ran to time and with their correct number of coaches.

To conclude, I give a story of the one-and-only time when an Oxted line train was provided for my exclusive use, although ultimately I gained no benefit from it. One evening in September 1980 the 8.19 pm from London Bridge to East Grinstead was delayed at London Bridge waiting for a relieving guard, who on the up run had allegedly got out at Eridge to relieve *himself* and the train had set off without him. The 8.19 pm was eventually announced at London Bridge as cancelled, as by 9.05 the stock for the 9.19 pm to East Grinstead had arrived. However, the driver of the 8.19 was ready to take his train and suddenly said to me 'Jump in!' So I did, and this train (officially empty coaching stock) left London Bridge at 9.09 pm, running non-stop to Oxted in 33½ minutes and conveying, in the front saloon, an unofficial passenger. At Oxted the rear unit (1315) was detached, and I assumed the front unit in which I was riding (1319) would continue to East Grinstead. Instead Unit 1319 drew forward on to the viaduct, reversed over the south crossover and ran into the up platform! Clearly the driver had forgotten I was still in the train, but I thought it would be a good idea to get out then. The driver said that the train *was* originally going to East Grinstead, but Control had changed its mind and instead the unit would form the 10.10 pm up from Oxted, East Grinstead not having had a train for two hours. So in the end I didn't get home any earlier than the other passengers who were on the 9.19 pm from London Bridge; all were delayed an hour, including the one who had enjoyed a ride in an 'empty' train.

The Oxted line has certainly had its moments.

Acknowledgements and Bibliography

This book contains material from *The Oxted Line* by R.W. Kidner, published by Oakwood Press in 1972. I am very much indebted to Mr Kidner for his permission to use the results of his own researches, on which the present work leans rather heavily in places. Thanks are also due to T.G. Burnham and Denis Cullum for rendering assistance in other areas.

Several magazine articles have dealt with the Oxted line. These include:

'Oxted line relived' (D.A. Bone): *Railway Magazine* Vol.117 p.358 (1971)

'Working with 'H' class tanks at Tunbridge Wells West' (R.W. Coomber): *Bluebell News* Vol.23 p.114 (1981) and Vol.24 p.21 (1982)

'The London, Brighton and South Coast Railway in East Sussex' (J. Francis): *Railway Magazine* Vol.35 pp.157, 226 (1914)

'The Croydon and Oxted Joint Railway' (H.L. Hopwood) *Railway Magazine* Vol.43 p.237 (1918)

'The Marsh 'I3' class tanks (N. Harvey): *Railway World* Vol.21 p.259 (1960)

'The Brighton Scotsmen' (N. Harvey): *Railway World* Vol.23 p.400 (1962)

'The Northern Extension of 1884' (K. Marx): *Bluebell News* Vol.27 p.24 (1985)

'The Croydon & Oxted Joint and Woodside & South Croydon Railways' (W.J. Rugman): *Railway World* Vol.35 p.512 (1974)

'Upper Warlingham Southern Region' (E.B. Trotter): *Model Railway News* Vol.33 p.160 (1957)

'Terriers and Tunbridge Wells topics' (B.C. Vigor): *Bluebell News* Vol.15 p.100 (1973)

'Crowborough-Tunbridge Wells 1916-1921' (B.C. Vigor): *Bluebell News* Vol. 27 p.116 (1985)

'The Evolution of Train Services on the Southern's Oxted line' (H.P.White): *Trains Illustrated* Vol.13 pp. 661, 730 (1960)

The series of locomotive histories by D.L. Bradley, published by the Railway Correspondence & Travel Society, has been consulted, including

The Locomotives of the London Brighton & South Coast Railway: Part 1 (1969), Part 2 (1972) and Part 3 (1974)

Locomotives of the Southern Railway: Part 1 (1975) and Part 2 (1976)

The Locomotives of the South Eastern and Chatham Railway (1961)

The Locomotives of the South Eastern Railway (1963)

Newspapers

The East Grinstead Courier
The East Grinstead Observer
The Sussex Express

Various documents in the Public Record Office, including working timetables and Board of Trade files and the CO&EGR Minute Book (LBS1 200).

Index

† Indicates map.